MW00607935

React Projects

Build 12 real-world applications from scratch using React,
React Native, and React 360

Roy Derks

BIRMINGHAM - MUMBAI

React Projects

Copyright © 2019 Packt Publishing

All rights reserved. No part of this book may be reproduced, stored in a retrieval system, or transmitted in any form or by any means, without the prior written permission of the publisher, except in the case of brief quotations embedded in critical articles or reviews.

Every effort has been made in the preparation of this book to ensure the accuracy of the information presented. However, the information contained in this book is sold without warranty, either express or implied. Neither the author, nor Packt Publishing or its dealers and distributors, will be held liable for any damages caused or alleged to have been caused directly or indirectly by this book.

Packt Publishing has endeavored to provide trademark information about all of the companies and products mentioned in this book by the appropriate use of capitals. However, Packt Publishing cannot guarantee the accuracy of this information.

Commissioning Editor: Pavan Ramchandani
Acquisition Editor: Ashitosh Gupta
Content Development Editor: Akhil Nair
Senior Editor: Martin Whittemore
Technical Editor: Suwarna Patil
Copy Editor: Safis Editing
Project Coordinator: Kinjal Bari
Proofreader: Safis Editing
Indexer: Pratik Shirodkar
Production Designer: Arvindkumar Gupta

First published: December 2019

Production reference: 1191219

Published by Packt Publishing Ltd.
Livery Place
35 Livery Street
Birmingham
B3 2PB, UK.

ISBN 978-1-78995-493-7

www.packt.com

Packt.com

Subscribe to our online digital library for full access to over 7,000 books and videos, as well as industry leading tools to help you plan your personal development and advance your career. For more information, please visit our website.

Why subscribe?

- Spend less time learning and more time coding with practical eBooks and Videos from over 4,000 industry professionals

- Improve your learning with Skill Plans built especially for you

- Get a free eBook or video every month

- Fully searchable for easy access to vital information

- Copy and paste, print, and bookmark content

Did you know that Packt offers eBook versions of every book published, with PDF and ePub files available? You can upgrade to the eBook version at www.packt.com and as a print book customer, you are entitled to a discount on the eBook copy. Get in touch with us at customercare@packtpub.com for more details.

At www.packt.com, you can also read a collection of free technical articles, sign up for a range of free newsletters, and receive exclusive discounts and offers on Packt books and eBooks.

Contributors

About the author

Roy Derks is a serial start-up CTO, conference speaker, and developer from Amsterdam. He has been actively programming since he was a teenager, starting as a self-taught programmer using online tutorials and books. At the age of 14, he founded his first start-up, a peer-to-peer platform where users could trade DVDs with other users for free. This marked the start of his career in web development, which back then primarily consisted of creating web applications using an MVC architecture with the LAMP stack.

In 2015, he was introduced to React and GraphQL at a hackathon in Berlin, and after winning a prize for his project, he started to use these technologies professionally. Over the next few years, he helped multiple start-ups create cross-platform applications using React and React Native, including a start-up he co-founded. He also started giving workshops and talks at conferences around the globe. In 2019, he gave over 20 conference talks about React, React Native, and GraphQL, inspiring over 10,000 developers worldwide.

First, I'd like to thank the creators of React at Facebook for open-sourcing their library and making it available for everyone. Without their effort, my career would have looked very different and this book wouldn't have been written.

Second, a shoutout to all the developers that have created, maintained, or contributed to the packages used in this book. If it wasn't for all the hard work you've put into these libraries, frameworks, and tools, React would have been way less popular.

Finally, many thanks to the online communities that inspired and motivated me to write this book. Communities need dedicated people to thrive and trying to mention some of you personally would mean selling short all the people I might forget. So thank you ALL for making React great.

About the reviewers

Kirill Ezhemenskii is an experienced software engineer, frontend and mobile developer, solution architect, and a CTO at a healthcare company. He is also a functional programming advocate and an expert in React stack, GraphQL, and TypeScript. He is a React Native mentor.

Emmanuel Demey works with the JavaScript ecosystem on a daily basis. He spends his time sharing his knowledge with anyone and everyone. His first goal at work is to help the people he works with. He has spoken at French conferences (such as Devfest Nantes, Devfest Toulouse, Sunny Tech, and Devoxx France) about topics related to the web platform, such as JavaScript frameworks (Angular, React.js, Vue.js), accessibility, and Nest.js. He has been a trainer for 10 years at Worldline and Zenika (two French consulting companies). He also the co-leader of the Google Developer Group de Lille and the co-organizer of the Devfest Lille conference.

Packt is searching for authors like you

If you're interested in becoming an author for Packt, please visit `authors.packtpub.com` and apply today. We have worked with thousands of developers and tech professionals, just like you, to help them share their insight with the global tech community. You can make a general application, apply for a specific hot topic that we are recruiting an author for, or submit your own idea.

Table of Contents

Preface

This book will help you take your React knowledge to the next level by showing how to apply both basic and advanced React patterns to create cross-platform applications. The concepts of React are described in a way that's understandable to both new and experienced developers; no prior experience of React is required, although it would help.

In each of the 12 chapters of this book, you'll create a project with React, React Native, or React 360. The projects created in these chapters implement popular React features such as **Higher-Order Components (HOCs)** for re-using logic, the context API for state-management, and Hooks for life cycle. Popular libraries, such as React Router and React Navigation, are used for routing, while the JavaScript testing framework Jest is used to write unit tests for the applications. Also, some more advanced chapters involve a GraphQL server, and Expo is used to help you create React Native applications.

Who this book is for

The book is for JavaScript developers who want to explore React tooling and frameworks for building cross-platform applications. Basic knowledge of web development, ECMAScript, and React will assist in understanding key concepts covered in this book.

The supported React versions for this book are:

- React - v16.10.2
- React Native - v0.59
- React 360 - v1.1.0

What this book covers

Chapter 1, *Creating a Movie List Application in React*, will explore the foundation of building React projects that can scale. Best practices of how to structure your files, packages to use, and tools will be discussed and practiced. The best way to architect a React project will be shown by building a list of movies. Also, webpack and Babel are used to compile code.

Chapter 2, *Creating a Progressive Web Application with Reusable React Components*, will explain how to set up and re-use styling in React components throughout your entire application. We will build a GitHub Card application to see how to use CSS in JavaScript and re-use components and styling in your application.

Chapter 3, *Build a Dynamic Project Management Board with React and Suspense*, will cover how to create components that determine the dataflow between other components, so called HOCs. We will build a project management board to see the flow of data throughout an application.

Chapter 4, *Build a SSR-Based Community Feed Using React Router*, will discuss routing, ranging from setting up basic routes, dynamic route handling, and how to set up routes for server-side rendering.

Chapter 5, *Build a Personal Shopping List Application Using Context API and Hooks*, will show you how to use the React context API with Hooks to handle the data flow throughout the application. We will create a personal shopping list to see how data can be accessed and changed from parent to child components and vice versa with Hooks and the context API.

Chapter 6, *Build an Application Exploring TDD Using Jest and Enzyme*, will focus on unit testing with assertions and snapshots. Also, test coverage will be discussed. We will build a hotel review application to see how to test components and data flows.

Chapter 7, *Build a Full Stack E-Commerce Application with React Native and GraphQL*, will use GraphQL to supply a backend to the application. This chapter will show you how to set up a basic GraphQL server and access the data on this server. We will build an e-commerce application to see how to create a server and send requests to it.

Chapter 8, *Build a House Listing Application with React Native and Expo*, will cover scaling and structuring React Native applications, which is slightly different from web applications created with React. This chapter will outline the differences in the development environment and tools such as Expo. We will build a house listing application to examine the best practices.

Chapter 9, *Build an Animated Game Using React Native and Expo*, will discuss animations and gestures, which are what truly distinguishes a mobile application from a web application. This chapter will explain how to implement them. Also, the differences in gestures between iOS and Android will be shown by building a card game application that has animations and that responds to gestures.

Chapter 10, *Creating a Real-Time Messaging Application with React Native and Expo*, will cover notifications, which are important for keeping the users of the application up to date. This chapter will show how to add notifications and send them from the GraphQL server using Expo. We will learn how to implement all this by building a message application.

Chapter 11, *Build a Full Stack Social Media Application with React Native and GraphQL*, will cover building a full-stack application with React Native and GraphQL. The flow of data between the server and the application will be demonstrated, along with how data are fetched from the GraphQL server.

Chapter 12, *Creating a Virtual Reality Application with React 360*, will discuss how to get started with React 360 by creating a panorama viewer that gives the user the ability to look around in the virtual world and create components inside it.

To get the most out of this book

All the projects in this book are created with React, React Native, or React 360 and require you to have prior knowledge of JavaScript. Although all the concepts of React and related technologies are described in this book, we advise you to refer to React docs if you want to find out more about a feature. In the following section, you can find some information about setting up your machine for this book and how to download the code for each chapter.

Set up your machine

For the applications that are created in this book, you'll need to have at least Node.js v10.16.3 installed on your machine so that you can run npm commands. If you haven't installed Node.js on your machine, please go to https://nodejs.org/en/download/, where you can find the download instructions for macOS, Windows, and Linux.

After installing Node.js, run the following commands in your command line to check the installed versions:

- For Node.js (should be v10.16.3 or higher):

    ```
    node -v
    ```

- For npm (should be v6.9.0 or higher):

    ```
    npm -v
    ```

Also, you should have installed the **React Developer Tools** plugin (for Chrome and Firefox) and added it to your browser. This plugin can be installed from the **Chrome Web Store** (https://chrome.google.com/webstore) or Firefox Addons (https://addons.mozilla.org).

Download the example code files

You can download the example code files for this book from your account at
www.packt.com. If you purchased this book elsewhere, you can visit
www.packtpub.com/support and register to have the files emailed directly to you.

You can download the code files by following these steps:

1. Log in or register at www.packt.com.
2. Select the **Support** tab.
3. Click on **Code Downloads**.
4. Enter the name of the book in the **Search** box and follow the onscreen
   instructions.

Once the file is downloaded, please make sure that you unzip or extract the folder using the
latest version of:

- WinRAR/7-Zip for Windows
- Zipeg/iZip/UnRarX for Mac
- 7-Zip/PeaZip for Linux

The code bundle for the book is also hosted on GitHub at https://github.com/
PacktPublishing/React-Projects. In case there's an update to the code, it will be updated
on the existing GitHub repository.

We also have other code bundles from our rich catalog of books and videos available
at https://github.com/PacktPublishing/. Check them out!

Download the color images

We also provide a PDF file that has color images of the screenshots/diagrams used in this
book. You can download it
here: https://static.packt-cdn.com/downloads/9781789954937_ColorImages.pdf.

Conventions used

There are a number of text conventions used throughout this book.

`CodeInText`: Indicates code words in text, database table names, folder names, filenames, file extensions, pathnames, dummy URLs, user input, and Twitter handles. Here is an example: "Since you're going to build a Movie List application in this chapter, name this directory `movieList`."

A block of code is set as follows:

```
{
    "name": "movieList",
    "version": "1.0.0",
    "description": "",
    "main": "index.js",
    "scripts": {
        "test": "echo \"Error: no test specified\" && exit 1"
    },
    "keywords": [],
    "author": "",
    "license": "ISC"
}
```

When we wish to draw your attention to a particular part of a code block, the relevant lines or items are set in bold:

```
import React from 'react';
import ReactDOM from 'react-dom';
+ import List from './containers/List';

const App = () => {
-    return <h1>movieList</h1>;
+    return <List />;
};

ReactDOM.render(<App />, document.getElementById('root'));
```

Any command-line input or output is written as follows:

```
npm init -y
```

Bold: Indicates a new term, an important word, or words that you see onscreen. For example, words in menus or dialog boxes appear in the text like this. Here is an example: "When the user clicks the **Close X** button, the display styling rule of the component will be set to none."

Warnings or important notes appear like this.

 Tips and tricks appear like this.

Get in touch

Feedback from our readers is always welcome.

General feedback: If you have questions about any aspect of this book, mention the book title in the subject of your message and email us at customercare@packtpub.com.

Errata: Although we have taken every care to ensure the accuracy of our content, mistakes do happen. If you have found a mistake in this book, we would be grateful if you would report this to us. Please visit www.packtpub.com/support/errata, selecting your book, clicking on the Errata Submission Form link, and entering the details.

Piracy: If you come across any illegal copies of our works in any form on the Internet, we would be grateful if you would provide us with the location address or website name. Please contact us at copyright@packt.com with a link to the material.

If you are interested in becoming an author: If there is a topic that you have expertise in and you are interested in either writing or contributing to a book, please visit authors.packtpub.com.

Reviews

Please leave a review. Once you have read and used this book, why not leave a review on the site that you purchased it from? Potential readers can then see and use your unbiased opinion to make purchase decisions, we at Packt can understand what you think about our products, and our authors can see your feedback on their book. Thank you!

For more information about Packt, please visit packt.com.

Creating a Movie List Application in React

When you bought this book, you'd probably heard of React before and probably even tried out some of the code examples that can be found online. This book is constructed in such a way that the code examples in each chapter gradually increase in complexity, so even if you feel your experience with React is limited, each chapter should be understandable if you've read the previous one. When you reach the end of this book, you will know how to work with React and its stable features, up until version 16.11, and you will also have experience with **React Native** and **React 360**.

This first chapter kicks off with us learning how to build a simple movie list application and provides you with an overview of popular movies that we'll fetch from an external source. The core concepts for getting started with React will be applied to this project, which should be understandable if you've got some prior experience in building applications with React. If you haven't worked with React before, that's no problem either; this book describes the React features that are used in the code examples along the way.

In this chapter, we'll cover the following topics:

- Setting up a new project with webpack and React
- Structuring a React project

Let's dive in!

Project overview

In this chapter, we will create a movie list application in React that retrieves data from a local JSON file and runs in the browser with webpack and Babel. Styling will be done using Bootstrap. The application that you'll build will return a list of the highest-grossing movies as of 2019, along with some more details and a poster for every movie.

The build time is 1 hour.

Getting started

The application for this chapter will be built from scratch and uses assets that can be found on GitHub at https://github.com/PacktPublishing/React-Projects/tree/ch1-assets. These assets should be downloaded to your computer so that you can use them later on in this chapter. The complete code for this chapter can be found on GitHub as well: https://github.com/PacktPublishing/React-Projects/tree/ch1.

For applications that are created in this book, you'll need to have at least Node.js v10.16.3 installed on your machine so that you can run npm commands. If you haven't installed Node.js on your machine, please go to https://nodejs.org/en/download/, where you can find the download instructions for macOS, Windows, and Linux.

After installing Node.js, run the following commands in your command line to check the installed versions:

- For Node.js (should be v10.16.3 or higher):

  node -v

- For npm (should be v6.9.0 or higher):

  npm -v

Also, you should have installed the **React Developer Tools** plugin (for Chrome and Firefox) and added it to your browser. This plugin can be installed from the **Chrome Web Store** (https://chrome.google.com/webstore) or Firefox Addons (https://addons.mozilla.org).

Creating a movie list application

In this section, we will create a new React application from scratch, starting with setting up a new project with webpack and Babel. Setting up a React project from scratch will help you understand the basic needs of a project, which is crucial for any project you create.

Setting up a project

Every time you create a new React project, the first step is to create a new directory on your local machine. Since you're going to build a movie list application in this chapter, name this directory movieList.

Inside this new directory, execute the following from the command line:

```
npm init -y
```

Running this command will create a package.json file with the bare minimum of information that npm needs about this project. By adding the -y flag to the command, we can automatically skip the steps where we set information such as the name, version, and description. After running this command, the following package.json file will be created:

```
{
    "name": "movieList",
    "version": "1.0.0",
    "description": "",
    "main": "index.js",
    "scripts": {
        "test": "echo \"Error: no test specified\" && exit 1"
    },
    "keywords": [],
    "author": "",
    "license": "ISC"
}
```

As you can see, there are no dependencies for npm packages since we haven't installed any yet. The first package we'll be installing and configuring is webpack, which we'll do in the next part of this section.

Setting up webpack

To run the React application, we need to install webpack 4 (while writing this book, the current stable version of webpack is version 4) and webpack CLI as **devDependencies**. Let's get started:

1. Install these packages from npm using the following command:

   ```
   npm install --save-dev webpack webpack-cli
   ```

2. The next step is to include these packages inside the package.json file and have them run in our start and build scripts. To do this, add the start and build scripts to our package.json file:

   ```
   {
       "name": "movieList",
       "version": "1.0.0",
       "description": "",
       "main": "index.js",
       "scripts": {
   _       "start": "webpack --mode development",
   +       "build": "webpack --mode production",
           "test": "echo \"Error: no test specified\" && exit 1"
       },
       "keywords": [],
       "author": "",
       "license": "ISC"
   }
   ```

 "+" symbol is used for the line which is added and "-" symbol is used for the line which is removed in the code.

The preceding configuration will add start and build scripts to our application using webpack. As you can see, npm start will run webpack in development mode and npm build will run webpack in production mode. The biggest difference is that running webpack in production mode will minimize our code to decrease the size of the project bundle.

3. Create a new directory inside our project called `src` and create a new file inside this directory called `index.js`. Later on, we'll configure webpack so that this file is the starting point for our application. Place the following line of code inside this newly created file:

```
console.log("movieList")
```

If we now run the `npm start` or `npm build` command at our command line, webpack will start up and create a new directory called `dist`. Inside this directory, there will be a file called `main.js` that includes our project code. Depending on whether we've run webpack in development or production mode, the code will be minimized in this file. You can check whether your code is working by running the following command:

```
node dist/main.js
```

This command runs the bundled version of our application and should return the `movieList` string as output in the command line. Now, we're able to run JavaScript code from the command line. In the next part of this section, we will learn how to configure webpack so that it works with React.

Configuring webpack to work with React

Now that we've set up a basic development environment with webpack for a JavaScript application, we can start installing the packages we need in order to run any React application. These are `react` and `react-dom`, where the former is the generic core package for React and the latter provides an entry point to the browser's DOM and renders React. Let's get started:

1. Install these packages by executing the following command in the command line:

```
npm install react react-dom
```

Merely installing the dependencies for React is not sufficient to run it since, by default, not every browser can read the format (such as ES2015+ or React) that your JavaScript code is written in. Therefore, we need to compile the JavaScript code into a readable format for every browser.

2. For this, we'll use Babel and its related packages, which can be installed as `devDependencies` by running the following command:

```
npm install --save-dev @babel/core @babel/preset-env @babel/preset-react babel-loader
```

Next to the Babel core, we'll also install `babel-loader`, which is a helper so that Babel can run with webpack and two preset packages. These preset packages help determine which plugins will be used to compile our JavaScript code into a readable format for the browser (`@babel/preset-env`) and to compile React-specific code (`@babel/preset-react`).

With the packages for React and the correct compilers installed, the next step is to make them work with webpack so that they are used when we run our application.

3. To do this, create a file called `webpack.config.js` in the root directory of the project. Inside this file, add the following code:

```
module.exports = {
    module: {
        rules: [
            {
                test: /\.js$/,
                exclude: /node_modules/,
                use: {
                    loader:'/babel-loader',
                },                    ← remove "
            },
        ],
    },
}
```

The configuration in this file tells webpack to use `babel-loader` for every file that has the `.js` extension and excludes `.js` files in the `node_modules` directory for the Babel compiler. The actual settings for `babel-loader` are placed in a separate file, called `.babelrc`.

4. We can also create the `.babelrc` file in the project's root directory and place the following code inside it, which configures `babel-loader` to use the `@babel/preset-env` and `@babel/preset-react` presets when it's compiling our code:

```
{
    "presets": [
        [
            "@babel/preset-env",
            {
                "targets": {
                    "node": "current"
                }
```

```
        }
    ],
    "@babel/react"
  ]
}
```

TIP

We can also declare the configuration for `babel-loader` directly inside the `webpack.config.js` file, but for better readability, we should place it in a separate `.babelrc` file. Also, the configuration for Babel can now be used by other tools that are unrelated to webpack.

The `@babel/preset-env` preset has options defined in it that make sure that the compiler uses the latest version of Node.js, so polyfills for features such as `async/await` will still be available. Now that we've set up webpack and Babel, we can run JavaScript and React from the command line. In the next part of this section, we'll create our first React code and make it run in the browser.

Rendering a React project

Now that we've set up React so that it works with Babel and webpack, we need to create an actual React component that can be compiled and run. Creating a new React project involves adding some new files to the project and making changes to the setup for webpack. Let's get started:

1. Let's edit the `index.js` file that already exists in our `src` directory so that we can use `react` and `react-dom`:

```
import React from 'react';
import ReactDOM from 'react-dom';

const App = () => {
    return <h1>movieList</h1>;
};

ReactDOM.render(<App />, document.getElementById('root'));
```

As you can see, this file imports the `react` and `react-dom` packages, defines a simple component that returns an `h1` element containing the name of your application, and has this component rendered with `react-dom`. The last line of code mounts the `App` component to an element with the `root` ID in your document, which is the entry point of the application.

2. We can create this file by adding a new file called index.html to the src directory with the following code inside it:

```
<!DOCTYPE html>
<html lang="en">
<head>
    <meta charset="UTF-8">
    <meta name="viewport" content="width=device-width, initial-scale=1.0">
    <meta http-equiv="X-UA-Compatible" content="ie=edge">
    <title>movieList</title>
</head>
<body>
    <section id="root"></section>
</body>
</html>
```

This adds an HTML heading and body. Within the head tag is the title of our application and inside the body tag is a section with the id property root. This matches with the element we've mounted the App component to in the src/index.js file.

3. The final step of rendering our React component is extending webpack so that it adds the minified bundle code to the body tags as scripts when running. Therefore, we should install the html-webpack-plugin package as a devDependency:

```
npm install --save-dev html-webpack-plugin
```

Add this new package to the webpack configuration in the webpack.config.js file:

```
const HtmlWebPackPlugin = require('html-webpack-plugin');

const htmlPlugin = new HtmlWebPackPlugin({
    template: './src/index.html',
    filename: './index.html',
});

module.exports = {
    module: {
        rules: [
            {
                test: /\.js$/,
                exclude: /node_modules/,
                use: {
```

```
                loader: 'babel-loader',
              },
            },
          ],
        },
        plugins: [htmlPlugin],
  };
```

In the configuration for `html-webpack-plugin`, we've set the entry point of the application as the `index.html.` file. That way, webpack knows where to add the bundle to the `body` tag.

 We can also add the configuration of the plugin directly inside the exported configuration for webpack by replacing the `htmlPlugin` constant in the exported configuration. As our application grows in size, this may make the webpack configuration less readable, depending on our preferences.

Now, if we run `npm start` again, webpack will start in development mode and add the `index.html` file to the `dist` directory. Inside this file, we'll see that, inside your `body` tag, a new `scripts` tag has been inserted that directs us to our application bundle, that is, the `dist/main.js` file. If we open this file in the browser or run `open dist/index.html` from the command line, it will return the `movieList` result directly inside the browser. We can do the same when running the `npm build` command to start Webpack in production mode; the only difference is that our code will be minified.

This process can be speeded up by setting up a development server with webpack. We'll do this in the final part of this section.

Creating a development server

While working in development mode, every time we make changes to the files in our application, we need to rerun the `npm start` command. Since this is a bit tedious, we will install another package called `webpack-dev-server`. This package adds the option to force webpack to restart every time we make changes to our project files and manages our application files in memory instead of by building the `dist` directory. The `webpack-dev-server` package can also be installed with `npm`:

```
npm install --save-dev webpack-dev-server
```

Also, we need to edit the `start` script in the `package.json` file so that it uses `webpack-dev-server` instead of webpack directly when running the `start` script:

```
{
    "name": "movieList",
    "version": "1.0.0",
    "description": "",
    "main": "index.js",
    "scripts": {
-       "start": "webpack --mode development",
+       "start": "webpack-dev-server --mode development --open",
        "build": "webpack --mode production"
    },
    "keywords": [],
    "author": "",
    "license": "ISC"


    . . .
}
```

The preceding configuration replaces webpack in the start scripts with `webpack-dev-server`, which runs webpack in development mode. This will create a local server that runs the application with the `--open` flag, which makes sure webpack is restarted every time an update is made to any of your project files.

> To enable hot reloading, replace the `--open` flag with the `--hot` flag. This will only reload files that have been changed instead of the entire project.

Now, we've created the basic development environment for our React application, which you'll develop and structure further in the next section of this chapter.

Structuring a project

With the development environment set up, it's time to start creating the movie list application. First let's have a look at the current structure of the project, where two of the directories within our project's root directory are important:

- The first directory is called `dist` and is where the output from webpack's bundled version of your application can be found

- The second one is called `src` and includes the source code of our application:

```
movieList
|-- dist
    |-- index.html
    |-- main.js
|-- node_modules
|-- src
    |-- index.js
    |-- index.html
.babelrc
package.json
webpack.config.js
```

Another directory that can be found in the root directory of our project is called `node_modules`. This is where the source files for every package that we install using `npm` are placed. It is recommended you don't make any manual changes to files inside this directory.

In the following subsections, we will learn how to structure our React projects. This structure will be used in the rest of the chapters in this book as well.

Creating new components

The official documentation for React doesn't state any preferred approach regarding how to structure our React project. Although two common approaches are popular within the community: either structuring your files by feature or route or structuring them by file type.

The movie list application will use a hybrid approach, where files are structured by file type first and by feature second. In practice, this means that there will be two types of components: top-level components, which are called containers, and low-level components, which relate to these top-level components. Creating these components requires that we add the following files and code changes:

1. The first step to achieve this structure is creating a new subdirectory of `src` called `containers`. Inside this directory, create a file called `List.js`. This will be the container for the list containing the movies and contains the following content:

```
import React, { Component } from 'react';

class List extends Component {
    render() {
```

```
      return <h1>movieList</h1>;
    }
};

export default List;
```

2. This container should be included in the entry point of our application so that it's visible. Therefore, we need to include it in the `index.js` file, inside the `src` directory, and refer to it:

```
import React from 'react';
import ReactDOM from 'react-dom';
+ import List from './containers/List';

const App = () => {
-     return <h1>movieList</h1>;
+     return <List />;
};

ReactDOM.render(<App />, document.getElementById('root'));
```

3. If we still have the development server running (if not, execute the `npm start` command again), we'll see that our application still returns the same result. Our application should have the following file structure:

```
movieList
|-- dist
    |-- index.html
    |-- main.js
|-- src
    |-- containers
        |-- List.js
    |-- index.js
    |-- index.html
.babelrc
package.json
webpack.config.js
```

4. The next step is to add a component to the `List` container, which we'll use later to display information about a movie. This component will be called `Card` and should be located in a new `src` subdirectory called `components`, which will be placed inside a directory with the same name as the component. We need to create a new directory called `components` inside the `src` directory, which is where we'll create another new directory called `Card`. Inside this directory, create a file called `Card.js` and add the following code block to the empty `Card` component:

```
import React from 'react';

const Card = () => {
    return <h2>movie #1</h2>;
};

export default Card;
```

5. Now, import this `Card` component into the container for `List` and return this component instead of the h1 element by replacing the `return` function with the following code:

```
import React, { Component } from 'react';
+ import Card from '../components/Card/Card';

class List extends Component {
    render() {
-        return <h1>movieList</h1>;
+        return <Card />;
    }
};

export default List;
```

Now that we've added these directories and the `Card.js` file, our application file's structure will look like this:

```
movieList
|-- dist
    |-- index.html
    |-- main.js
|-- src
    |-- components
        |-- Card
            |-- Card.js
    |-- containers
        |-- List.js
```

```
    |-- index.js
    |-- index.html
.babelrc
package.json
webpack.config.js
```

If we visit our application in the browser again, there will be no visible changes as our application still returns the same result. But if we open the React Developer Tools plugin in our browser, we'll notice that the application currently consists of multiple stacked components:

```
<App>
    <List>
        <Card>
            <h1>movieList</h1>
        </Card>
    </List>
</App>
```

In the next part of this section, you will use your knowledge of structuring a React project and create new components to fetch data about the movies that we want to display in this application.

Retrieving data

With both the development server and the structure for our project set up, it's time to finally add some data to it. If you haven't already downloaded the assets in the GitHub repository from the *Getting started* section, you should do so now. These assets are needed for this application and contain a JSON file with data about the five highest-grossing movies and their related image files.

The data.json file consists of an array with objects containing information about movies. This object has the title, distributor, year, amount, img, and ranking fields, where the img field is an object that has src and alt fields. The src field refers to the image files that are also included.

We need to add the downloaded files to this project's root directory inside a different subdirectory, where the `data.json` file should be placed in a subdirectory called `assets` and the image files should be placed in a subdirectory called `media`. After adding these new directories and files, our application's structure will look like this:

```
movieList
|-- dist
    |-- index.html
    |-- main.js
|-- src
    |-- assets
        |-- data.json
    |-- components
        |-- Card
            |-- Card.js
    |-- containers
        |-- List.js
    |-- media
        |-- avatar.jpg
        |-- avengers_infinity_war.jpg
        |-- jurassic_world.jpg
        |-- star_wars_the_force_awakens.jpg
        |-- titanic.jpg
    |-- index.js
    |-- index.html
.babelrc
package.json
webpack.config.js
```

This data will be retrieved in the top-level components only, meaning that we should add a `fetch` function in the `List` container that updates the state for this container and passes it down as props to the low-level components. The `state` object can store variables; every time these variables change, our component will rerender. Let's get started:

1. Before retrieving the data for the movies, the `Card` component needs to be prepared to receive this information. To display information about the movies, we need to replace the content of the `Card` component with the following code:

```
import React from 'react';

const Card = ({ movie }) => {
    return (
        <div>
            <h2>{`#${movie.ranking} - ${movie.title}
(${movie.year})`}</h2>
                <img src={movie.img.src} alt={movie.img.alt}
```

```
width='200' />
            <p>{`Distributor: ${movie.distributor}`}</p>
            <p>{`Amount: ${movie.amount}`}</p>
        </div>
    );
};

export default Card;
```

2. Now, the logic to retrieve the data can be implemented by adding a `constructor` function to the `List` component, which will contain an empty array as a placeholder for the movies and a variable that indicates whether the data is still being loaded:

```
. . .

class List extends Component {+
+    constructor() {
+        super()
+        this.state = {
+            data: [],
+            loading: true,
+        };
+    }

    return (
        . . .
```

3. Immediately after setting up the `constructor` function, we should set up a `componentDidMount` function, where we'll fetch the data after the `List` component is mounted. Here, we should use an `async/await` function since the `fetch` API returns a promise. After fetching the data, `state` should be updated by replacing the empty array for data with the movie information and the `loading` variable should be set to `false`:

```
. . .

class List extends Component {

    . . .

+    async componentDidMount() {
+        const movies = await fetch('../../assets/data.json');
+        const moviesJSON = await movies.json();

+        if (moviesJSON) {
+            this.setState({
```

```
+                    data: moviesJSON,
+                    loading: false,
+            });
+        }
+    }

    return (
        ...
```

The previous method that we use to retrieve information from JSON files using `fetch` doesn't take into account that the request to this file may fail. If the request fails, the `loading` state will remain `true`, meaning that the user will keep seeing the loading indicator. If you want to display an error message when the request doesn't succeed, you'll need to wrap the `fetch` method inside a `try...catch` block, which will be shown later on in this book.

4. Pass this state to the `Card` component, where it can ultimately be shown in the `Card` component that we changed in the first step. This component will also get a `key` prop, which is required for every component that is rendered within an iteration. Since this value needs to be unique, the `id` of the movie is used, as follows:

```
class List extends Component {

    ...

    render() {
-       return <Card />
+       const { data, loading } = this.state;

+       if (loading) {
+           return <div>Loading...</div>
+       }

+       return data.map(movie => <Card key={ movie.id } movie={
movie } />);
    }
}

export default List;
```

If we visit our application in the browser again, we'll see that it now shows a list of movies, including some basic information and an image. At this point, our application will look similar to the following screenshot:

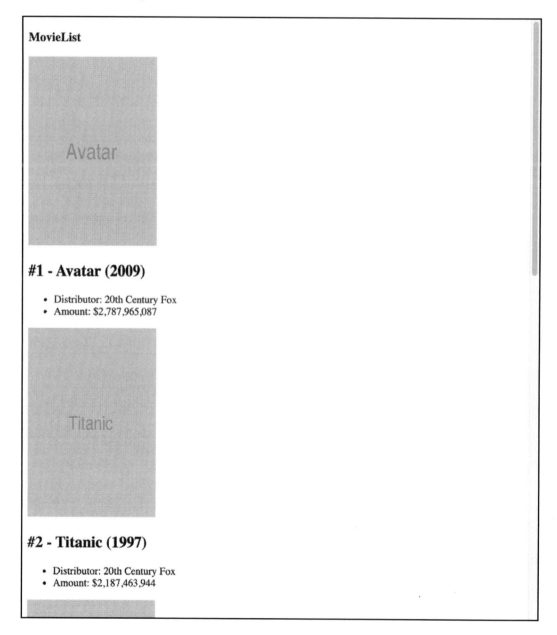

As you can see, limited styling has been applied to the application and it's only rendering the information that's been fetched from the JSON file. Styling will be added in the next part of this section using a package called **Bootstrap**.

Adding styling

Showing just the movie information isn't enough. We also need to apply some basic styling to the project. Adding styling to the project is done with the Bootstrap package, which adds styling to our components based on class names. Bootstrap can be installed from npm and requires the following changes to be used:

1. To use Bootstrap, we need to install it from npm and place it in this project:

   ```
   npm install --save-dev bootstrap
   ```

2. Also, import this file into the entry point of our React application, called index.js, so that we can use the styling throughout the entire application:

   ```
   import React, { Component } from 'react';
   import ReactDOM from 'react-dom';
   import List from './containers/List';
   + import 'bootstrap/dist/css/bootstrap.min.css';

   const App = () => {
       return <List />;
   }

   ReactDOM.render(<App />, document.getElementById('root'));
   ```

   If we try and run the development server again, we will receive an error saying `"You may need an appropriate loader to handle this file type."`. Because Webpack is unable to compile CSS files, we need to add the appropriate loaders to make this happen. We can install these by running the following command:

   ```
   npm install --save-dev css-loader style-loader
   ```

3. We need to add these packages as a rule to the webpack configuration:

   ```
   const HtmlWebPackPlugin = require('html-webpack-plugin');

   const htmlPlugin = new HtmlWebPackPlugin({
       template: './src/index.html',
       filename: './index.html',
   });
   ```

```
module.exports = {
    module: {
        rules: [
            {
                test: /\.js$/,
                exclude: /node_modules/,
                use: {
                    loader: "babel-loader"
                }
            },
+           {
+               test: /\.css$/,
+               use: ['style-loader', 'css-loader']
+           }
        ]
    },
    plugins: [htmlPlugin]
};
```

The order in which loaders are added is important since `css-loader` handles the compilation of the CSS file and `style-loader` adds the compiled CSS files to the React DOM. Webpack reads these settings from right to left and the CSS needs to be compiled before it's attached to the DOM.

4. The application should run in the browser correctly now and should have picked up some small styling changes from the default Bootstrap stylesheet. Let's make some changes to the `index.js` file first and style it as the container for the entire application. We need to change the `App` component that is rendered to the DOM and wrap the `List` component with a `div` container:

```
. . .

const App = () => {
    return (
+       <div className='container-fluid'>
            <List />
        </div>
    );
};

ReactDOM.render(<App />, document.getElementById('root'));
```

5. Inside the `List` component, we need to set the grid to display the `Card` components, which display the movie information. Wrap the `map` function and the `Card` component with the following code:

```
...

class List extends Component {

    ...

    render() {
        const { data, loading } = this.state;

        if (loading) {
            return <div>Loading...</div>;
        }

        return (
+           <div class='row'>
                {data.map(movie =>
+                   <div class='col-sm-2'>
                        <Card key={ movie.id } movie={ movie } />
+                   </div>
                )}
+           </div>
        );
    }
}

export default List;
```

6. The code for the `Card` component is as follows. This will add styling for the `Card` component using Bootstrap:

```
import React from 'react';

const Card = ({ movie }) => {
    return (
        <div className='card'>
            <img src={movie.img.src} className='card-img-top'
alt={movie.img.alt} />
            <div className='card-body'>
                <h2 className='card-title'>{`#${movie.ranking} -
${movie.title} (${movie.year})` }</h2>
            </div>
            <ul className='list-group list-group-flush'>
                <li className='list-group-item'>{`Distributor:
```

```
${movie.distributor}`}</li>
                    <li className='list-group-item'>{`Amount:
${movie.amount}`}</li>
                </ul>
            </div>
        );
    };

    export default Card;
```

7. To add the finishing touches, open the `index.js` file and insert the following code to add a header that will be placed above our list of movies in the application:

```
    ...

    const App = () => {
        return (
            <div className='container-fluid'>
    _           <h1>movieList</h1>
    +           <nav className='navbar sticky-top navbar-light bg-
    dark'>
    +               <h1 className='navbar-brand text-
    light'>movieList</h1>
    +           </nav>

                <List />
            </div>
        );
    };

    ReactDOM.render(<App />, document.getElementById('root'));
```

If we visit the browser again, we'll see that the application has had styling applied through Bootstrap, which will make it look as follows:

The style rules from Bootstrap have been applied to our application, making it look far more complete then it did before. In the final part of this section, we'll add the ESLint package to the project, which will make maintaining our code easier by synchronizing patterns across the project.

Adding ESLint

Finally, we will add ESLint to the project to make sure our code meets certain standards, for instance, that our code follows the correct JavaScript patterns. Adding ESLint requires the following changes:

1. Install ESLint from npm by running the following command:

   ```
   npm install --save-dev eslint eslint-loader eslint-plugin-react
   ```

   The first package, called `eslint`, is the core package and helps us identify any potentially problematic patterns in our JavaScript code. `eslint-loader` is a package that is used by Webpack to run ESLint every time we update our code. Finally, `eslint-plugin-react` adds specific rules to ESLint for React applications.

2. To configure ESLint, we need to create a file called `.eslintrc.js` in the project's root directory and add the following code to it:

   ```
   module.exports = {
       "env": {
           "browser": true,
           "es6": true
       },
       "parserOptions": {
           "ecmaFeatures": {
               "jsx": true
           },
           "ecmaVersion": 2018,
           "sourceType": "module"
       },
       "plugins": [
           "react"
       ],
       "extends": ["eslint:recommended", "plugin:react/recommended"]
   };
   ```

   The `env` field sets the actual environment our code will run in and will use `es6` functions in it, while the `parserOptions` field adds extra configuration for using `jsx` and modern JavaScript. Where things get interesting, however, is the `plugins` field, which is where we specify that our code uses `react` as a framework. The `extends` field is where the `recommended` settings for `eslint` are used, as well as framework-specific settings for React.

We can run the `eslint --init` command to create custom settings, but using the preceding settings is recommended, so that we ensure the stability of our React code.

3. If we look at our command line or browser, we will see no errors. However, we have to add the `eslint-loader` package to the webpack configuration. In the `webpack.config.js` file, add `eslint-loader` next to `babel-loader`:

```
...

module.exports = {
    module: {
        rules: [
            {
                test: /\.js$/,
                exclude: /node_modules/,
+               use: ['babel-loader', 'eslint-loader']
            },
            {
                test: /\.css$/,
                use: ['style-loader', 'css-loader']
            }
        ]
    },
    plugins: [htmlPlugin]
};
```

By restarting the development server, webpack will now use ESLint to check whether our JavaScript code complies with the configuration of ESLint. In our command line (or Console tab in the browser), the following error should be visible:

```
movieList/src/components/Card/Card.js
    3:17   error 'movie' is missing in props validation   react/prop-types
```

When using React, it's recommended that we validate any props we send to components since JavaScript's dynamic type system may lead to situations where variables are undefined or have an incorrect type. Our code will work without us having to validate the props, but to fix this error we have to install the `prop-types` package, which used to be a feature of React but was later deprecated. Let's get started:

1. The package that we use to check for prop types can be installed from npm:

```
npm install --save prop-types
```

2. Now, we can validate `propTypes` in our component by importing the package into the `Card` component and adding the validation to the bottom of this file:

```
  import React from 'react';
+ import PropTypes from 'prop-types';

  const Card = ({ movie }) => {
      ...
  };

+ Card.propTypes = {
+     movie: PropTypes.shape({}),
+ };

  export default Card;
```

3. If we look at the command line again, we'll see that the missing `propTypes` validation error has disappeared. However, the validation for our props still isn't very specific. We can make this more specific by also specifying the `propTypes` of all the fields of the `movie` prop:

```
  ...

  Card.propTypes = {
-     movie: PropTypes.shape({}),
+     movie: PropTypes.shape({
+       title: PropTypes.string,
+       distributor: PropTypes.string,
+       year: PropTypes.number,
+       amount: PropTypes.string,
+       img: PropTypes.shape({
+         src: PropTypes.string,
+         alt: PropTypes.string
+       }),
+       ranking: PropTypes.number
+     }).isRequired
  };
```

We can also indicate which props are required for React to render the component by adding `isRequired` to the `propTypes` validation.

Congratulations! You have created a basic React application from scratch using React, ReactDom, webpack, Babel, and ESLint.

Summary

In this chapter, you've created a movie list application for React from scratch and learned about core React concepts. This chapter started with you creating a new project with webpack and Babel. These libraries help you compile and run your JavaScript and React code in the browser with minimal setup. Then, we described how to structure a React application. This structure will be used throughout this book. The principles that were applied provided you with the basics from which to create React applications from nothing and structure them in a scalable way.

If you've been working with React before, then these concepts probably weren't that hard to grasp. If you haven't, then don't worry if some concepts felt strange to you. The upcoming chapters will build upon the features that you used in this chapter, giving you enough time to fully understand them.

The project you'll build in the next chapter will focus on creating reusable React components with more advanced styling. This will be available offline since it will be set up as a **Progressive Web Application (PWA)**.

Further reading

- Thinking in React https://reactjs.org/docs/thinking-in-react.html
- Bootstrap https://getbootstrap.com/docs/4.3/getting-started/introduction/
- ESLint https://eslint.org/docs/user-guide/getting-started

2
Creating a Progressive Web Application with Reusable React Components

Do you already feel familiar with React's core concepts after completing the first chapter? Great! This chapter will be no problem for you! If not, don't worry – most of the concepts you came across in the previous chapter will be repeated. However, if you want to get more experience with webpack and Babel, it's recommended that you try creating the project in Chapter 1, *Creating a Movie List Application in React*, again since this chapter won't be covering those topics.

In this chapter, you'll work with Create React App, a starter kit (created by the React core team to get you started with React quickly) that can be used as a **Progressive Web App (PWA)** – a web application that behaves like a mobile application. It will make the configuration of module bundlers and compilers such as webpack and Babel unnecessary as this will be taken care of in the Create React App package. This means you can focus on building your GitHub portfolio application as a PWA that reuses React components and styling.

Alongside setting up Create React App, the following topics will be covered in this chapter:

- Creating a Progressive Web App
- Building reusable React components
- Styling in React with `styled-components`

Can't wait? Let's continue!

Project overview

In this chapter, we will create a PWA that has reusable React components and styling using Create React App and `styled-components`. The application will use data fetched from the public GitHub API.

The build time is 1.5-2 hours.

Getting started

The project you'll create in this chapter will use the public API from GitHub, which you can find at `https://developer.github.com/v3/`. To be able to use this API, you need to have a GitHub account, since you'll want to retrieve information from a GitHub user account. If you don't have a GitHub account yet, you can create one by registering on its website. Also, you need to download the GitHub logo pack from here: `https://github-media-downloads.s3.amazonaws.com/GitHub-Mark.zip`. The complete source code for this application can also be found on GitHub: `https://github.com/PacktPublishing/React-Projects/tree/ch2`.

GitHub portfolio application

In this section, we will learn how to create a new React project using Create React App and set it up as a PWA that reuses React components and styling with `styled-components`.

Creating a PWA with Create React App

Having to configure webpack and Babel every time we create a new React project can be quite time-consuming. Also, the settings for every project can change and it becomes hard to manage all of these configurations when we want to add new features to our project.

Therefore, the React core team introduced a starter kit known as Create React App and released a stable version of it, 2.0, in 2018. By using Create React App, we no longer have to worry about managing compile and build configurations, even when newer versions of React are released, which means we can focus on coding instead of configurations. Also, it has features we can use to easily create a PWA.

A PWA is usually faster and more reliable than regular web applications as it focuses on an offline/cache-first approach. This makes it possible for users to still open our application when they have no or a slow internet connection due to its focus on caching. Also, users can add our application to the home screen of their smartphone or tablet and open it like a native application.

This section will show us how to create a React application with PWA features, starting with setting up a new application with Create React App.

Installing Create React App

Create React App can be installed by using the command line, where we should install it globally so that the package is available everywhere on our local computer and not just in a specific project:

```
npm install -g create-react-app
```

Now that the `create-react-app` package has been installed, we're ready to create our first Create React App project. There are multiple ways to set up a new project, but since we're already familiar with `npm`, there are only two methods we need to learn about. Let's get started:

1. The first method is to create a new project with `npm` by running the following command:

   ```
   npm init react-app github-portfolio
   ```

   You can replace `github-portfolio` with any other name you want to use for this project.

2. Alternatively, we can use `npx`, a tool that comes preinstalled with `npm` (v5.2.0 or higher) and simplifies the way we execute `npm` packages:

   ```
   npx create-react-app github-portfolio
   ```

Both methods will start the installation process for Create React App, which can take several minutes, depending on your hardware. Although we're only executing one command, the installer for Create React App will install the packages we need to run our React application. Therefore, it will install `react`, `react-dom`, and `react-scripts`, where the last package includes all the configuration for compiling, running, and building React applications.

If we move into the project's root directory, which is named after our project name, we will see that it has the following structure:

```
github-portfolio
|-- node_modules
|-- public
    |-- favicon.ico
    |-- index.html
    |-- manifest.json
|-- src
    |-- App.css
    |-- App.js
    |-- App.test.js
    |-- index.css
    |-- index.js
    |-- logo.svg
    |-- serviceWorker.js
.gitignore
package.json
```

This structure looks a lot like the one we set up in the first chapter, although there are some slight differences. The public directory includes all the files that shouldn't be included in the compile and build process, and the files inside this directory are the only files that can be directly used inside the index.html file. The manifest.json file contains the default configuration for a PWA, which is something we'll learn more about later on in this chapter.

In the other directory, called src, we will find all the files that will be compiled and built when we execute any of the scripts inside the package.json file. There is a component called App, which is defined by the App.js, App.test.js, and App.css files, and a file called index.js, which is the entry point for Create React App. The serviceWorker.js file is needed to set up the PWA and is also something that will be discussed in the next part of this section.

If we open the package.json file, we'll see that three scripts have been defined: start, build, and test. Since testing is something that isn't yet handled at this point yet, we can ignore this script for now. To be able to open the project in the browser, we can simply type in the following command into the command line, which runs package react-scripts in development mode:

```
npm start
```

If we visit `http://localhost:3000/`, the default Create React App page will look as follows:

Since `react-scripts` supports hot reloading by default, any changes we make to the code will result in a page reload. If we run the build script, a new directory called `build` will be created in the projects' root directory, where the minified bundle of our application can be found.

With the basic installation of Create React App in place, the next part of this section will show us how to enable the features that turn this application into a PWA.

Creating a PWA

Create React App comes with a configuration for that supports PWA, generated when we initiate the build script. We can set up our Create React App project as a PWA by accessing the `src/index.js` file and changing the last line, which will register the `serviceWorker`:

```
import React from 'react';
import ReactDOM from 'react-dom';
import './index.css';
import App from './App';
import * as serviceWorker from './serviceWorker';

ReactDOM.render(<App />, document.getElementById('root'));

// If you want your app to work offline and load faster, you can change
// unregister() to register() below. Note this comes with some pitfalls.
// Learn more about service workers: http://bit.ly/CRA-PWA
```

```
- //serviceWorker.register();
+ serviceWorker.register();
```

Now, when we run the build script, the minified bundle of our application will use the offline/cache first approach. Under the hood, `react-scripts` uses a package called `workbox-webpack-plugin`, which works together with webpack 4 to serve our application as a PWA. It doesn't only cache local assets placed in the `public` directory; it also caches navigation requests so that our application acts more reliably on unstable mobile networks.

The other file that plays a part in setting up the PWA using Create React App is `manifest.json`. Most of the configuration for our PWA is placed here, which we can see if we open the `public/manifest.json` file. In this configuration JSON file, we will find the most important pieces for operating systems and browsers. Let's break this down:

1. This file contains the `short_name` and `name` fields, which describe how our application should be identified to users:

    ```
    {
      "short_name": "React App",
      "name": "Create React App Sample",

    . . .
    ```

    The `short_name` field should be no longer than 12 characters and will be shown underneath the application icon on the user's home screen. For the `name` field, we can use up to 45 characters. This is the main identifier for our application and can be seen during the process of adding the application to the home screen.

2. Which particular icon users see when they add our application to the home screen can be configured in the `icons` field:

    ```
    "icons": [
      {
        "src": "favicon.ico",
        "sizes": "64x64 32x32 24x24 16x16",
        "type": "image/x-icon"
      }
    ],
    ```

As you can see, the `favicon.ico` file is used as the only icon and is served in multiple sizes in `image/x-icon` format. As we mentioned previously, the same rule for `index.html` applies to `manifest.json`. Only files that are placed in the public directory can be referred to from this file.

3. Finally, using the `theme_color` and `background_color` fields, we can set the colors (in HEX format) for the top bar when our application is opened from the home screen on a mobile device:

```
...
"theme_color": "#000000",
"background_color": "#ffffff"
}
```

The default toolbar with the URL box isn't displayed; instead, a top bar is shown. This behavior is similar to native mobile applications.

 Another thing we can handle with this configuration file is internalization, which is useful when our application serves content in different languages. We can also add versioning to this file if there are multiple versions of our application in production.

The changes we made here configured the application so that it functions as a PWA, but don't make these features available to the user just yet. In the next part of this section, we'll learn how to serve this PWA and make it visible in the browser.

Serving the PWA

With the configuration of our PWA in place, it's time to see how this will affect the application. If you still have your Create React App running (if not, execute the `npm start` command again), visit the project at `http://localhost:3000/`. We will see that nothing has changed yet. As we mentioned previously, the PWA will only be visible when the build version of our application is open. To do this, execute the following command in the projects' root directory:

```
npm run build
```

This will initiate the build process, which minifies our application to a bundle that's stored inside the build directory. This built version of our application can be served from our local machine. If we look at the output of the build process on the command line, we will see that Create React App suggested how we should serve this build version:

```
npm install -g serve
serve -s build
```

The npm install command installs the serve package, which is used to serve built static sites or, in this case, JavaScript applications. After installing this package, we can use it to deploy the build directory on our server or local machine by running the following:

```
serve -s build
```

 The -s flag is used to redirect any navigation requests that aren't found back to our index.js file.

If we visit our project in the browser at http://localhost:5000/, we'll see that everything looks exactly like the version we're running on http://localhost:3000/. There is one big difference, however: the build version is running as a PWA. This means that if our internet connections fails, the application will still be shown. We can try this out by disconnecting our internet connection or stopping the serve package from the command line. If we refresh the browser on http://localhost:5000/, we will see the exact same application.

How does this work? If we open up the **Developer tools** in our browser (Chrome or Firefox) and visit the **Application** tab, we'll see items in the sidebar. The one we should open first is called **Service Workers**. The result will look similar to what's shown in the following screenshot if you're using Chrome as your browser:

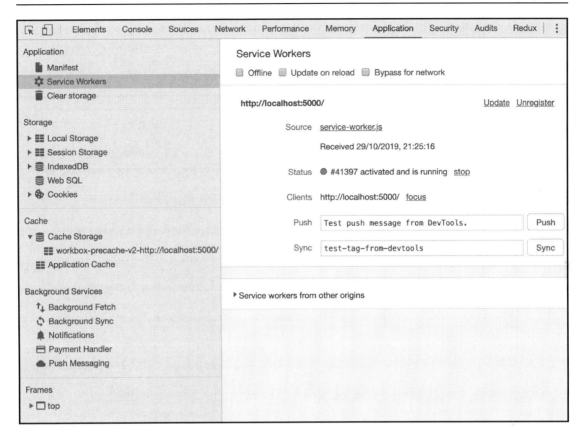

If we click on the **Service Worker** sidebar item, we will see a list of all the service workers that are running. For `localhost`, there's one active service worker that has `service-worker.js` as its source – the same file that is inside our project. This file makes sure that a cached version of our application is served if there is no or a slow internet connection.

The service worker shouldn't be active when we have a local instance of our application running with `npm start`. Since the service worker will cache our application, we won't be able to see any of the changes that we've made since the cached version will be a server.

These cache files are stored inside the browser cache and can also be found in this toolbar under **Cache Storage**. Here, we may see multiple cache locations, which are created by the `workbox-webpack-plugin` package when we build the application.

The one that's relevant to serving our application is called `workbox-precache-v2-http://localhost:5000/` and consists of all the cached files for our application:

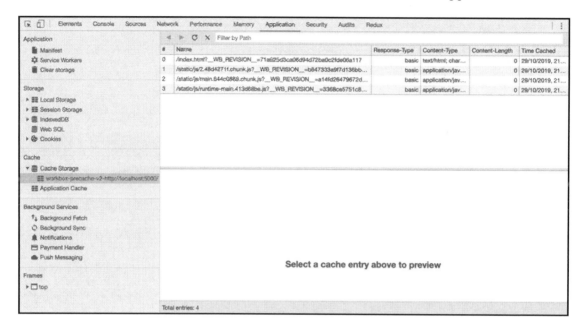

In the preceding screenshot, we can see which files are being cached by the browser for our application, where the `index.html` file is the entry point of the application and files starting with `static/` are created during the build process and represent the minified bundle of our application. As we can see, it consists of minified `.js`, `.css`, and `.svg` files, which are stored inside the browser cache. Each time a user loads our application, it will try to serve those files first before looking for an internet connection.

With our first PWA created and with Create React App in place, we will start looking at creating the components for our project and styling them.

Building reusable React components

Creating React components with JSX was briefly discussed in the previous chapter, but in this chapter, we'll explore this topic further by creating components that we can reuse throughout our application. First, let's look at how to structure our application, which builds upon the contents of the previous chapter.

Structuring our application

To begin, we'll need to structure our application in the same way that we did in the first chapter. This means that we need to create two new directories called `components` and `containers` inside the `src` directory. The files for the `App` component can be moved to the `container` directory, and the `App.test.js` file can be deleted since testing hasn't been covered yet.

After creating the directories and moving the files, our application structure will look as follows:

```
github-portfolio
|-- node_modules
|-- public
    |-- favicon.ico
    |-- index.html
    |-- manifest.json
|-- src
    |-- components
    |-- containers
    |-- App.css
    |-- App.js
    |-- index.css
    |-- index.js
    |-- serviceWorker.js
.gitignore
package.json
```

Don't forget to change the location of the import for the `App` component in `src/index.js`:

```
import React from 'react';
import ReactDOM from 'react-dom';
import './index.css';
- import App from './App';
+ import App from './containers/App';
import * as serviceWorker from './serviceWorker';

ReactDOM.render(<App />, document.getElementById('root'));

...
```

Do the same for the location of the React `logo` in `src/containers/App.js`:

```
import React, { Component } from 'react';
- import logo from './logo.svg';
+ import logo from '../logo.svg';
import './App.css';
```

```
class App extends Component {

  ...
```

If we run `npm start` again and visit the project in the browser, there will be no visible changes since we've only changed the structure of the project and none of its content.

Our project still consists of only one component, which doesn't make it very reusable. The next step will be to divide our `App` component into `Components` as well. If we look at the source code for this component in `App.js`, we'll see that there's already a CSS `header` element in the return function. Let's change that `header` element into a React component:

1. First, create a new directory called `Header` inside the `components` directory and copy the styling for `classNames`, `App-header`, `App-logo`, and `App-link` into a new file called `Header.css`:

```css
.App-logo {
  height: 40vmin;
  pointer-events: none;
}

.App-header {
  background-color: #282c34;
  display: flex;
  flex-direction: column;
  align-items: center;
  justify-content: center;
  font-size: calc(10px + 2vmin);
  color: white;
}

.App-link {
  color: #61dafb;
}

@keyframes App-logo-spin {
  from {
    transform: rotate(0deg);
  }
  to {
    transform: rotate(360deg);
  }
}
```

2. Now, create a file called `Header.js` inside this directory. This file should return the same content as the `<header>` element:

```
import React from 'react';
import './Header.css';

const Header = () => (
  <header className='App-header'>
      <img src={logo} className='App-logo' alt='logo' />
      <p>
        Edit <code>src/App.js</code> and save to reload.
      </p>
      <a
        className='App-link'
        href='https://reactjs.org'
        target='_blank'
        rel='noopener noreferrer'
      >
        Learn React
      </a>
  </header>
);

export default Header;
```

3. Import this `Header` component inside your `App` component and add it to the `return` function:

```
import React, { Component } from 'react';
+ import Header from '../components/App/Header';
import logo from '../logo.svg';
import './App.css';

class App extends Component {
  render() {
    return (
      <div className='App'>
-        <header className='App-header'>
-          <img src={logo} className='App-logo' alt='logo' />
-          <p>Edit <code>src/App.js</code> and save to reload.</p>
-          <a
-            className='App-link'
-            href='https://reactjs.org'
-            target='_blank'
-            rel='noopener noreferrer'
-          >
-            Learn React
-          </a>
```

```
-        </header>
+        <Header />
       </div>
     );
   }
 }

 export default App;
```

When we visit our project in the browser again, we'll see an error saying that the value for the logo is undefined. This is because the new `Header` component can't reach the `logo` constant that's been defined inside the `App` component. From what we've learned in the first chapter, we know that this logo constant should be added as a prop to the `Header` component so that it can be displayed. Let's do this now:

1. Send the `logo` constant as a prop to the `Header` component
   in `src/container/App.js`:

```
...
class App extends Component {
 render() {
   return (
     <div className='App'>
-        <Header />
+        <Header logo={logo} />
     </div>
   );
 }
}

export default App;
```

2. Get the `logo` prop so that it can be used by the `img` element as an `src` attribute
   in `src/components/App/Header.js`:

```
import React from 'react';

- const Header = () => (
+ const Header = ({ logo }) => (
 <header className='App-header'>
   <img src={logo} className='App-logo' alt='logo' />
   ...
```

In the previous chapter, the use of the `prop-types` package was demonstrated but this is something that isn't used in this chapter. If you'd like to use `prop-types` in this chapter as well, you can install the package from `npm` using `npm install prop-types` and import it inside the files where you want to use it.

Here, we won't see any visible changes when we open the project in the browser. But if we open up the React Developer Tools, we will see that the project is now divided into an `App` component and a `Header` component. This component receives the `logo` prop in the form of a `.svg` file, as shown in the following screenshot:

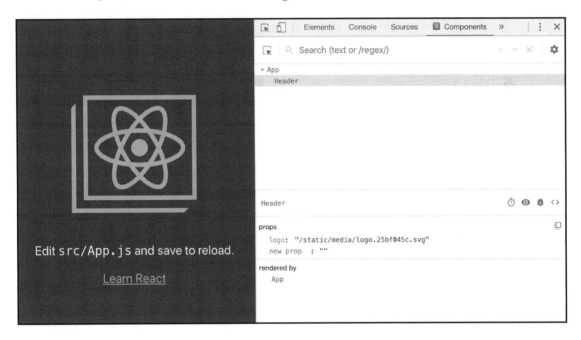

The `Header` component is still divided into multiple elements that can be split into separate components. Looking at the `img` and `p` elements, they look pretty simple already. However, the `a` element looks more complicated and takes attributes such as `url`, `title`, `className`, and so in. To change this `a` element into a component we can reuse, it needs to be moved to a different location in our project.

To do this, create a new directory called `Link` inside the `components` directory. Inside this directory, create a new file called `Link.js`. This file should return the same `a` element that we've already got inside our `Header` component. Also, we can send both the `url` and `title` to this component as a prop. Let's do this now:

1. Delete the styling for the `App-link` class from `src/components/Header/Header.css` and place this inside a file called `Link.css`:

   ```
   .App-link {
       color: #61dafb;
   }
   ```

2. Create a new component called `Link` that takes the `url` and `title` props. This component adds these props as attributes to the `<a>` element in `src/components/Link/Link.js`:

   ```
   import React from 'react';
   import './Link.css';

   const Link = ({ url, title }) => (
     <a
       className='App-link'
       href={url}
       target='_blank'
       rel='noopener noreferrer'
     >
       {title}
     </a>
   );

   export default Link;
   ```

3. Import this `Link` component and place it inside the `Header` component in `src/components/Header/Header.js`:

   ```
   import React from 'react';
   + import Link from '../Link/Link';

   const Header = ({ logo }) => (
    <header className='App-header'>
      <img src={logo} className='App-logo' alt='logo' />
      <p>Edit <code>src/App.js</code> and save to reload.</p>
   -  <a
   -    className='App-link'
   -    href='https://reactjs.org'
   ```

```
-       target='_blank'
-       rel='noopener noreferrer'
-     >
-       Learn React
-     </a>
+     <Link url='https://reactjs.org' title='Learn React' />
    </header>
  );

export default Header;
```

Our code should now look like the following, meaning that we've successfully split the directories into `containers` and `components`, where the components are placed in separate subdirectories that have been named after the components:

```
github-portfolio
|-- node_modules
|-- public
    |-- favicon.ico
    |-- index.html
    |-- manifest.json
|-- src
    |-- components
        |-- Header
            |-- Header.js
            |-- Header.css
        |-- Link
            |-- Link.js
            |-- Link.css
    |-- containers
        |-- App.css
        |-- App.js
    |-- index.css
    |-- index.js
    |-- serviceWorker.js
.gitignore
package.json
```

However, if we take a look at the project in the browser, no visible changes are present. In React Developer Tools, however, the structure of our application has already taken shape. The `App` component is shown as the parent component in the component tree, while the `Header` component is a child component that has `Link` as a child.

In the next part of this section, we'll add more components to the component tree of this application and make these reusable throughout the application.

Reusing components in React

The project we're building in this chapter is a GitHub portfolio page; it will show our public information and a list of public repositories. Therefore, we need to fetch the official GitHub REST API (v3) and pull information from two endpoints. Fetching data is something we did in the first chapter, but this time, the information won't come from a local JSON file. The method to retrieve the information is almost the same. We'll use the fetch API to do this.

We can retrieve our public GitHub information from GitHub by executing the following command. Replace the `username` at the end of the bold section of code with your own `username`:

```
curl 'https://api.github.com/users/username'
```

 If you don't have a GitHub profile or haven't filled out all the necessary information, you can also use the `octocat` username. This is the username of the GitHub `mascotte` and is already filled with sample data.

This request will return the following output:

```
{
  "login": "octocat",
  "id": 1,
  "node_id": "MDQ6VXNlcjE=",
  "avatar_url": "https://github.com/images/error/octocat_happy.gif",
  "gravatar_id": "",
  "url": "https://api.github.com/users/octocat",
  "html_url": "https://github.com/octocat",
  "followers_url": "https://api.github.com/users/octocat/followers",
  "following_url":
"https://api.github.com/users/octocat/following{/other_user}",
  "gists_url": "https://api.github.com/users/octocat/gists{/gist_id}",
  "starred_url":
"https://api.github.com/users/octocat/starred{/owner}{/repo}",
  "subscriptions_url":
"https://api.github.com/users/octocat/subscriptions",
  "organizations_url": "https://api.github.com/users/octocat/orgs",
  "repos_url": "https://api.github.com/users/octocat/repos",
  "events_url": "https://api.github.com/users/octocat/events{/privacy}",
  "received_events_url":
"https://api.github.com/users/octocat/received_events",
  "type": "User",
  "site_admin": false,
  "name": "monalisa octocat",
```

```
    "company": "GitHub",
    "blog": "https://github.com/blog",
    "location": "San Francisco",
    "email": "octocat@github.com",
    "hireable": false,
    "bio": "There once was...",
    "public_repos": 2,
    "public_gists": 1,
    "followers": 20,
    "following": 0,
    "created_at": "2008-01-14T04:33:35Z",
    "updated_at": "2008-01-14T04:33:35Z"
}
```

Multiple fields in the JSON output are highlighted since these are the fields we'll use in the application. These are `avatar_url`, `html_url`, `repos_url`, `name`, `company`, `location`, `email`, and `bio`, where the value of the `repos_url` field is actually another API endpoint that we need to call to retrieve all the repositories of this user. This is something we'll do later in this chapter.

Since we want to display this result in the application, we need to do the following:

1. To retrieve this public information from GitHub, create a new container called `Profile` and add the following code to `src/containers/Profile.js`:

```
import React, { Component } from 'react';

class Profile extends Component {
  constructor() {
    super();
    this.state = {
      data: {},
      loading: true,
    }
  }
  async componentDidMount() {
    const profile = await
fetch('https://api.github.com/users/octocat');
    const profileJSON = await profile.json();

    if (profileJSON) {
      this.setState({
        data: profileJSON,
        loading: false,
      })
    }
  }
```

```
    render() {
      return (
        <div></div>
      );
    }
  }

  export default Profile;
```

This new component contains a `constructor`, where the initial value for `state` is set and a `componentDidMount` life cycle method, which is used asynchronously, sets a new value for `state` when the fetched API returns a result. No result has been rendered yet since we still need to create new components to display the data.

Now, import this new component into the `App` component:

```
import React, { Component } from 'react';
+ import Profile from './Profile';
import Header from '../components/Header/Header';
import logo from '../logo.svg';
import './App.css';

class App extends Component {
  render() {
    return (
      <div className='App'>
        <Header logo={logo} />
+       <Profile />
      </div>
    );
  }
}

export default App;
```

2. A quick look at the browser where our project is running shows that this new `Profile` component isn't visible yet. This is because the `Header.css` file has a `height` attribute with a `view-height` of `100`, meaning that the component will take up the entire height of the page. To change this, open the `scr/components/App/Header.css` file and change the following highlighted lines:

```
.App-logo {
- height: 40vmin;
+ height: 64px;
```

```
  pointer-events: none;
}

.App-header {
  background-color: #282c34;
- min-height: 100vh;
+ height: 100%;
  display: flex;
  flex-direction: column;
  align-items: center;
  justify-content: center;
  font-size: calc(10px + 2vmin);
  color: white;
}

...
```

3. There should be enough free space on our page to display the
   Profile component, so we can open the scr/containers/Profile.js file
   once more and display the
   avatar_url, html_url, repos_url, name, company, location, email and bi
   o fields that were returned by the Github API:

```
  ...

render() {
+    const { data, loading } = this.state;

+    if (loading) {
+        return <div>Loading...</div>;
+    }

    return (
      <div>
+        <ul>
+          <li>avatar_url: {data.avatar_url}</li>
+          <li>html_url: {data.html_url}</li>
+          <li>repos_url: {data.repos_url}</li>
+          <li>name: {data.name}</li>
+          <li>company: {data.company}</li>
+          <li>location: {data.location}</li>
+          <li>email: {data.email}</li>
+          <li>bio: {data.bio}</li>
+        </ul>
      </div>
    );
  }
```

```
  }

  export default Profile;
```

Once we've saved this file and visited our project in the browser, we will see a bulleted list of the GitHub information being displayed, as shown in the following screenshot:

Since this doesn't look very pretty and the header doesn't match with the content of the page, let's make some changes to the `styling` files for these two components:

1. Change the code for the `Header` component, remove the React logo, and replace it with the GitHub logo. We no longer need to take `logo` as a prop from the `App` component. Also, the `Link` component can be deleted from here as we'll be using it in a `Profile` component later on:

```
import React from 'react';
- import logo from '../logo.svg';
+ import logo from '../../GitHub-Mark-Light-64px.png';
- import Link from '../components/Link';
import './Header.css';

- const Header = ({ logo }) => (
+ const Header = () => (
  <header className='App-header'>
    <img src={logo} className='App-logo' alt='logo' />
-   <p>
+   <h1>
-     Edit <code>src/App.js</code> and save to reload.
```

```
+       My Github Portfolio
-       </p>
+       </h1>
+       <Link url='https://reactjs.org' title='Learn React' />
    </header>
  );

  export default Header;
```

2. Change the highlighted lines in `scr/containers/Profile.js`, where we'll separate the avatar image from the bulleted list and add a `strong` element around the field names. Remember the `Link` component we created previously? This will be used to create a link to our profile on the GitHub website:

```
import React, { Component } from 'react';
+ import Link from '../components/Link/Link';
+ import './Profile.css';

class Profile extends Component {

    ...

        return (
-           <div>
+           <div className='Profile-container'>
+               <img className='Profile-avatar' src={data.avatar_url}
alt='avatar' />
-               <ul>
-                   ...
-               </ul>
+               <ul>
+                   <li><strong>html_url:</strong> <Link
url={data.html_url} title='Github URL' /></li>
+                   <li><strong>repos_url:</strong> {data.repos_url}</li>
+                   <li><strong>name:</strong> {data.name}</li>
+                   <li><strong>company:</strong> {data.company}</li>
+                   <li><strong>location:</strong> {data.location}</li>
+                   <li><strong>email:</strong> {data.email}</li>
+                   <li><strong>bio:</strong> {data.bio}</li>
+               </ul>
+           </div>
        );
    }
}

export default Profile;
```

3. Don't forget to create the `src/containers/Profile.css` file and paste the following code into it. This defines the styling for the `Profile` component:

```css
.Profile-container {
  width: 50%;
  margin: 10px auto;
}

.Profile-avatar {
  width: 150px;
}

.Profile-container > ul {
 list-style: none;
 padding: 0;
 text-align: left;
}

.Profile-container > ul > li {
 display: flex;
 justify-content: space-between;
}
```

Finally, we can see that the application is starting to look like a GitHub portfolio page, with a header showing the GitHub logo icon and a title, followed by our GitHub avatar and a list of our public information. This results in an application that looks similar to what's shown in the following screenshot:

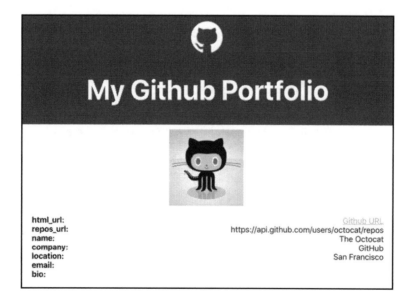

If we take a look at the code in the Profile component, we'll see that there is a lot of duplicate code, so we need to transform the list that's displaying our public information into a separate component. Let's get started:

1. Create a new file called List.js inside the new src/components/List directory:

```
import React from 'react';

const List = () => (
  <ul></ul>
);

export default List;
```

2. In the Profile component, which can be found in the src/containers/Profile.js file, we can import this new List component, construct a new array containing all the items we want to display inside this list, and send it as a prop. For the html_url field, we'll be sending the Link component as a value instead of the value that was returned from the GitHub API:

```
import React, { Component } from 'react';
import Link from '../components/Link/Link';
+ import List from '../components/List/List';

class Profile extends Component {

...

render() {
  const { data, loading } = this.state;

  if (loading) {
    return <div>Loading...</div>;
  }

+ const items = [
+   { label: 'html_url', value: <Link url={data.html_url}
title='Github URL' /> },
+   { label: 'repos_url', value: data.repos_url },
+   { label: 'name', value: data.name},
+   { label: 'company', value: data.company },
+   { label: 'location', value: data.location },
+   { label: 'email', value: data.email },
+   { label: 'bio', value: data.bio }
```

```
+ ]

    return (
      <div className='Profile-container'>
        <img className='Profile-avatar' src={data.avatar_url}
alt='avatar' />
-       <ul>
-         <li><strong>html_url:</strong> <Link url={data.html_url}
title='Github URL' /></li>
-         <li><strong>repos_url:</strong> {data.repos_url}</li>
-         <li><strong>name:</strong> {data.name}</li>
-         <li><strong>company:</strong> {data.company}</li>
-         <li><strong>location:</strong> {data.location}</li>
-         <li><strong>email:</strong> {data.email}</li>
-         <li><strong>bio:</strong> {data.bio}</li>
-       </ul>
+       <List items={items} />
      </div>
    );
  }
}

export default Profile;
```

3. In the `List` component, we can now map over the `items` prop and return the list items with styling:

```
import React from 'react';

- const List = () => (
+ const List = ({ items }) => (
  <ul>
+   {items.map(item =>
+     <li key={item.label}>
+       <strong>{item.label}</strong>{item.value}
+     </li>
+   )}
  </ul>
);

export default List;
```

Assuming we executed the preceding steps correctly, your application shouldn't have changed aesthetically. However, if we take a look at the React Developer Tools, we will see that some changes have been made to the component tree.

In the next section, we'll style these components using `styled-components` instead of CSS and add repositories that are linked to our GitHub account.

Styling in React with styled-components

So far, we've been using CSS files to add styling to our React components. However, this forces us to import these files across different components, which makes our code less reusable. Therefore, we'll add the `styled-components` package to the project, which allows us to write CSS inside JavaScript (so-called **CSS-in-JS**) and create components.

By doing this, we'll get more flexibility out of styling our components, will be able to prevent duplication or overlapping of styles due to `classNames`, and we'll add dynamic styling to components with ease. All of this can be done using the same syntax we used for CSS, right inside our React components.

The first step is installing `styled-components` using npm:

```
npm install styled-components
```

 If you look at the official documentation of `styled-components`, you will notice that they strongly advise you to use the Babel plugin for this package as well. But since you're using Create React App to initialize your project, you don't need to add this plugin as all the compilation your application needs has already been taken care of by `react-scripts`.

After installing `styled-components`, let's try to delete the CSS file from one of our components. A good start would be the `Link` component since this is a very small component with limited functionality:

1. Start by importing the `styled-components` package and creating a new styled component called `InnerLink`. This component extends an `a` element and takes the CSS rules we already got for the `className App-link`:

```
import React from 'react';
+ import styled from 'styled-components';
import './Link.css';

+ const InnerLink = styled.a`
+   color: #61dafb;
+ `;

const Link = ({ url, title }) => (
  <a className='App-link'
```

```
            href={url}
            target='_blank'
            rel='noopener noreferrer'
        >
          {title}
        </a>
);

export default Link;
```

2. Once we've added this component, we can replace the existing <a> element with this styled component. Also, we no longer have to import the Link.css file since all the styling is now being done inside this JavaScript file:

```
import React from 'react';
import styled from 'styled-components';
- import './Link.css';

const InnerLink = styled.a`
 color: #61dafb;
`;

const Link = ({ url, title }) => (
- <a className='App-link'
+ <InnerLink
        href={url}
        target='_blank'
        rel='noopener noreferrer'
    >
      {title}
- </a>
+ </InnerLink>
);

export default Link;
```

If we visit our project in the browser after running npm start again, we'll see that our application still looks the same after deleting the CSS file. The next step is to replace all the other components that import CSS files for styling:

1. Add styled-components and delete the CSS file for the Header component inside src/components/Header/Header.js:

```
import React from 'react';
+ import styled from 'styled-components';
import logo from '../../GitHub-Mark-Light-64px.png';
- import './Header.css'
```

```
+ const HeaderWrapper = styled.div`
+   background-color: #282c34;
+   height: 100%;
+   display: flex;
+   flex-direction: column;
+   align-items: center;
+   justify-content: center;
+   font-size: calc(10px + 2vmin);
+   color: white;
+ `;

+ const Logo = styled.img`
+   height: 64px;
+   pointer-events: none;
+ `;

const Header = ({ logo }) => (
-   <header className='App-header'>
+   <HeaderWrapper>
      <Logo src={logo} alt='logo' />
      <h1>My Github Portfolio</h1>
-   </header>
+   </HeaderWrapper>
);

export default Header;
```

2. Add `styled-components` and delete the CSS file for the `App` component inside `src/containers/App.js`:

```
import React, { Component } from 'react';
+ import styled from 'styled-components';
import Profile from './Profile';
import Header from '../components/App/Header';
- import './App.css';

+ const AppWrapper = styled.div`
+   text-align: center;
+ `;

class App extends Component {
  render() {
    return (
-     <div className="App">
+     <AppWrapper>
        <Header />
        <Profile />
-     </div>
```

```
+     </AppWrapper>
    );
  }
}

export default App;
```

3. Add some styled components for the ul, li, and strong elements inside the List component:

```
import React from 'react';
+ import styled from 'styled-components';

+ const ListWrapper = styled.ul`
+   list-style: none;
+   text-align: left;
+   padding: 0;
+ `;

+ const ListItem = styled.li`
+   display: flex;
+   justify-content: space-between;
+ `;

+ const Label = styled.span`
+   font-weight: strong;
+ `;

const List = ({ items }) => (
- <ul>
+ <ListWrapper>
    {items.map(item =>
-     <li key={item.label}>
+     <ListItem key={item.label}>
-       <strong>{item.label}</strong>{item.value}
+       <Label>{item.label}</Label>{item.value}
-     </li>
+     </ListItem>
    )}
- </ul>
+ </ListWrapper>
);

export default List;
```

4. Finally, delete the `Profile.css` file from the `Profile` component by converting the last two elements with `classNames` into styled components:

```
import React, { Component } from 'react';
+ import styled from 'styled-components';
import Link from '../components/Link/Link';
import List from '../components/List/List';
- import './Profile.css';

+ const ProfileWrapper = styled.div`
+   width: 50%;
+   margin: 10px auto;
+ `;

+ const Avatar = styled.img`
+   width: 150px;
+ `;

class Profile extends Component {

...

  return (
-     <div className='Profile-container'>
+     <ProfileWrapper>
-       <img className='Profile-avatar' src={data.avatar_url}
alt='avatar' />
+       <Avatar src={data.avatar_url} alt='avatar' />
        <List items={items} />
-     </div>
+     </ProfileWrapper>
  );
  }
}

export default Profile;
```

Now, open the project in the browser again; our application should still look the same. All of our components have been converted so that they use `styled-components` and no longer use CSS files and `classNames` for styling. Don't forget to delete the `.css` files inside the `containers` and `components` directories and subdirectories.

However, there is still one CSS file in the project located directly inside the `src` directory. This CSS file contains the styling for the `<body>` element, which exists inside the `public/index.html` file and has been imported into the `src/index.js` file. To also delete this CSS file, we can use the `createGlobalStyle` function from `styled-components` to add styling for the `<body>` element to our application.

We can create a styled component for global styles inside the `App` component and paste the CSS styling for the `body` element inside it. Since this component should be at the same hierarchy in the component tree as our `AppWrapper` component, we need to use **React Fragments** since JSX components should be wrapped inside an enclosing tag:

```
  import React, { Component } from 'react';
- import styled from 'styled-components';
+ import styled, { createGlobalStyle } from 'styled-components';
  import Profile from './Profile';
  import Header from '../components/App/Header';

+ const GlobalStyle = createGlobalStyle`
+   body {
+     margin: 0;
+     padding: 0;
+     font-family: -apple-system, BlinkMacSystemFont, "Segoe UI", "Roboto",
"Oxygen",
+       "Ubuntu", "Cantarell", "Fira Sans", "Droid Sans", "Helvetica Neue",
+       sans-serif;
+     -webkit-font-smoothing: antialiased;
+     -moz-osx-font-smoothing: grayscale;
+   }
+ `;

  ...

  class App extends Component {
   render() {
     return (
+      <>
+      <GlobalStyle />
       <AppWrapper>
         <Header />
         <Profile />
       </AppWrapper>
```

```
+    </>
  );
  }
}

export default App;
```

 The <> tag is shorthand for <React.Fragment>. These React Fragments are used to list children components inside a single enclosing tag without the need to add extra nodes to the DOM.

Now, we should be able to delete the last CSS file in the project, that is, `src/index.css`. We can confirm this by looking at the project in the browser. We will see no changes to the `body` font that was being set by the `src/index.css` file.

The very last step is to display the repositories from our Github profile on this Github Portfolio page. The API endpoint that retrieves these repositories was also returned by the endpoint to retrieve our user information. To display these repositories, we can reuse the `List` component we created earlier:

1. Load the repository list from the API endpoint and add it to `state` in `src/containers/Profile.js`:

```
...

class Profile extends Component {
  constructor() {
    super();
    this.state = {
      data: {},
+     repositories: [],
      loading: true,
    }
  }

  async componentDidMount() {
    const profile = await
fetch('https://api.github.com/users/octocat');
    const profileJSON = await profile.json();

    if (profileJSON) {
+     const repositories = await fetch(profileJSON.repos_url);
+     const repositoriesJSON = await repositories.json();

      this.setState({
```

```
            data: profileJSON,
+           repositories: repositoriesJSON,
            loading: false,
          })
      }
    }

  render() {
-    const { data, loading } = this.state;
+    const { data, loading, repositories } = this.state;

    if (loading) {
      return <div>Loading...</div>
    }

    const items = [
      ...
    ];

+    const projects = repositories.map(repository => ({
+      label: repository.name,
+      value: <Link url={repository.html_url} title='Github URL' />
+    }));

  ...
```

2. Next, return a `List` component for the repositories and send a prop called `title` to this list. We're doing this since we want to show the difference between the two lists:

```
  ...

  render() {

  ...

    const projects = repositories.map(repository => ({
      label: repository.name,
      value: <Link url={repository.html_url} title='Github URL' />
    }));

    return (
      <ProfileWrapper>
        <Avatar src={data.avatar_url} alt='avatar' />
-        <List items={items} />
+        <List title='Profile' items={items} />
+        <List title='Projects' items={projects} />
      </ProfileWrapper>
```

```
      );
    }
  }

  export default Profile;
```

3. Make changes to the `List` component in `src/components/List/List.js` and display the title at the top of each list. In this scenario, we'll use React Fragments to prevent unnecessary nodes being added to the DOM:

```
  import React from 'react';
  import styled from 'styled-components';

+ const Title = styled.h2`
+   padding: 10px 0;
+   border-bottom: 1px solid lightGrey;
+ `;

  ...

- const List = ({ items }) => (
+ const List = ({ items, title }) => (
+   <>
+     <Title>{title}</Title>
      <ListWrapper>
        {items.map(item =>
          <ListItem key={item.label}>
            <Label>{item.label}</Label>{item.value}
          </ListItem>
        )}
      </ListWrapper>
+   </>
  );

  export default List;
```

Now, if we visit the project in the browser again, we will see the GitHub portfolio page we created in the chapter. This application will look something like what's shown in the following screenshot, where the default GitHub user from the previous section is used to fetch the data:

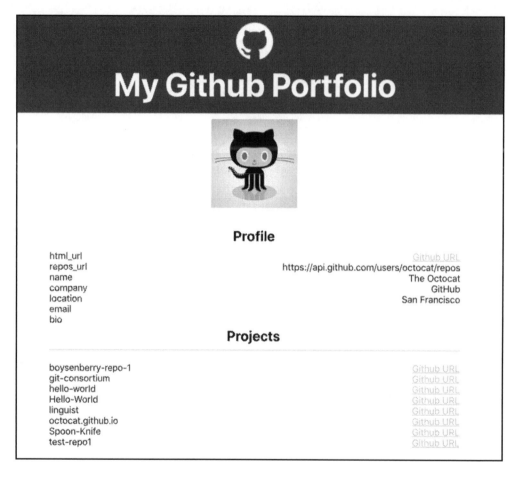

Now that we've used Create React App and enabled the project to be set up as a PWA, we should be able to see a cached version when we visit the build version of the project. To build the project, run the following command:

```
npm run build
```

Then, serve the build version by running the following command:

```
serve -s build
```

We can view the `build` version of our application by going to `http://localhost:5000/`. However, we'll probably see the very first version of our application. This is because the project has been created as a PWA and therefore a cached version of the application will be shown. We can restart the Service Worker and cache a fresh version of our application by going to the `Application` tab in the Developer Tools of our browser:

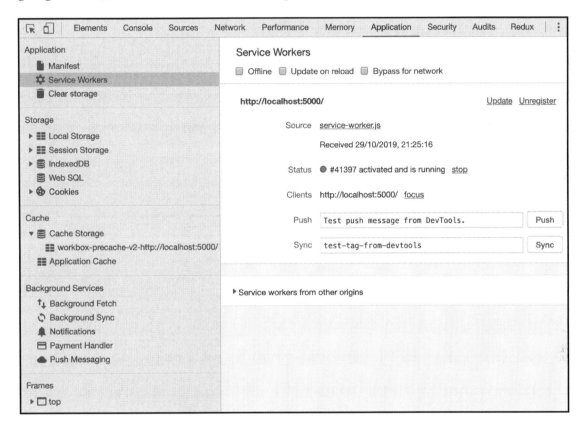

On this page, select **Service Workers** in the sidebar. From here, we can update the service worker for `localhost` by pressing the **Update** button. The `service-worker.js` file will be called again and the currently cached version will be replaced by a new one. We can also test how our application will respond when the internet connection fails by checking the `Offline` checkbox.

As we can see, the `Header` component has been cached properly, but no information from GitHub is being displayed. Instead, the `Profile` component displays a `Loading...` message since no information is being returned from the API request. If we open the Developer Tools in our browser and look at the console, we'll see an error message. We can catch this error to display the reason why our application contains no content:

1. To do this, we need to change the `src/containers/Profile.js` file and add a variable called `error` to `state`:

```
...

class Profile extends Component {
  constructor() {
    super();
    this.state = {
      data: {},
      repositories: [],
      loading: false,
+     error: '',
    }
  }

  async componentDidMount() {
    ...
```

2. This variable will either be an empty string or will contain the error message that's returned by the `try...catch` method:

```
...

  async componentDidMount() {
+   try {
      const profile = await
fetch('https://api.github.com/users/octocat');
      const profileJSON = await profile.json();

      if (profileJSON) {
        const repositories = await fetch(profileJSON.repos_url);
        const repositoriesJSON = await repositories.json();

        this.setState({
          data: profileJSON,
          repositories: repositoriesJSON,
          loading: false,
        });
      }
```

```
      }
+   catch(error) {
+     this.setState({
+       loading: false,
+       error: error.message,
+     });
+   }
+ }

    ...
```

3. When the component is rendered, the error state should also be taken from the state and displayed instead of the loading state if an error occurs:

```
    ...

render() {
-   const { data, loading, repositories } = this.state;
+   const { data, loading, repositories, error } = this.state;

-   if (loading) {
-     return <div>Loading...</div>;
+   if (loading || error) {
+     return <div>{loading ? 'Loading...' : error}</div>;
    }

    ...

export default Profile;
```

With these changes, the state now has an initial value for the loading state, which displays the `Loading...` message when the application first mounts. The GitHub endpoint is wrapped in a `try...catch` statement, meaning that we can catch the error message when the `fetch` function fails. If this happens, the value for `loading` will be replaced by the error message.

We can check whether these changes are working by building our application again and running it locally, like so:

```
npm run build
serve -s build
```

When we visit the project at `http://localhost:5000` and set the application to offline mode in the `Application` tab inside the browser's Developer Tools, we will see a `Failed to fetch` message being displayed. Now, we know that our users will see this message if they are using our application without an active internet connection.

Summary

In this chapter, you used Create React App to create your starter project for a React application, which comes with an initial configuration for libraries such as Babel and webpack. By doing this, you didn't have to configure these libraries yourself and don't have to worry about how your React code will run in the browser. Also, Create React App comes with a default setup for PWA, which you can use by registering a service worker. This makes your application run smoothly when there's no internet connection or when it's on a mobile device. Remember how you had to style your applications with CSS before? This chapter showed you how the `styled-components` package can be used to create components that are reusable and styled without importing any CSS files since it uses the CSS-in-JS principle.

Upcoming chapters will all feature projects that are created with Create React App, meaning that these projects don't require you to make changes to webpack or Babel. Did you enjoy using `styled-components` in this chapter? Then you're in for a treat as most of the projects in this book are styled with this package, including the next chapter.

In the next chapter, we will build upon this chapter by creating a dynamic project management board with React that uses features such as **Suspense**.

Further reading

- Create React App: `https://facebook.github.io/create-react-app/`
- Using npx: `https://medium.com/@maybekatz/introducing-npx-an-npm-package-runner-55f7d4bd282b`
- PWA with Create React App `https://facebook.github.io/create-react-app/docs/making-a-progressive-web-app`
- About the `manifest.json` file: `https://developers.chrome.com/apps/manifest`
- Styled components: `https://www.styled-components.com/docs/basics`

3
Build a Dynamic Project Management Board with React and Suspense

In the first two chapters of this book, you've already created two React projects all by yourself, and you should, by now, have a solid understanding of the core concepts of React. The concepts you've used so far will also be used in this chapter to create your third project with React, including some new and more advanced concepts that will show you the strength of using React. Again, if you feel you may lack some of the knowledge you'll need to finalize the contents of this chapter, you can always repeat what you have built so far.

This chapter will once again use Create React App, which you used in the previous chapter. During the development of the project management board application for this chapter, you'll use reusable components that have been created using `styled-components`. Following this, you'll use more advanced React techniques to control the dataflow throughout your components. Furthermore, HTML5 Web APIs will be used to dynamically drag and drop components that function as **Higher-Order Components (HOC)**.

The following topics will be covered in this chapter:

- React Suspense and code-splitting
- Using HOC
- Dynamic data flow

Project overview

In this chapter, we will create a **Progressive Web Application** (**PWA**) that has reusable React components and styling using Create React App and `styled-components`. The application will feature a dynamic drag and drop interface that uses the HTML5 Drag and Drop API.

The build time is 1.5-2 hours.

Getting started

The project that we'll create in this chapter builds upon an initial version that you can find on GitHub: `https://github.com/PacktPublishing/React-Projects/tree/ch3-initial`. The complete source code can also be found on GitHub: `https://github.com/PacktPublishing/React-Projects/tree/ch3`.

After downloading the initial application from GitHub, we can start by moving into its root directory and running the `npm install` command. This will install the core packages from Create React App (`react`, `react-dom`, and `react-scripts`) next to the `styled-components` package, which we used in the previous chapter. After the installation, we can start the application by executing the `npm start` command and visit the project in the browser by visiting `http://localhost:3000`.

We can also build the application by executing `npm run build` and subsequently `serve -s build`. The minified version of the application can now be visited at `http://localhost:5000`. Since it's been set up as a PWA, it will also work without any internet connection.

It's possible that you'll see a different application than when you ran the project locally, if you've built and served a Create React App PWA before. This is due to the service worker of the PWA that has stored a cached version of that application in the browser. You can delete any previous application from the browser cache by opening `devTools` and opening the **Application** tab, where you can click on the **Clear site data** button in the **Clear storage** section.

As shown in the following screenshot, the application has a basic header with a title and is divided into four columns. These columns are the lanes for the **Project Management Board** and will contain the individual tickets once we've connected the project to the data file:

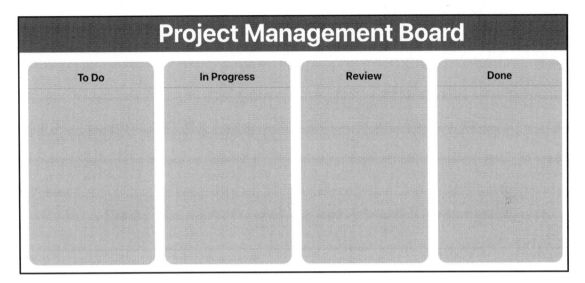

As we mentioned in `Chapter 2`, *Creating a Progressive Web Application with Reusable React Components*, we can check whether our application is running when there is no internet connection by visiting the **Service Workers** section of the **Application** tab. On this page, we can check the **Offline** checkbox and try refreshing the browser.

If we look at the project's structure, we'll see that it's structured in the same way as the projects in the previous chapters. The entry point of the application is the `src/index.js` file, which renders a component called `App`, which holds two other components called `Header` and `Board`. The first one is the actual header of the application, while the `Board` component holds the four columns we can see in the application. These columns are represented by the `Lane` component.

Also, in the `assets` directory, we will see a file called `data.json`, which contains data that we can display on the project management board:

```
project-management-board
|-- assets
    |-- data.json
|-- node_modules
|-- public
    |-- favicon.ico
```

```
            |-- index.html
            |-- manifest.json
    |-- src
        |-- components
            |-- Header
                |-- Header.js
            |-- Lane
                |-- Lane.js
        |-- containers
            |-- App.js
            |-- Board.js
        |-- index.js
        |-- serviceWorker.js
    .gitignore
    package.json
```

Creating a project management board application

In this section, we'll create a project management board PWA that uses React APIs such as Suspense and the HTML5 Drag and Drop API. We're going to use a Create React App, which we can find in the GitHub repository for this chapter.

Handling the data flow

With the initial version of the application in place, the next step is to fetch the data from the data file and handle its flow through the components. For this, we will use React Suspense and memo. With Suspense, we can access the React lazy API to dynamically load components and, with memo, we can control which components should rerender when their props change.

The first part of this section will show us how to load data from a data source using React life cycle methods and display this in React components.

Loading and displaying the data

Loading and displaying data that is retrieved from a data source is something we did in the previous chapter. This section will explore this further. Follow these steps to get started:

1. We will start by fetching the project data from the data file. To do this, we need to add the necessary functions to the `Board` component. We need these to access the React life cycles. These are `constructor`, where the initial state is set, and `componentDidMount`, where the data will be fetched:

```
. . .
class Board extends Component {
+ constructor() {
+   super();
+   this.state = {
+     data: [],
+     loading: true,
+     error: '',
+   }
+ }

+ async componentDidMount() {
+   try {
+     const tickets = await fetch('../../assets/data.json');
+     const ticketsJSON = await tickets.json();

+     if (ticketsJSON) {
+       this.setState({
+         data: ticketsJSON,
+         loading: false,
+       });
+     }
+   } catch(error) {
+     this.setState({
+       loading: false,
+       error: error.message,
+     });
+   }
+ }

  render() {
    . . .
  }
}

export default Board;
```

In the `componentDidMount` life cycle function, the data is fetched inside a `try..catch` statement. This statement catches any errors that are being returned from the data fetching process and replaces the error state with this message.

2. Now, we can distribute the tickets over the corresponding lanes:

```
...
class Board extends Component {
  ...
  render() {
+   const { data, loading, error } = this.state;

    const lanes = [
      { id: 1, title: 'To Do' },
      { id: 2, title: 'In Progress' },
      { id: 3, title: 'Review' },
      { id: 4, title: 'Done' },
    ];

    return (
      <BoardWrapper>
        {lanes.map(lane =>
          <Lane
            key={lane.id}
            title={lane.title}
+           loading={loading}
+           error={error}
+           tickets={data.filter(ticket => ticket.lane ===
            lane.id)}
          />
        )}
      </BoardWrapper>
    );
  }
}

export default Board;
```

In the preceding code, we can see that, inside `render`, the `data`, `loading`, and `error` constants have been destructured from the state object. Inside the function that iterates over the `lanes` constant, these values should be passed as props to the `Lane` component. For the data state, something special is going on since the `filter` function is being used to only return tickets from the `data` state that match the lane ID.

3. Next, we need to make some changes to the `Lane` component:

```
import React from 'react';
import styled from 'styled-components';
+ import Ticket from '../Ticket/Ticket';


...


+ const TicketsWrapper = styled.div`
+   padding: 5%;
+ `;

+ const Alert = styled.div`
+   text-align: center;
+ `;

- const Lane = ({ title }) => (
+ const Lane = ({ tickets, loading, error, title }) => (
    <LaneWrapper>
      <Title>{title}</Title>
+       {(loading || error) && <Alert>{loading ? 'Loading...' :
        error}</Alert>}
+       <TicketsWrapper>
+         {tickets.map(ticket => <Ticket key={ticket.id}
          ticket={ticket} />)}
+       </TicketsWrapper>
    </LaneWrapper>
);

export default Lane;
```

4. The `Lane` component now takes three other props, that is, `tickets`, `loading`, and `error`, where `tickets` contains the array of tickets from the `data` state, `loading` indicates whether the loading message should be displayed, and `error` contains the error message when there is one. We can see that a wrapper has been created and that, inside the `map` function, the `Ticket` component that displays the ticket information will be rendered. This `Ticket` component is also something we need to create in the `src/components` directory:

```
import React from 'react';
import styled from 'styled-components';

const TicketWrapper = styled.div`
  background: darkGray;
  padding: 20px;
  border-radius: 20px;

  &:not(:last-child) {
    margin-bottom: 5%;
  }
`;

const Title = styled.h3`
  width: 100%;
  margin: 0px;
`;

const Body = styled.p`
  width: 100%;
`;

const Ticket = ({ ticket }) => (
  <TicketWrapper>
    <Title>{ticket.title}</Title>
    <Body>{ticket.body}</Body>
  </TicketWrapper>
);

export default Ticket;
```

If we visit our application in a web browser at `http://localhost:3000`, we will see the following:

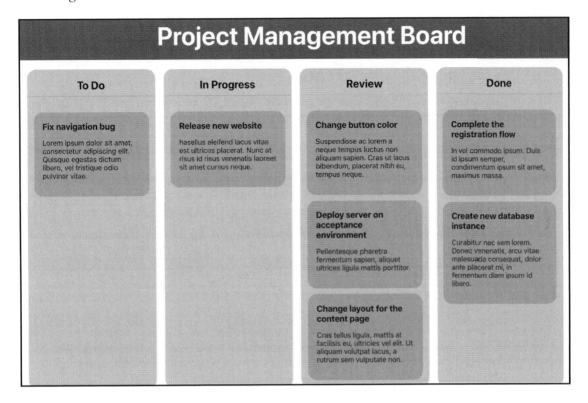

As this application has been set up as a PWA, we can build the project again and restart the service worker. In offline mode, the project should still display the header and the four columns, with a message inside these columns that displays **Failed to fetch**.

To build and serve the PWA, we need to run `npm run` and `serve -s build` after the build process has completed. Now, we can visit the project at `http://localhost:5000`. We may need to restart the service worker, which we can do in the `devTools` on the **Application** tab, and select the **Service Worker** section. On the right-hand side of this section, next to the service worker, press **Update**. To check out the application in offline mode, we need to check the **Offline** checkbox.

Fetching data from a data source is logic that can be reused throughout our application. In the next section, we will explore how this logic can be reused across multiple components with HOC.

Getting started with HOC

HOCs are advanced features in React that focus on the reusability of our components. They aren't part of the official React APIs, but introduce a pattern that is popular among the core team and many libraries, such as Redux.

In the first part of this section, we'll create our first HOC, which uses logic to retrieve data from the data source that we created in the previous section.

Creating HOC

As we mentioned previously, HOCs focus on reusing components. Therefore, it can best be described as follows:

"A HOC is a function that takes a component and returns a new component."

To explain what this means in practice, let's create an example. Our project has a `Board` component, which fetches and renders all the lanes. There is logic in this component in the form of a `constructor`, a `componentDidMount`, and information about how each `Lane` component is being rendered. How would we handle a situation where we just want to show a board without lanes, but only tickets? Do we just send different props to the `Board` component? Sure, that's possible, but, in React, that's what HOCs are used for.

A `Board` component without lanes wouldn't map over all the lanes and render the corresponding lane with the tickets as a prop. Instead, it would map over all the tickets and render them directly. Although the rendered components are different, the logic to set the initial state, fetch the data, and render the component(s) could be reused. The HOC should be able to add the life cycles to the `Board` component just by sending this component to it, along with some additional props.

To create the HOC, place a new file called `withDataFetching.js` inside the `src` directory. Now, follow these steps:

1. First, we need to import React and create a new function for the HOC which becomes the default export. Since this HOC will add the life cycles for data fetching, let's call this HOC `withDataFetching` and have it take a component as a parameter. This function should return another component:

```
+ import React from 'react';

+ export default function withDataFetching(WrappedComponent) {
+   return class extends React.Component {

+ }
```

2. Inside this returned component, add the `constructor` component, which has almost the same structure as the `Board` component:

```
    ...

  export default function withDataFetching(WrappedComponent) {
    return class extends React.Component {
+     constructor(props) {
+       super(props);
+       this.state = {
+         data: [],
+         loading: true,
+         error: '',
+       };
+     }
    ...
```

3. Next, we need to create the `componentDidMount` function, which is where the data fetching will be done. The `dataSource` prop is used as the location to fetch from. Also, notice that the constant names are now more generic and no longer specify a single use:

```
  export default function withDataFetching(WrappedComponent) {
    return class extends React.Component {

    ...

+   async componentDidMount() {
+     try {
+       const data = await fetch(this.props.dataSource);
+       const dataJSON = await data.json();
```

```
+       if (dataJSON) {
+         this.setState({
+           data: dataJSON,
+           loading: false,
+         });
+       }
+     } catch(error) {
+       this.setState({
+         loading: false,
+         error: error.message,
+       });
+     }
+   }

    ...
```

4. In the `render` function, we can return the `WrappedComponent` that was inserted into the function and pass the `data`, `loading`, and `error` state as props. It's important to understand that it also takes any additional props that are spread with `{...this.props}`:

```
export default function withDataFetching(WrappedComponent) {
  return class extends React.Component {

    ...

+   render() {
+     const { data, loading, error } = this.state;

+     return (
+       <WrappedComponent
+         data={data}
+         loading={loading}
+         error={error}
+         {...this.props}
+       />
+     );
+   }
  };
}
```

Congratulations! You've created your very first HOC! However, it needs a component to return a component that supports data fetching. Therefore, we need to refactor our `Board` component into a function component. Let's get started:

1. Import the HOC from the `src/withDataFetching.js` file:

```
import React, { Component } from 'react';
import styled from 'styled-components';
+ import withDataFetching from '../withDataFetching';
import Lane from '../components/Lane/Lane';

const BoardWrapper = styled.div`
  display: flex;
  justify-content: space-between;
  flex-direction: row;
  margin: 5%;

  @media (max-width: 768px) {
    flex-direction: column;
  }
`;

...
```

2. Subsequently, we can delete the entire class component, that is, `Board`, from this file and create a new function component that returns the JSX we declared in the `return` function for the refactored class component. This function component will take `lanes`, `loading`, `error`, and `data` as props:

```
import React, { Component } from 'react';
import styled from 'styled-components';
import withDataFetching from '../withDataFetching';
import Lane from '../components/Lane/Lane';

const BoardWrapper = ...;

+ const Board = ({ lanes, loading, error, data }) => (
+   <BoardWrapper>
+     {lanes.map(lane =>
+       <Lane
+         key={lane.id}
+         title={lane.title}
+         loading={loading}
+         error={error}
+         tickets={data.filter(ticket => ticket.lane === lane.id)}
+       />
+     )}
```

```
+   </BoardWrapper>
+ );

export default Board;
```

3. Finally, export the function component along with the HOC function:

```
...
const Board = ({ lanes, loading, error, data }) => (
  <BoardWrapper>
    {boards.map(lane =>
      <Lane
        key={lane.id}
        title={lane.title}
        loading={loading}
        error={error}
        tickets={data.filter(ticket => ticket.lane === lane.id)}
      />
    )}
  </BoardWrapper>
);

- export default Board;
+ export default withDataFetching(Board);
```

But where do these props come from? If we open the application and open up the browser, we will see the following error:

TypeError: Cannot read property 'map' of undefined

This is because our `Board` component tries to map over the `lanes` prop, but, in the HOC, `WrappedComponent` receives the `data`, `loading`, and `error` props. Luckily, we've also added the option to spread over any additional props that are sent to the component. If we open the `App` component where the `Board` component is being opened, we can pass the `lanes` prop with the `lane` constant that was declared in the `Board` component previously:

```
...

class App extends Component {
  render() {
+   const lanes = [
+     { id: 1, title: 'To Do' },
+     { id: 2, title: 'In Progress' },
+     { id: 3, title: 'Review' },
+     { id: 4, title: 'Done' },
+   ]
```

```
    return (
        <>
          <GlobalStyle />
            <AppWrapper>
            <Header />
-           <Board />
+           <Board lanes={lanes} />
            </AppWrapper>
        </>
    );
  }
}

export default App;
```

Now, if we take a look at our project in the browser, we'll see that the application has been rendered again. However, it displays an error message from the `try...catch` statement in the HOC. This HOC needs the `dataSource0` prop, which we also need to pass to the `Board` component:

```
...
class App extends Component {
  render() {

    ...

    return (
        <>
          <GlobalStyle />
            <AppWrapper>
            <Header />
-           <Board lanes={lanes} />
+           <Board lanes={lanes} dataSource={'../../assets/data.json'} />
            </AppWrapper>
        </>
    );
  }
}

export default App;
```

Finally, we can see the `Board` component being rendered by the HOC in the browser. However, as we mentioned previously, a HOC is supposed to reuse logic. In the next section, we'll learn how to do this by adding the HOC to a different component.

Using the HOC

With the very first HOC in place it's time to think of other components you can create with this HOC, such as a component that is displaying only tickets. The process to create this component consists of two steps: creating the actual component and importing the component and passing the required props to it. Let's get started:

1. Inside the directory containers, we need to create a new file called `Tickets.js` and place the following code inside it. Where we imported the HOC, set some basic styling with `styled-components` and create a function component that we can export with the HOC:

```javascript
import React from 'react';
import styled from 'styled-components';
import withDataFetching from '../withDataFetching';
import Ticket from '../components/Ticket/Ticket';

const TicketsWrapper = styled.div`
  display: flex;
  justify-content: space-between;
  flex-direction: row;
  margin: 5%;

  @media (max-width: 768px) {
    flex-direction: column;
  }
`;

const Alert = styled.div`
    text-align: center;
`;

const Tickets = ({ loading, data, error }) => (
  <TicketsWrapper>
    {(loading || error) && <Alert>{loading ? 'Loading... :
     error}</Alert>}
    {data.map(ticket => <Ticket key={ticket.id} ticket={ticket}
/>)}
  </TicketsWrapper>
);

export default withDataFetching(Tickets);
```

2. In the `App` component, we can import this component and pass a `dataSource` prop to it:

```
import React, { Component } from 'react';
import styled, { createGlobalStyle } from 'styled-components';
import Board from './Board';
+ import Tickets from './Tickets';
import Header from '../components/Header/Header';


...


class App extends Component {
  render() {
    ...
    return (
      <>
        <GlobalStyle />
        <AppWrapper>
        <Header />
        <Board boards={boards}
          dataSource={'../../assets/data.json'} />
+       <Tickets dataSource={'../../assets/data.json'} />
        </AppWrapper>
      </>
    );
  }
}

export default App;
```

Something that seems a bit off is how the tickets are displayed next to each other without any margin. We could change this in the actual `Ticket` component, but that would also change the margin for the tickets that are displayed in the lanes. What we can do to solve this problem is pass a prop that is being used by `styled-components` to this component. To do this, we need to make changes to the `Tickets` component where we render the tickets and the `Ticket` component where the styling is defined. Let's get started:

1. Pass a new prop called `marginRight` to the `Ticket` components inside the `map` function. This prop is just a Boolean and takes no value:

```
...

const Tickets = ({ loading, data, error }) => (
  <TicketsWrapper>
    {(loading || error) && <Alert>{loading ? 'Loading...' :
      error}</Alert>}
```

```
-    {data.map(ticket => <Ticket key={ticket.id} ticket={ticket}
/>)}
+    {data.map(ticket => <Ticket key={ticket.id} marginRight
ticket={ticket} />)}
  </TicketsWrapper>
);

export default withDataFetching(Tickets);
```

2. In the `Ticket` component, we need to destructure this prop and pass it to the `TicketWrapper` we created with `styled-components`:

```
import React from 'react';
import styled from 'styled-components';

const TicketWrapper = styled.div`
  background: darkGray;
  padding: 20px;
  border-radius: 20px;

  &:not(:last-child) {
    margin-bottom: 5%;
+    margin-right: ${props => !!props.marginRight ? '1%' : '0'};
  }
`;

...

- const Ticket = ({ ticket }) => (
+ const Ticket = ({ marginRight, ticket }) => (
-    <TicketWrapper>
+    <TicketWrapper marginRight={marginRight}>
      <Title>{ticket.title}</Title>
      <Body>{ticket.body}</Body>
    </TicketWrapper>
);

export default Ticket;
```

Now, we can control the `margin-right` property for this `TicketWrapper` just by sending props to the `Ticket` component. If we view our application in a browser, we'll see how, right below our `Board` component with the four lanes, another component rendering a `Ticket` component is being displayed:

Project Management Board

To Do	In Progress	Review	Done
Fix navigation bug Lorem ipsum dolor sit amet, consectetur adipiscing elit. Quisque egestas dictum libero, vel tristique odio pulvinar vitae.	**Release new website** hasellus eleifend lacus vitae est ultrices placerat. Nunc at risus id risus venenatis laoreet sit amet cursus neque.	**Change button color** Suspendisse ac lorem a neque tempus luctus non aliquam sapien. Cras ut lacus bibendum, placerat nibh eu, tempus neque.	**Complete the registration flow** In vel commodo ipsum. Duis id ipsum semper, condimentum ipsum sit amet, maximus massa.
		Deploy server on acceptance environment Pellentesque pharetra fermentum sapien, aliquet ultrices ligula mattis porttitor.	**Create new database instance** Curabitur nec sem lorem. Donec venenatis, arcu vitae malesuada consequat, dolor ante placerat mi, in fermentum diam ipsum id libero.
		Change layout for the content page Cras tellus ligula, mattis at facilisis eu, ultricies vel elit. Ut aliquam volutpat lacus, a rutrum sem vulputate non.	

Another thing we can customize is how the components that are returned by the HOC are named by the React developer tools. Open up the application in the browser and have a look at the component tree. Here, we can see the components that we've created without the HOC have a readable naming convention such as `App` or `Header`. The components that have been created by the HOC are named `<_class />`. To make this component tree more clear, we can easily have our HOC add this naming convention to the components it creates. Usually, we would use the name of the component that is created by the HOC. In our case, however, the HOC is called `withDataFetching` and when we insert a component called `Board`, the name that's displayed in the React developer tools would be `withDataFetching(Board)`. To set this up, we need to make a few changes to the `withDataFetching.js` file. Let's get started:

1. Remove `return` before declaring the class component and give the class component a name. For this, use the name of the HOC and change the first character to a capital letter. This results in `WithDataFetching`:

```
import React from 'react';

export default function withDataFetching(WrappedComponent) {
```

```
- return class extends React.Component {
+ class WithDataFetching extends React.Component {
  ...
```

2. In the last few lines of this file, we can take the name of the WrappedComponent that has been inserted into the HOC and use it to name the HOC by setting the displayName of the returned component. Don't forget to return the WithDataFetching class component at the end of this file:

```
import React from 'react';

export default function withDataFetching(WrappedComponent) {
  class WithDataFetching extends React.Component {
    ...

    render() {
      const { data, loading, error } = this.state;

      return (
        <WrappedComponent
          data={data}
          loading={loading}
          error={error}
          {...this.props}
        />
      );
    }
  };

+ WithDataFetching.displayName =
`WithDataFetching(${WrappedComponent.name})`;

+ return WithDataFetching;
}
```

Looking at the React developer tools again, we can see that these changes have resulted in a more readable naming convention for the components that have been created by the HOC.

All the tickets that are displayed in the lanes are only in one part of our application since we want to be able to drag and drop these tickets into different lanes. We'll learn how to do this in the next section, where we'll add dynamic functionalities to the board.

Making the board dynamic

One of the things that usually gives project management boards great user interaction is the ability to drag and drop tickets from one lane into another. This is something that can easily be accomplished using the HTML5 Drag and Drop API, which is available in every modern browser, including IE11.

The HTML5 Drag and Drop API makes it possible for us to drag and drop elements across our project management board. To make this possible, it uses drag events. `onDragStart`, `onDragOver`, and `onDrop` will be used for this application. These events should be placed on both the `Lane` and the `Ticket` components. Let's get started:

1. First, we need to make the `Board` component a class component instead of a functional component. We're doing this because the ticket data needs to be added to the state and the `Board` component is the most logical place to do this since we may want the `Lane` component to be reused somewhere else. We can do this by changing the definition of the `Board` constant, like so:

```
...

- const Board = ({ lanes, loading, data, error }) => (
+ class Board extends React.Component {
+   render() {
+     const { lanes, loading, data, error } = this.props;
+     return (
        <BoardWrapper>
          {lanes.map(lane =>
            <Lane
              key={lane.id}
              title={lane.title}
              loading={loading}
              error={error}
              tickets={data.filter(ticket => ticket.lane ===
              lane.id)}
            />
          )}
        </BoardWrapper>
      );
+   }
+ }

export default withDataFetching(Board);
```

2. Now, we can add the initial value for the tickets to the state. We're doing this since we want to change the key of the lane it should be placed on. By adding this data to the state, we can mutate it dynamically with the setState function:

```
...
class Board extends React.Component {
+ constructor() {
+   super();
+   this.state = {
+     tickets: [],
+   };
+ }

  render() {
  ...
```

3. Since the data needs to be loaded from the source and isn't available when the application first mounts, we need to check whether the props for these components have changed. If they have, we need to add the ticket data to the state. To do this, use the componentDidUpdate life cycle method, which can take the previous props as a parameter:

```
...

class Board extends React.Component {
  constructor() {
    super()
    this.state = {
      tickets: [],
    };
  }

+ componentDidUpdate(prevProps) {
+   if (prevProps.data !== this.props.data) {
+     this.setState({ tickets: this.props.data });
+   }
+ }

  render() {
  ...
```

4. Finally, show the tickets from the state:

```
...
render() {
-   const { lanes, data, loading, error } = this.props;
+   const { lanes, loading, error } = this.props;

    return (
      <BoardWrapper>
        {lanes.map(lane =>
          <Lane
            key={lane.id}
            title={lane.title}
            loading={loading}
            error={error}
-           tickets={data.filter(ticket => ticket.lane ===
            lane.id)}
+           tickets={this.state.tickets.filter(ticket =>
            ticket.lane === lane.id)}
          />
        )}
      </BoardWrapper>
    );
  }
}

export default withDataFetching(Board);
```

If we take at the project in the browser now, no visible changes should be present. The only difference is the data for the tickets is now loaded from the state, instead of being loaded from the props.

In this same file, let's add the functions that respond to the drop events, which need to be sent to the `Lane` and `Ticket` components:

1. Start by adding the event handler function for the `onDragStart` event, which fires when the dragging operation is started, to the `Board` component. This function needs to be passed to the `Lane` component, where it can be passed on to the `Ticket` component. This function sets an ID for the ticket that is being dragged to the `dataTransfer` object of the element, which is used by the browser to identify the drag element:

```
...
class Board extends React.Component {
  constructor() {
    super();
```

```
        this.state = {
          tickets: [],
        };
      }

      componentDidUpdate(prevProps) {
        if (prevProps.data !== this.props.data) {
          this.setState({ tickets: this.props.data });
        }
      }

+   onDragStart = (e, id) => {
+     e.dataTransfer.setData('id', id);
+   };

      render() {
        const { lanes, loading, error } = this.props;

        return (
          <BoardWrapper>
            {lanes.map(lane =>
              <Lane
                key={lane.id}
                title={lane.title}
                loading={loading}
                error={error}
+               onDragStart={this.onDragStart}
                tickets={this.state.tickets.filter(ticket =>
                ticket.lane === lane.id)}
              />
            )}
          </BoardWrapper>
        );
      }
    }

    export default withDataFetching(Board);
```

2. In the `Lane` component, we need to pass this event handler function to the `Ticket` component:

```
...
- const Lane = ({ tickets, loading, error, title }) => (
+ const Lane = ({ tickets, loading, error, onDragStart, title }) =>
(
  <LaneWrapper>
    <Title>{title}</Title>
    {(loading || error) && <Alert>{loading ? 'Loading...' :
    error}</Alert>}
    <TicketsWrapper>
-     {tickets.map(ticket => <Ticket key={ticket.id}
      ticket={ticket} />)}
+     {tickets.map(ticket => <Ticket key={ticket.id}
      onDragStart={onDragStart} ticket={ticket} />)}
    </TicketsWrapper>
  </LaneWrapper>
);

export default Lane;
```

3. Now, we can invoke this function in the `Ticket` component, where we also need to add the `draggable` attribute to `TicketWrapper`. Here, we send the element and the ticket ID as a parameter to the event handler:

```
...
- const Ticket = ({ marginRight, ticket }) => (
+ const Ticket = ({ marginRight, onDragStart, ticket }) => (
  <TicketWrapper
+   draggable
+   onDragStart={e => onDragStart(e, ticket.id)}
    marginRight={marginRight}
  >
    <Title>{ticket.title}</Title>
    <Body>{ticket.body}</Body>
  </TicketWrapper>
);

export default Ticket;
```

After making these changes, we should be able to see each ticket can be dragged around. But don't drop them anywhere yet—the other drop events and event handlers that update the state should be added as well. Dragging a ticket from one lane to another can be done by clicking on a ticket without releasing the mouse and dragging it to another lane, as shown in the following screenshot:

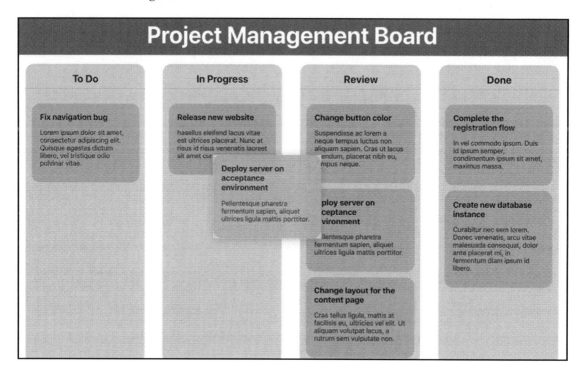

With the `onDragStart` event implemented, the `onDragOver` and `onDrop` events can be implemented as well. Let's get started:

1. By default, it's impossible to drop elements into another element; for example, a `Ticket` component into the `Lane` component. This can be prevented by calling the `preventDefault` method for the `onDragOver` event:

```
...

+  onDragOver = e => {
+    e.preventDefault();
+  };

  render() {
    const { lanes, loading, error } = this.props;
```

```
        return (
          <BoardWrapper>
            {lanes.map(lane =>
              <Lane
                key={lane.id}
                title={lane.title}
                loading={loading}
                error={error}
                onDragStart={this.onDragStart}
+               onDragOver={this.onDragOver}
                tickets={this.state.tickets.filter(ticket =>
                  ticket.lane === lane.id)}
              />
            )}
          </BoardWrapper>
        );
      }
    }
```

2. This event handler needs to be placed on the Lane component:

```
    ...
-   const Lane = ({ tickets, loading, error, title }) => (
+   const Lane = ({ tickets, loading, error, onDragOver, title }) =>
    (
-       <LaneWrapper>
+       <LaneWrapper
+         onDragOver={onDragOver}
+       >
          <Title>{title}</Title>
          {(loading || error) && <Alert>{loading ? 'Loading...' :
           error}</Alert>}
          <TicketsWrapper>
            {tickets.map(ticket => <Ticket onDragStart={onDragStart}
             ticket={ticket} />)}
          </TicketsWrapper>
        </LaneWrapper>
    );

    export default Lane;
```

The onDrop event is where things get interesting since, this event makes it possible for us to mutate the state after we've finished the drag operation.

The event handler function for this event should be placed on the `Ticket` component, but defined in the `Board` component, since the `setState` function can only be invoked in the same file as the initial value for the state:

```
   ...
 +  onDrop = (e, laneId) => {
 +    const id = e.dataTransfer.getData('id');
 +
 +    const tickets = this.state.tickets.filter(ticket => {
 +      if (ticket.id === id) {
 +        ticket.board = boardId;
 +      }
 +      return ticket;
 +    });
 +
 +    this.setState({
 +      ...this.state,
 +      tickets,
 +    });
 +  };

   render() {
     const { lanes, loading, error } = this.props;

     return (
       <BoardWrapper>
         {lanes.map(lane =>
           <Lane
             key={lane.id}
 +           laneId={lane.id}
             title={lane.title}
             loading={loading}
             error={error}
             onDragStart={this.onDragStart}
             onDragOver={this.onDragOver}
 +           onDrop={this.onDrop}
             tickets={this.state.tickets.filter(ticket => ticket.lane ===
             lane.id)}
           />
         )}
       </BoardWrapper>
     );
   }
 }

 export default withDataFetching(Board);
```

This `onDrop` event handler function takes an element and ID of the lane as a parameter, because it needs the ID of the dragged element and the new lane it should be placed in. With this information, the function uses a `filter` function to find the ticket that needs to be moved and changes the ID of the lane. This new information will replace the current object for the tickets in the state with the `setState` function. Since the `onDrop` event gets fired from the `Lane` component, it is passed as a prop to this component. Also, the ID of the lane is added as a prop because this needs to be passed to the `onDrop` event handler function from the `Lane` component:

```
...
- const Lane = ({ tickets, loading, error, onDragStart, onDragOver, title
}) => (
+ const Lane = ({ laneId, tickets, loading, error, onDragStart, onDragOver,
onDrop, title }) => (
  <LaneWrapper
    onDragOver={onDragOver}
+   onDrop={e => onDrop(e, laneId)}
  >
    <Title>{title}</Title>
    {(loading || error) && <Alert>{loading ? 'Loading...' : error}</Alert>}
    <TicketsWrapper>
      { tickets.map(ticket => <Ticket onDragStart={onDragStart}
        ticket={ticket} />)}
    </TicketsWrapper>
  </LaneWrapper>
);

export default Lane;
```

With this, we're able to drag and drop tickets onto other lanes in our board.

Summary

In this chapter, you created a project management board that lets you move and drag and drop tickets from one lane to another using React Suspense and the HTML5 Drag and Drop API. The data flow of this application is handled using local state and life cycles and determines which tickets are displayed in the different lanes. This chapter also introduced the advanced React pattern of **Higher-Order Components (HOCs)**. With HOCs, you can reuse state logic from class components across your applications.

This advanced pattern will be also be used in the next chapter, which will handle routing and **Server-Side Rendering (SSR)** in React applications. Have you ever tried using Stack Overflow to find a solution to a programming issue you once had? I have!

In the next chapter, we will be building a community feed that uses Stack Overflow as a data source and React to render the application.

Further reading

- Drag and Drop API: `https://developer.mozilla.org/en-US/docs/Web/API/HTML_Drag_and_Drop_API`.
- HOC: `https://medium.com/@dan_abramov/mixins-are-dead-long-live-higher-order-components-94a0d2f9e750`.
- DataTransfer: `https://developer.mozilla.org/en-US/docs/Web/API/DataTransfer`.
- React DnD: `https://github.com/react-dnd/react-dnd`.

Build a SSR-Based Community Feed Using React Router

4

So far, you've learned how React applications are typically **Single-Page Applications (SPAs)** that can be used as a **Progressive Web App (PWA)**. This means the application is rendered client-side, making it load in the browser when the user visits your application. But did you know React also supports **Server-Side Rendering (SSR)**, as you might remember from back in the old days when code only rendered from a server?

In this chapter, you'll add declarative routing to a Create React App using `react-router` and have components dynamically loaded from the server instead of the browser. To enable SSR, the React feature, Suspense, will be used with `ReactDOMServer`. If you're interested in **Search Engine Optimization (SEO)**, this chapter will use React Helmet to add metadata to the page so your application can be better indexed by search engines.

The following topics will be covered in this chapter:

- Declarative routing
- Server-side rendering
- SEO in React

Project overview

In this chapter, we will create a PWA with declarative routing using `react-router` that supports SSR and therefore is loaded from the server rather than the browser. Also, the application is optimized for search engines using React Helmet.

The build time is 2 hours.

Getting started

The project that we'll create in this chapter builds upon an initial version that you can find on GitHub: `https://github.com/PacktPublishing/React-Projects/tree/ch4-initial`. The complete source code can also be found on GitHub: `https://github.com/PacktPublishing/React-Projects/tree/ch4`. Also, this project uses the publicly available Stack Overflow API to fill the application with data. This is done by fetching questions that are posted to Stack Overflow. More information about this API can be found at: `https://api.stackexchange.com/docs/questions#order=descsort=hottagged=reactjsfilter=defaultsite=stackoverflowrun=true`.

After downloading the initial project from GitHub, you need to move into the root directory for this project and run `npm install`. As this project is built on top of Create React App, running this command will install `react`, `react-dom`, and `react-scripts`. Also, `styled-components` is used to handle the styling of all of the components in the application. When the installation process has finished, you can execute the `npm` command start to be able to visit the project in the browser at `http://localhost:3000`.

As the project is set up as a PWA, the service workers are registered to make it possible to visit the application even when there is no internet connection. You can check this by running `npm run build` first and `serve -s build` once the build process is completed. The build version of the application can now be visited at `http://localhost:5000`. As mentioned in a previous chapter, you can check whether the application is still available when there is no internet connection by visiting the **Application** tab in the Developer Tools of your browser. Inside this tab, you can find **Service Workers** in the menu on the left; after clicking this link, you can select the **Offline** checkbox on the page that appears.

You may see a different application than when you ran the project locally if you've built and served a Create React App PWA before. You can delete any previous application from the browser cache by opening the browser's Developer Tools and open the **Application** tab where you can click on the **Clear site data** button on the **Clear Storage** section.

The initial application that is available at `http://localhost:3000` consists of a simple header and a list of cards—as seen in the following screenshot. These cards have a title and meta information such as view count, answer count, and information about the user who asked this question:

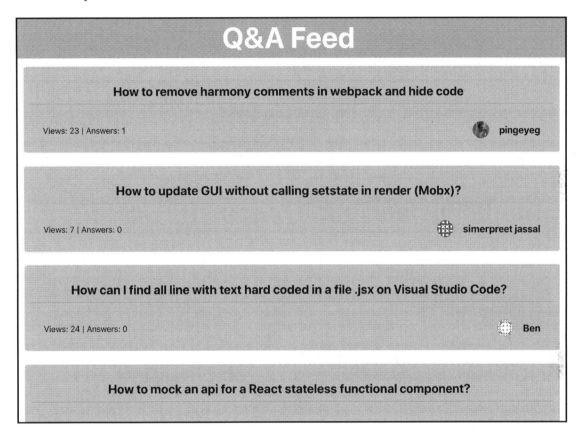

If you look at the project's structure, it uses the same structure as the projects you've created before. The entry point of this application is a file called `src/index.js`, which renders a container component called `App` that contains the `Header` and `Feed` components. The `Header` component only displays the title of the project, while `Feed` is a class component that has life cycle methods, calls the Stack Overflow API, and renders the `Card` components containing the Stack Overflow questions:

```
community-feed
|-- node_modules
|-- public
    |-- favicon.ico
    |-- index.html
```

```
        |-- manifest.json
  |-- src
      |-- components
          |-- Header
              |-- Header.js
          |-- Card
              |-- Card.js
          |-- Owner
              |-- Owner.js
      |-- containers
          |-- App.js
          |-- Feed.js
      |-- index.js
      |-- serviceWorker.js
  .gitignore
  package.json
```

Community feed application

In this section, you'll build a community feed application with declarative routing that has SSR enabled. For SEO, a package called React Helmet will be used. In this community feed, you can see an overview of recent questions on Stack Overflow that have the `reactjs` tag, and click on them to see more information and the answers. The starting point will be a project that is created using Create React App.

Declarative routing

With the `react-router` package, you can add declarative routing to a React application, just by adding components. These components can be divided into three types: router components, route matching components, and navigation components.

Setting up routing with `react-router` consists of multiple steps:

1. To use these components, you need to install the web package of `react-router`, called `react-router-dom`, by executing the following:

   ```
   npm install react-router-dom
   ```

2. After installing `react-router-dom`, the next step is to import the routing and route matching components from this package in the component that is the entry point of your application. In this case, that is the `App` component, which is inside the `src/containers` directory:

```
import React, { Component } from 'react';
import styled, { createGlobalStyle } from 'styled-components';
+ import { BrowserRouter as Router, Route } from 'react-router-
dom';
import Header from '../components/Header/Header';
import Feed from './Feed';

const GlobalStyle = createGlobalStyle`...`;

const AppWrapper = styled.div`...`;

class App extends Component {
    ...
```

3. The actual routes must be added to the `return` function of this component, where all of the route matching components (`Route`) must be wrapped in a routing component, `Router`. When your URL matches a route defined in any of the iterations of `Route`, this component will render the JSX component that is added as a `component` prop:

```
...
class App extends Component {
  render() {
    return (
        <>
          <GlobalStyle />
          <AppWrapper>
            <Header />
+           <Router>
+             <Route path='/' component={Feed} />
+           </Router>
          </AppWrapper>
        </>
    );
  }
}

export default App;
```

4. If you now visit the project in the browser again at `http://localhost:3000`, the `Feed` component showing all the questions will be rendered. Also, if you type `http://localhost:3000/feed` in the browser, the `Feed` component will still be rendered. This is because the `/` route matches every possible URL, as you didn't define that an exact match should be made. Therefore, add the `exact` attribute to `Route`:

```
...
class App extends Component {
  render() {
    return (
      <>
        <GlobalStyle />
        <AppWrapper>
          <Header />
          <Router>
-           <Route path='/' component={Feed} />
+           <Route exact path='/' component={Feed} />
          </Router>
        </AppWrapper>
      </>
    );
  }
}

export default App;
```

Now, you shouldn't be able to see the `Feed` component being rendered if you visit any route other than `/`.

If you want these routes to display, for example, a specific question, you'd need to send parameters to a route. How you can do this is shown in the next part of this section.

Routes with parameters

With the first route in place, other routes can be added to the router component. A logical one is having a route for individual questions, that has an extra parameter that specifies which question should be displayed. Therefore, a new container component called `Question` must be created, which contains the logic for fetching a question from the Stack Overflow API. This component is rendered when the path matches `/question/:id`, where `id` stands for the ID of the question that is clicked on from the feed:

1. Create a new class component called `Question` in the `src/containers` directory, and add a `constructor` and `render` method to this file:

```
import React, { Component } from 'react';
import styled from 'styled-components';

const QuestionWrapper = styled.div`
  display: flex;
  justify-content: space-between;
  flex-direction: column;
  margin: 5%;
`;

const Alert = styled.div`
  text-align: center;
`;

class Question extends Component {
  constructor() {
    super();
    this.state = {
      data: [],
      loading: true,
      error: '',
    };
  }

  render() {
    const { data, loading, error } = this.state;

    if (loading || error) {
      return <Alert>{loading ? 'Loading...' : error}</Alert>;
    }

    return (
      <QuestionWrapper></QuestionWrapper>
```

```
            );
        }
    }

    export default Question;
```

2. To make this route available, you need to import this component inside the
   `App` component and define a route for it:

```
import React, { Component } from 'react';
import styled, { createGlobalStyle } from 'styled-components';
import { BrowserRouter as Router, Route } from 'react-router-dom';
import Header from '../components/Header/Header';
import Feed from './Feed';
+ import Question from './Question';
...
class App extends Component {
  render() {
    return (
        <>
          <GlobalStyle />
          <AppWrapper>
            <Header />
            <Router>
              <Route exact path='/' component={Feed} />
+             <Route path='/questions/:id' component={Question} />
            </Router>
          </AppWrapper>
        </>
    );
  }
}

export default App;
```

If you now visit `http://localhost:3000/questions/55366474`, the
`Loading...` message will be displayed as no data fetching is implemented yet. The
`Route` component passes props to the component that it renders, in this case, `Question`;
these props are `match`, `location`, and `history`. You can see this by opening the React
Developer Tools and searching for the `Question` component, which will return the
following result:

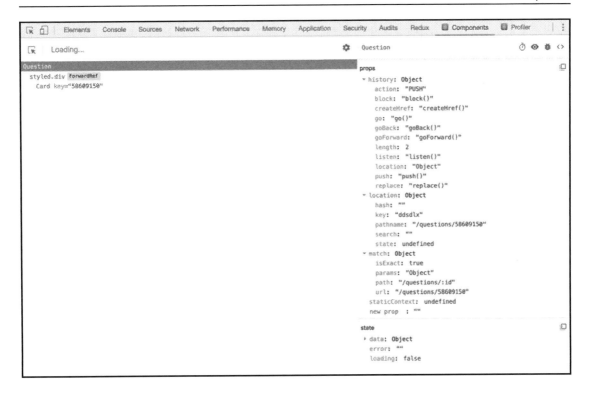

The match prop is the most interesting, as this contains the value of the id parameter. The location and history props have information about the current and past location of your application.

You can also access the react-router props by using the withRouter **Higher-Order Component (HOC)**, which passes the match, location, and history props to the wrapped component each time it renders. That way, you can use methods such as history.goBack or history.push from anywhere in your application. In Chapter 3, *Build a Dynamic Project Management Board with React and Suspense*, you've seen an example of using a HOC; the withRouter HOC is implemented in the same manner.

To implement data fetching on the `Question` component, you need to check for the `id` parameter and fetch the corresponding question from the Stack Overflow API:

1. Therefore, a `componentDidMount` method should be added to `Question`, which fetches the API using this parameter:

```
...

+ const ROOT_API = 'https://api.stackexchange.com/2.2/';

class Question extends Component {
  constructor(props) { ... }

+ async componentDidMount() {
+   const { match } = this.props;
+   try {
+     const data = await fetch(
+
`${ROOT_API}questions/${match.params.id}?site=stackoverflow`,
+     );
+     const dataJSON = await data.json();

+     if (dataJSON) {
+       this.setState({
+         data: dataJSON,
+         loading: false,
+       });
+     }
+   } catch(error) {
+     this.setState({
+       loading: true,
+       error: error.message,
+     });
+   }
+ }

  render() {
    ...
```

2. The data that is being fetched can then be displayed inside a `Card` component. Bear in mind that the Stack Overflow API returns an array instead of a single object when making this request:

```
import React, { Component } from 'react';
import styled from 'styled-components';
+ import Card from '../components/Card/Card';
```

```
...

class Question extends Component {
  ...
  render() {
    const { data, loading, error } = this.state;

    if (loading || error) {
      return <Alert>{loading ? 'Loading...' : error}</Alert>;
    }

    return (
      <QuestionWrapper>
+       <Card key={data.items[0].question_id} data={data.items[0]}
/>
      </QuestionWrapper>
    );
  }
}

export default Question;
```

3. If you now refresh `http://localhost:3000/questions/55366474`, a
   `Card` component showing information about this specific question is displayed.
   To be able to navigate to this page from the `Feed` component, a `Link` navigation
   should be added to wrap `Card`:

```
import React, { Component } from 'react';
import styled from 'styled-components';
+ import { Link } from 'react-router-dom';
import Card from '../components/Card/Card';

...

class Feed extends Component {
  ...
  render() {
    const { data, loading, error } = this.state;

    if (loading || error) {
      return <Alert>{loading ? 'Loading...' : error}</Alert>;
    }

    return (
      <FeedWrapper>
        {data.items.map(item =>
+         <Link key={item.question_id}
```

```
        to={`/questions/${item.question_id}`}>
-               <Card key={item.question_id} data={item} />
+               <Card data={item} />
+           </Link>
+         )}
        </FeedWrapper>
      );
    }
  }

export default Feed;
```

4. As you might notice when visiting `http://localhost:3000/`, the
   `Card` components are now clickable and link to a new page showing the question
   you've just clicked on. The styling for the `Card` components has also changed, as
   the `Link` navigation component is an `a` element; it adds an underline and
   changes the padding. You must make the following changes to fix these styling
   changes:

```
  ...
+ const CardLink = styled(Link)`
+   text-decoration: none;
+   color: inherit;
+ `;

const ROOT_API = 'https://api.stackexchange.com/2.2/';

class Feed extends Component {
  ...
  render() {
    const { data, loading, error } = this.state;

    if (loading || error) {
      return <Alert>{loading ? 'Loading...' : error}</Alert>;
    }

    return (
      <FeedWrapper>
        {data.items.map(item => (
-         <Link key={item.question_id}
to={`/questions/${item.question_id}`}>
+         <CardLink key={item.question_id}
to={`/questions/${item.question_id}`}>
            <Card data={item} />
-         </Link>
+         </CardLink>
        ))}
```

```
            </FeedWrapper>
          );
        }
      }

      export default Feed;
```

Now, the styling should be restored and you're able to navigate to the question routes to view individual questions. But next to parameters, there are other ways to use the routes for filtering or pass data to it, which are query strings. These are investigated in the next part of this chapter.

Handling query strings

Being able to navigate to individual questions is only one piece of the cake when you want to add routing a project, and pagination could be another one. For this, it would be a good idea to move the overview of all of the questions to another route that is called `/questions`. To do this, you need to add another `Route` that refers to the `Feed` component within `Router` in your `App` component:

```
      ...
      class App extends Component {
        render() {
          return (
            <>
              <GlobalStyle />
              <AppWrapper>
                <Header />
                <Router>
                  <Route exact path='/' component={Feed} />
+                 <Route path='/questions' component={Feed} />
                  <Route path='/questions/:id' component={Question} />
                </Router>
              </AppWrapper>
            </>
          );
        }
      }

      export default App;
```

However, if you now visit the project and try clicking on any of the questions, you will see both the rendered component and URL haven't changed. Because of the way `react-router` is set up, it will navigate to any route that matches the current URL. To solve this problem, you need to add a `Switch` route matching component, which works as a switch statement and will render the first `Route` that matches the current location:

1. You can import `Switch` from the `react-router-dom` package in the `scr/containers/App.js` file:

```
import React, { Component } from 'react';
import styled, { createGlobalStyle } from 'styled-components';
- import { BrowserRouter as Router, Route } from 'react-router-
dom';
+ import { BrowserRouter as Router, Route, Switch } from 'react-
router-dom';

. . .
```

2. And place this `Switch` within `Router`, where the order of the routes must be changed to make sure that, whenever there is an `id` parameter, this route will be rendered first:

```
    . . .
    class App extends Component {
      render() {
        return (
          <>
            <GlobalStyle />
            <AppWrapper>
              <Header />
              <Router>
+               <Switch>
                  <Route exact path='/' component={Feed} />
-                 <Route path='/questions' component={Feed} />
                  <Route path='/questions/:id' component={Question} />
+                 <Route path='/questions' component={Feed} />
+               </Switch>
              </Router>
            </AppWrapper>
          </>
        );
      }
    }

    export default App;
```

Both the `/questions` and `/questions/:id` routes will now return the correct component, which is either the `Feed` or `Question` component. With this in place, the next step is to add the pagination. If you look at the API response, the object that is being returned has a field called `has_more`. If this field has the value `true`, which means you can request more questions by adding the `page` query string to the API request.

You can try and add this query string to the URL in the browser, by visiting `http://localhost:3000/questions?page=2`. This query string is now available as a prop on the `Feed` component in the `location` object under the `search` field, which you can see in the output of the React Developer Tools:

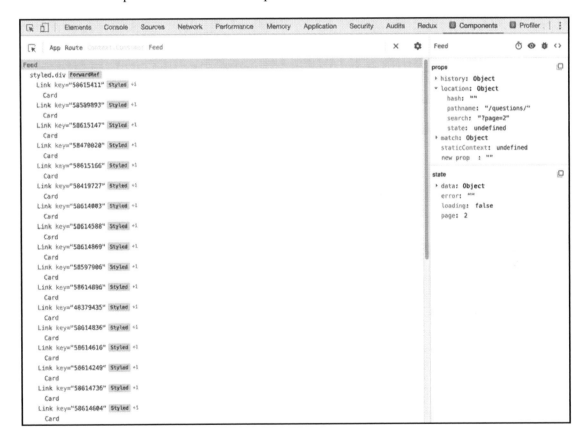

Unfortunately, `react-router` doesn't come with a standard solution to easily grasp the value of the `location.search` prop. Therefore, you need to install the `query-string` package using npm:

```
npm install query-string
```

This package is created to parse a query string, in this case, `location.search`, to an object you can use in your application:

1. You can do this by importing the package in the `Feed` component:

    ```
    import React, { Component } from 'react';
    import styled from 'styled-components';
    + import queryString from 'query-string';

        . . .
    ```

2. Now, you can parse the value for the `page` query string in the `constructor` method, and add this parsed value to `state`. Make sure to use the JavaScript `parseInt` function, so the page will become an integer and not a string. If there is no page query string available, it's assumed you're visiting the first page:

    ```
        . . .
    class Feed extends Component {
    - constructor() {
    -     super();
    + constructor(props) {
    +     super(props);
    +     const query = queryString.parse(props.location.search);
        this.state = {
          data: [],
    +     page: (query.page) ? parseInt(query.page) : 1,
          loading: true,
          error: '',
        };
    }
        . . .
    ```

3. And if there is a value for the `page` query string in `state`, you can send this to the API to get the questions for the page number you specify:

```
...
async componentDidMount() {
+ const { page } = this.state;
  try {
-     const data = await fetch(
-       `${ROOT_API}questions/${match.params.id}?site=stackoverflow`,
-     );
+     const data = await fetch(
+
`${ROOT_API}questions?order=desc&sort=activity&tagged=reactjs&site=
stackoverflow${(page) ? `&page=${page}` : ''}`,
+     );
      const dataJSON = await data.json();

      if (dataJSON) {
        this.setState({
          data: dataJSON,
          loading: false,
        });
      }
    } catch(error) {
      this.setState({
        loading: false,
        error: error.message,
      });
    }
  }
}
...
```

You can test whether this is working by changing the query string for `page` with different numbers, such as `http://localhost:3000/questions?page=1` or `http://localhost:3000/questions?page=3`. To make the application more user-friendly, let's add pagination buttons to the bottom of the page.

4. Create the `PaginationBar` component, which holds two `Button` components that are styled `Link` components from `react-router`:

```
...

+ const PaginationBar = styled.div`
+   width: 100%;
+   display: flex;
+   justify-content: space-between;
+ `;
```

```
+ const PaginationLink = styled(Link)`
+   padding: 1%;
+   background: lightBlue;
+   color: white;
+   text-decoration: none
+   border-radius: 5px;
+ `;

const ROOT_API = 'https://api.stackexchange.com/2.2/';

class Feed extends Component {
  ...
```

5. You can now add these to the bottom of `FeedWrapper`:

```
  ...
  render() {
    const { data, loading, error } = this.state;

      if (loading || error) {
        return <Alert>{loading ? 'Loading...' : error}</Alert>;
      }

      return (
        <FeedWrapper>
          {data.items.map(item => (
            <CardLink key={item.question_id}
to={`/questions/${item.question_id}`}>
              <Card data={item} />
            </CardLink>
          ))}
+         <PaginationBar>
+           <PaginationLink>Previous</PaginationLink>
+           <PaginationLink>Next</PaginationLink>
+         </PaginationBar>
        </FeedWrapper>
      );
    }
  }
}

export default Feed;
```

6. These `PaginationLink` components should link to somewhere for the user to be able to navigate to different pages. For this, the current URL can be taken from the `match` prop and the current page number is available in `state`. Be aware that the previous button should only be shown when the page number is above 1, and the next button only when the API response indicates that there are more results than the ones that are returned:

```
...

render() {
-   const { data, loading } = this.state;
+   const { data, page, loading } = this.state;
+   const { match } = this.props;

    if (loading || error) {
      return <Alert>{loading ? 'Loading...' : error}</Alert>;
    }

    return (
      <FeedWrapper>
        {data.items.map(item => (
          <CardLink key={item.question_id}
to={`/questions/${item.question_id}`}>
            <Card data={item} />
          </CardLink>
        ))}
        <PaginationBar>
-         <PaginationLink>Previous</PaginationLink>
-         <PaginationLink>Next</PaginationLink>
+         {page > 1 && <PaginationLink to={`${match.url}?page=${page
- 1}`}>Previous</PaginationLink>}
+         {data.has_more && <PaginationLink
to={`${match.url}?page=${page + 1}`}>Next</PaginationLink>}
        </PaginationBar>
      </FeedWrapper>
    );
  }
}

export default Feed;
```

However, if you now try and click on the next (or previous) button the URL will change, the questions that are being displayed don't change. By using the `componentDidMount` method, the API will only be called after your application mounts for the first time. To watch for any changes to `props` or `state` when your application is already mounted, you need to use another life cycle method called `componentDidUpdate`. This method can watch for changes to `props` or `state`, as it can access the values of `props` and `state` before they were updated. They are scoped within the `componendDidUpdate` method as the `prevProps` and `prevState` parameters, which you can compare to check whether you need to fetch the API again when any `props` or `state` have changed.

7. The first step in achieving this is creating a function that fetches the API and that can also be used outside of the `componentDidMount` method. This function should take the `page` number as a parameter, so it can fetch the correct page:

```
...
+ async fetchAPI(page) {
+    try {
+      const data = await
fetch(`${ROOT_API}questions?order=desc&sort=activity&tagged=reactjs
&site=stackoverflow${(page) ? `&page=${page}` : ''}`);
+      const dataJSON = await data.json();
+
+      if (dataJSON) {
+        this.setState({
+          data: dataJSON,
+          loading: false,
+        });
+      }
+    } catch(error) {
+      this.setState({
+        loading: false,
+        error: error.message,
+      });
+    }
+  }

async componentDidMount() {
  ...
```

8. After creating this function, it can be called in the `componentDidMount` method, which no longer needs to be an asynchronous function as this is already handled by the new `fetchAPI` function. Therefore, the method can be deleted and replaced by the following:

```
    . . .

-   async componentDidMount() { ... }

+   componentDidMount() {
+     const { page } = this.state;
+     this.fetchAPI(page);
+   }

    render() {
      . . .
```

9. Directly after the `componentDidMount` method, you need to add the new `componentDidUpdate` life cycle method. As mentioned before, this can take `prevProps` and `prevState` as parameters, but as navigating to a new URL only changes `props`, the prior is used. Here, you need to check whether the query strings have changed. If they have changed, you need to update `state` with the new parsed value for the `page` query string and call the `fetchAPI` function to get the results for this page:

```
    . . .
    componentDidMount() {
      const { page } = this.state;
      this.fetchAPI(page);
    }

+   componentDidUpdate(prevProps) {
+     if (prevProps.location.search !== this.props.location.search) {
+       const query = queryString.parse(this.props.location.search);
+       this.setState({ page: parseInt(query.page) }, () =>
+         this.fetchAPI(this.state.page),
+       );
+     }
+   }

    render() {
      . . .
```

When using the `componentDidUpdate` life cycle method, you should always make sure to compare either `prevProps` or `prevState` to the current `props` or `state`. The `componentDidUpdate` method is invoked continuously and when you don't compare any values, you could end up with an infinite loop that crashes your application.

You have now implemented the parsing of the query string to dynamically change the route for your application. In the next section, you'll explore another thing you can do with React, which is SRR that enables you to serve your application from the server instead of rendering it in runtime.

Enable SSR

Using SSR can be helpful if you're building an application that needs to render very quickly or when you want certain information to be loaded before the web page is visible. Although most search engines are now able to render SPA, this can still be an improvement if you want users to share your page on social media.

Creating an express server with react-router

There is no standard pattern to enable SSR for your React application, but the starting point is to create a Node.js server that's serving the entry for running the build version for your application. For this, you'll use a minimal API framework for Node.js called `express`. Also, the packets that you've already used, such as `react-router` and `styled-components`, can work with SSR as well:

1. You can start by installing `express` by running the following:

   ```
   npm install express
   ```

2. Now, you must create a new directory called `server` in the projects' root directory and place a new file called `server.js` inside. In this file, you can place the following code block to import packages you need to run the Node.js server, `react`, and `react-dom/server`—which is used to render your application from a server:

   ```
   import path from 'path';
   import fs from 'fs';
   import express from 'express';
   import React from 'react';
   import ReactDOMServer from 'react-dom/server';
   ```

3. Directly below these imports, you need to import the entry point of the application that should be rendered by the server:

```
import path from 'path';
import fs from 'fs';
import express from 'express';
import React from 'react';
import ReactDOMServer from 'react-dom/server';

+ import App from '../src/containers/App';
```

4. After having defined the entry point, the code to set up the Node.js server with `express` and have it listen to all of the endpoints on the server can be added. First, you need to set a port on which `express` will be running, after which, you define that all of the routes matching the `/*` wildcard should return a static version of your application that is being rendered by `ReactDOMServer` as a string. That is done by getting the contents of the `index.html` build file and replacing the `<div id="root"></div>` tags with new tags that contain the server-rendered version of the `App` component:

```
...
const PORT = 8080;
const app = express();

app.get('/*', (req, res) => {
  const context = {};
  const app = ReactDOMServer.renderToString(<App />);

  const indexFile = path.resolve('./build/index.html');
  fs.readFile(indexFile, 'utf8', (err, data) => {
    if (err) {
      console.error('Something went wrong:', err);
      return res.status(500).send('Oops, better luck next time!');
    }

    data = data.replace('<div id="root"></div>', `<div
id="root">${app}</div>`);

    return res.send(data);
  });
});
```

5. And have this `express` server listen to the `8080` port you've defined, by adding this code block to the bottom of this file:

```
...
app.listen(PORT, () => {
  console.log(`Server-Side Rendered application running on port
${PORT}`);
});
```

6. Finally, you need to change the way your `App` component is rendered from the entry point of the application in `src/index.js`. In this file, `ReactDOM.render` needs to be replaced by `ReactDOM.hydrate` as the Node.js server tries to change the markup of the `index.html` build file by injecting the server-rendered version:

```
import React from 'react';
import ReactDOM from 'react-dom';
import App from './containers/App';
import * as serviceWorker from './serviceWorker';

+ ReactDOM.hydrate(<App />, document.getElementById('root'));

...
```

However, this Node.js server isn't able to use any of the webpack configuration that is being used by your React application, as its code isn't placed in the `src` directory. To be able to run this Node.js server, you need to configure Babel for the `server` directory and install some of the Babel packages. This is something you've done before in the first chapter:

1. The Babel packages that should be installed are `@babel/polyfill`, which compiles functions such as `async/await`; `@babel/register` to tell Babel it should transform files with the `.js` extension; and `@babel/preset-env` and `@babel/preset-react` to configure Babel to work with React:

```
npm install @babel/polyfill @babel/register @babel/preset-env
@babel/preset-react
```

2. In a new file called `index.js` inside the `server` directory, you can now require these packages and have this file serve as an entry point to the `server.js` file:

```
require('@babel/polyfill');

require('@babel/register')({
  presets: ['@babel/preset-env', '@babel/preset-react'],
```

```
});

require('./server');
```

3. You should be able to run the `server/index.js` file with Node.js, by executing the `node server/index.js` command. So, let's make a shortcut for this command in `package.json` within the scripts field:

```
...
"scripts": {
  "start": "react-scripts start",
  "build": "react-scripts build",
  "test": "react-scripts test",
  "eject": "react-scripts eject",
+ "ssr": "node server/index.js"
},
```

Before running the `npm run ssr` command, you should always execute `npm run build` before as the Node.js server is using the build version. If you run the `npm run ssr` command now, though, you will receive an error saying `BrowserRouter needs to a DOM to render`. Because of the way `react-router` is set up, you need to use the `StaticRouter` component when using SSR instead of `BrowserRouter`:

1. When the application is running client-side (using `npm start`), it will still need to use `BrowserRouter`, so therefore the wrapping of the `Route` components should be moved from `App` to the `src/index.js` file:

```
import React from 'react';
import ReactDOM from 'react-dom';
+ import { BrowserRouter as Router } from 'react-router-
dom';
import App from './containers/App';
import * as serviceWorker from './serviceWorker';

ReactDOM.hydrate(
+   <Router>
      <App />
+   </Router>,
    document.getElementById('root'),
);
```

2. And, of course, it's deleted from the `App` component:

```
import React, { Component } from 'react';
import styled, { createGlobalStyle } from 'styled-components';
- import { BrowserRouter as Router, Route, Switch } from 'react-
router-dom';
+ import { Route, Switch } from 'react-router-dom';
import Header from '../components/Header/Header';
import Feed from './Feed';
import Question from './Question';

...

class App extends Component {
  render() {
    return (
      <>
        <GlobalStyle />
        <AppWrapper>
          <Header />
-         <Router>
          <Switch>
            <Route exact path='/' component={Feed} />
            <Route path='/questions/:id' component={Question} />
            <Route path='/questions' component={Feed} />
          </Switch>
-         </Router>
        </AppWrapper>
      </>
    );
  }
}

export default App;
```

3. To get the Node.js server to now use the `StaticRouter` component from `react-router`, you need to add this in `server/index.js` and wrap the `App` component that is being rendered by `ReactDOMServer` with `StaticRouter`. For `react-router` to know which route to load, you must pass the current URL as a `location` prop, and (in this case) an empty `context` prop as `StaticRouter` should always have this to handle redirects:

```
import path from 'path';
import fs from 'fs';
import express from 'express';
import React from 'react';
import ReactDOMServer from 'react-dom/server';
```

```
+ import { StaticRouter } from 'react-router-dom';

import App from '../src/containers/App';

const PORT = 8080;
const app = express();

app.get('/*', (req, res) => {
  const context = {};
  const app = ReactDOMServer.renderToString(
-   <Router>
+   <Router location={req.url} context={context}>
    <App />
  </Router>,
  );

  ...
```

With this last step done, you can go and execute `npm run build` again. After the build has finished, you can start the Node.js server by running `npm run ssr` to view your server-rendered React application on `http://localhost:8080`. This application looks the same, as SSR doesn't change anything to the appearance of your application.

Another advantage of SSR is that your application can be discovered by search engines more effectively. In the next part of this section, you'll add the tags that make your application discoverable by these engines.

Adding head tags using React Helmet

Assuming you want your application to be indexed by search engines, you need to set head tags for the crawlers to identify the content on your page. This is something you want to do dynamically for each route route, as each route will have different content. A popular package for setting these head tags in React applications is React Helmet, which has support for SSR. You can install React Helmet with `npm`:

```
npm install react-helmet
```

React Helmet can define the head tags in any component that is rendered by your application, and if nested, the lowest definition of a `Helmet` component in the component tree will be used. That's why you can create a `Helmet` component in your `Header` component for all routes and in each of the components that are being rendered on a route, you can overwrite these tags:

1. Import the `react-helmet` package in the `src/components/App/Header.js` file, and create a `Helmet` component that sets `title` and meta `description`:

```
import React from 'react';
import styled from 'styled-components';
+ import Helmet from 'react-helmet';

...

const Header = () => (
+   <>
+     <Helmet>
+       <title>Q&A Feed</title>
+       <meta name='description' content='This is a Community Feed
project build with React' />
+     </Helmet>
      <HeaderWrapper>
        <Title>Q&A Feed</Title>
      </HeaderWrapper>
+   </>
);

export default Header;
```

2. Also, create a `Helmet` component in `src/containers/Feed.js` that only sets a title for this route, so it will use the meta `description` of `Header`. This component is placed within Fragments before the `Alert` component as this is available when the application first renders:

```
import React, { Component } from 'react';
import styled from 'styled-components';
import queryString from 'query-string'
import { Link } from 'react-router-dom';
+ import Helmet from 'react-helmet';
import Card from '../components/Card/Card';

...

    render() {
```

```
      const { data, page, loading, error } = this.state;
      const { match } = this.props;

      if (loading || error) {
        return
+         <>
+           <Helmet>
+             <title>Q&A Feed - Questions</title>
+           </Helmet>
            <Alert>{loading ? 'Loading...' : error}</Alert>
+         </>
      }
      ...
```

3. Do the same for the `src/containers/Question.js` file, where you can also take the ID of the question from the `match` props to make the page title more dynamic:

```
import React, { Component } from 'react';
import styled from 'styled-components';
+ import Helmet from 'react-helmet';
import Card from '../components/Card/Card';

    ...

  render() {
+    const { match } = this.props;
    const { data, loading, error } = this.state;

    if (loading || error) {
      return
+         <>
+           <Helmet>
+             <title>{`Q&A Feed - Question
#${match.params.id}`}</title>
+           </Helmet>
            <Alert>{loading ? 'Loading...' : error}</Alert>
+         </>
    }

    ...
```

4. These head tags will now be used when you're running your application client-side by executing the `npm start` command. But to support SSR, React Helmet should also be configured on the Node.js server. For this, you can use the `Helmet.renderStatic` method, which transforms the `Helmet` components in your code the same way as `ReactDOMserver.renderToString` does for other components. Open the `server/server.js` file and add the following lines of code:

```
import path from 'path';
import fs from 'fs';
import express from 'express';
import React from 'react';
import ReactDOMServer from 'react-dom/server';
import { StaticRouter as Router } from 'react-router-dom';
+ import Helmet from 'react-helmet';

...

app.get('/*', (req, res) => {
  const context = {};
  const app = ReactDOMServer.renderToString(
    <Router location={req.url} context={context}>
      <App />
    </Router>,
  );
+   const helmet = Helmet.renderStatic();

  const indexFile = path.resolve('./build/index.html');
  fs.readFile(indexFile, 'utf8', (err, data) => {
    if (err) {
      console.error('Something went wrong:', err);
      return res.status(500).send('Oops, better luck next time!');
    }

    data = data.replace('<div id="root"></div>', `<div
id="root">${app}</div>`);
+     data = data.replace('<meta name="helmet"/>',
`${helmet.title.toString()}${helmet.meta.toString()}`);

    return res.send(data);
  });
});

...
```

5. On one of the last lines of this file, you've now defined that the `<meta name="helmet" />` element should be replaced by the `title` and `meta` tags created by React Helmet. To make it possible to replace this element with these tags, add this element to `index.html` in the `public` directory. Also, you must delete the `title` element that is already being created by React Helmet now:

```
<!DOCTYPE html>
<html lang="en">
  <head>
    <meta charset="utf-8" />
    <link rel="shortcut icon" href="%PUBLIC_URL%/favicon.ico" />
    <meta
      name="viewport"
      content="width=device-width, initial-scale=1, shrink-to-fit=no"
    />
    <meta name="theme-color" content="#000000" />
    <link rel="manifest" href="%PUBLIC_URL%/manifest.json" />
+   <meta name="helmet" />
-   <title>React App</title>
  </head>
...
```

With these last changes, you can now run `npm run build` again to create a new build version of your application. After this process has finished, you execute the `npm run ssr` command to start the Node.js server and visit your React SSR application in the browser on `http://localhost:8080`.

Summary

In this chapter, you've added dynamic routing to a Create React App using `react-router`, making it possible for users to open your application on a specific page. By using the React feature Suspense, components are loaded dynamically on the client-side. This way, you lower the amount of time before your user first gets in contact with your application. The project you created in this chapter also supports SSR, and React Helmet is used to add dynamic head tags to the application for SEO purposes.

After completing this chapter, you must already feel like an expert with React! The next chapter will for sure take your skill to the next level as you'll learn how to handle state management using the context API. With the context API, you can share state and data between multiple components in your application, no matter whether they're direct children of the parent component or not.

Further reading

- React Helmet: `https://github.com/nfl/react-helmet`
- ReactDOMServer: `https://reactjs.org/docs/react-dom-server.html`

5

Build a Personal Shopping List Application Using Context API and Hooks

State management is a very important part of modern web and mobile applications and is something that React is very good at. Handling state management in React applications can be quite confusing, as there are multiple ways you can handle the current state of your application. The projects you created in the first four chapters of this book haven't been focusing on state management too much, something that will be investigated much more in this chapter.

This chapter will show how you can handle state management in React, by creating a global state for your application that is accessible from every component. Before React v16.3, you needed third-party packages to handle global state in React, but with the renewed version of the context API, this is no longer mandatory. Also, with the release of React Hooks, more ways to mutate this Context were introduced. Using an example application, the methods to handle global state management for your application are demonstrated.

The following topics will be covered in this chapter:

- Using the context API for state management
- **Higher-Order Components (HOC)** and Context
- Mutating Context with Hooks

Project overview

In this chapter, we will create a **Progressive Web App (PWA)** with declarative routing using `react-router`, which handles global state management using Context and React Hooks. Also, HOC is used to access data throughout the application.

Build time is 2.5 hours.

Getting started

The project that we'll create in this chapter builds upon an initial version that you can find on GitHub: `https://github.com/PacktPublishing/React-Projects/tree/ch5-initial`. The complete source code can also be found on GitHub: `https://github.com/PacktPublishing/React-Projects/tree/ch5`.

After downloading the initial application, make sure that you run `npm install` from the project's root directory. This project is created using Create React App and installs the `react`, `react-dom`, `react-scripts`, `styled-components`, and `react-router` packages, which you've already seen in previous chapters. After finishing the installation process, you can run `npm start` from the same tab in Terminal and view the project in your browser (`http://localhost:3000`).

As the project is created with Create React App, the service workers are registered to have the application run as a PWA. You can check this by running `npm run build` first and `serve -s build` once the build process is completed. The build version of the application can now be visited at `http://localhost:5000`. In case you visit the application on this URL and see a different one, it might be that the built version of an application you've created in any of the preceding chapters is still being served. This might be due to the browser cache created by a service worker. You can clear any previous application from the browser cache by opening **Developer Tools** on your browse and open the **Application** tab, where you can click on the **Clear site data** button on the **Clear Storage** section.

To check whether the application is really still available when there is no internet connection, you can have the browser simulate an offline situation. The option to enable this can be found in the **Application** tab in the browser's **Developer Tools**. Inside this tab, you can find **Service Workers** in the menu on the left and, after clicking this link, you can select the **Offline** checkbox on the page that appears.

The initial application for this section is available at `http://localhost:3000` and is a bit more advanced than in any of the previous chapters. When you open the application, a screen displaying a header, a subheader, and two lists is being rendered. If you, for example, click on the first list that is displayed here, a new page will open that displays the items of this list. On this page, you can click on the **Add List** button at the top-right to open a new page, which has a form to add a new list and looks like this:

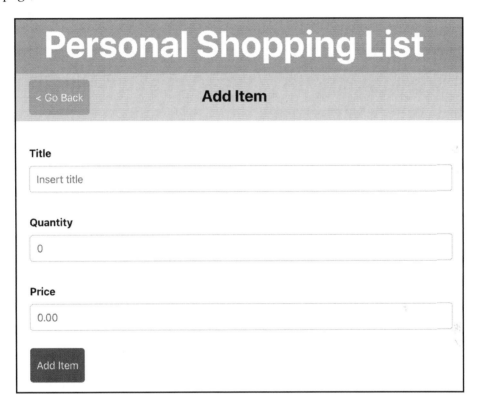

This form is rendered by the `Form` component and has no functionality yet, as you'll add this later on. When you click on the left button, it redirects you to the previously visited page, using the `history.goBack` method from `react-router`.

When you try to submit the form to either add a new list or add a new item to a list, nothing happens yet. The functionality of these forms will be added in this section later on, for which you'll use the context API and React Hooks.

The project is structured in the same manner as with the applications you've created before. A distinction between reusable function components in the components directory and class components in the containers directory is made. The class components are wrapped with a HOC called withDataFetching, which adds data fetching and life cycles (componentDidMount) to these components.

> The withDataFetching HOC is a slightly modified version of the HOC you created in Chapter 2, *Creating a Progressive Web Application with Reusable React Components*, which was also called withDataFetching.js. This modified version is a curried component, meaning it takes multiple arguments at once. In the case of a HOC, this means that you can't only use a component as an argument, but you also need to use the props for this component as an argument.

The following is an overview of the complete structure of the project:

```
shopping-list
|-- node_modules
|-- public
    |-- favicon.ico
    |-- index.html
    |-- manifest.json
|-- src
    |-- components
        |-- Button
            |-- Button.js
        |-- FormItem
            |-- FormItem.js
        |-- Header
            |-- Header.js
            |-- Subheader.js
        |-- ListItem
            |-- ListItem.js
    |-- containers
        |-- App.js
        |-- Form.js
        |-- List.js
        |-- Lists.js
    |-- index.js
    |-- serviceWorker.js
.gitignore
db.json
package.json
```

The entry point of this application is the `src/index.js` file that renders the `App` class component within a `Router` component from `react-router`.

The `App` component contains a `Header` component and a `Switch` router component that defines four routes. These routes are as follows:

- `/`: Renders `Lists`, with an overview of all of the lists
- `/list/:id`: Renders `List`, with an overview of all items from a specific list
- `/list/:id/new`: Renders `Form`, with a form to add new items to a specific list

The data is fetched from a mock server that was created using the free service, **My JSON Server**, which creates a server from the `db.json` file in the root directory of your project in GitHub. This file consists of a JSON object that has two fields, `items` and `lists`, which creates multiple endpoints on a mock server. The ones you'll be using in this chapter are as follows:

- `https://my-json-server.typicode.com/<your-username>/<your-repo>/items`
- `https://my-json-server.typicode.com/<your-username>/<your-repo>/lists`

The `db.json` file must be present in the master branch (or default branch) of your GitHub repository for the **My JSON Server** to work. Otherwise, you'll receive a **404 Not Found** message when trying to request the API endpoints.

Personal shopping list

In this section, you'll build a personal shopping list application that has global state management using Context and React Hooks. With this application, you can create shopping lists that you can add items to, along with their quantities and prices. The starting point of this section is an initial application that has routing and local state management already enabled.

Using the context API for state management

State management is very important, as the current state of the application holds data that is valuable to the user. In previous chapters, you've already used local state management by setting an initial state in `constructor` and updating this with the `this.setState` method. This pattern is very useful when the data in the state is only of importance to the component you're setting the state in. As passing down the state as props through several components can become confusing, you'd need a way to access props throughout your application even when you're not specifically passing them as props. For this, you can use the context API from React, which is also used by packages you've already used in previous chapters such as `styled-components` and `react-router`.

To share state across multiple components, a React feature called Context will be explored, starting in the first part of this section.

Creating Context

When you want to add Context to your React application, you can do this by creating a new Context with the `createContext` method from React. This creates a Context object that consists of two React components, called **Provider** and **Consumer**. The Provider is where the initial (and subsequently current) value of the Context is placed, which can be accessed by components that are present within the Consumer.

This is done in the `App` component in `src/containers/App.js`, as you want the Contexts for the lists to be available in every component that is rendered by `Route`:

1. Let's start by creating a Context for the lists and make it exportable so that the list data can be used everywhere. For this, you can create a new file called `ListsContextProvider.js` inside a new directory, `src/Context`. In this file, you can add the following code:

```
import React from 'react';
import withDataFetching from '../withDataFetching';

export const ListsContext = React.createContext();

const ListsContextProvider = ({ children, data }) => (
  <ListsContext.Provider value={{ lists: data }}>
    {children}
  </ListsContext.Provider>
);

export default withDataFetching({
```

```
        dataSource:
'https://my-json-server.typicode.com/PacktPublishing/React-Projects
/lists',
})(ListsContextProvider);
```

The previous code creates a Provider based on a Context component that is
passed as a prop and sets a value based on the return from the
withDataFetching HOC that is fetching all of the lists. Using the children
prop, all of the components that will be wrapped inside the
ListsContextProvider component can retrieve the data for the value from a
Consumer.

2. This ListsContextProvider component and the Context can be imported
   inside your App component in src/containers/App.js, where it should
   subsequently be placed around the Switch component. The ListsContext
   object is also imported, as, you can't create the Consumer later on:

```
import React from 'react';
import styled, { createGlobalStyle } from 'styled-components';
import { Route, Switch } from 'react-router-dom';
+ import ListsContextProvider, { ListsContext } from
'../Context/ListsContextProvider';

...

const App = () => (
 <>
   <GlobalStyle />
   <AppWrapper>
     <Header />
+     <ListsContextProvider>
       <Switch>
         <Route exact path='/' component={Lists} />
         <Route path='/list/:id/new' component={Form} />
         <Route path='/list/:id' component={List} />
       </Switch>
+     </ListsContextProvider>
   </AppWrapper>
 </>
);

export default App;
```

3. This way, you're now able to add a Consumer for `ListsContext`, which is nested within the `ListsContextProvider` component that holds the Provider for `ListsContext`. This Consumer returns the value from the Provider, which contains the list data that was fetched before:

```
...

const App = () => (
  <>
    <GlobalStyle />
      <AppWrapper>
      <Header />
        <ListsContextProvider>
+         <ListsContext.Consumer>
+           {({ lists }) => (
              <Switch>
                <Route exact path='/' component={Lists} />
                <Route path='/list/:id/new' component={Form} />
                <Route path='/list/:id' component={List} />
              </Switch>
+           )}
+         </ListsContext.Consumer>
        </ListsContextProvider>
      </AppWrapper>
  </>
);

export default App;
```

4. To actually pass this list data to any of the components rendered by `Route`, you should change the way the component is passed to the `Route` component. Instead of telling `Route` which component to render, you can also use the `RenderProps` pattern for React. This pattern refers to a technique for sharing code between React components using a prop whose value is a function that returns a component. In this case, you want the `Route` component to render a component and not just add the `react-router` props to it but also the list data from `ListsContext`:

```
      ...
      <ListsContextProvider>
        <ListsContext.Consumer>
          {({ lists }) => (
            <Switch>
-             <Route exact path='/' component={Lists} />
+             <Route exact path='/' render={props => lists && <Lists
lists={lists} {...props} /> } />
```

```
                <Route path='/list/:id/new' component={Form} />
                <Route path='/list/:id' component={List} />
            </Switch>
          )}
        </ListsContext.Consumer>
      </ListsContextProvider>
      ...
```

5. If you now look at the **Network** tab in the browser's **Developer Tools**, you can see the API is fetched twice. As the lists are now also being fetched by `ListsContextProvider`, the `Lists` component itself doesn't have to fetch the API anymore as it's now sent as a prop. Therefore, you can make the following changes to `src/containers/Lists.js`:

```
import React from 'react';
import styled from 'styled-components';
import { Link } from 'react-router-dom';
- import withDataFetching from '../withDataFetching';
import SubHeader from '../components/SubHeader/SubHeader';

...

- const Lists = ({ data, loading, error, match, history }) => (
+ const Lists = ({ lists, loading = false, error = false, match,
history }) => (
  <>
    {history && <SubHeader title='Your Lists' openForm={() =>
history.push('/new')} /> }
    <ListWrapper>
      {(loading || error) && <Alert>{loading ? 'Loading...' :
error}</Alert>}
-     {data.lists && data.lists.map(list => (
+     {lists && lists.map(list => (
        <ListLink key={list.id} to={`list/${list.id}`}>
          <Title>{ list.title }</Title>
        </ListLink>
      ))}
    </ListWrapper>
  </>
);

- export default withDataFetching({
-   dataSource:
'https://github.com/PacktPublishing/React-Projects/lists',
})(Lists);
+ export default Lists;
```

Now you've removed the `withDataFetching` HOC from `Lists`, no duplicate requests to the API are sent anymore. The data for the lists is fetched from `ListsContextProvider` and is passed by `ListsContext.Consumer` to `Lists`. If you open the application in the browser by going to `http://localhost:3000/`, you can see the lists are being rendered just as before.

Something else you can do is to send the list data to the `List` component as well, so you could, in the example, display the name of the selected lists when you click on a list from the home page:

1. For this, you use the `RenderProps` pattern again, this time for `Route`, which renders `List`. This makes sure `lists` is available and renders the `List` component afterward, which also takes all of the `react-router` props:

```
...
<ListsContextProvider>
  <ListsContext.Consumer>
    {({ lists }) => (
      <Switch>
        <Route exact path='/' render={props => lists && <Lists
lists={lists} {...props} /> } />
        <Route path='/list/:id/new' component={Form} />
-       <Route path='/list/:id' component={List} />
+       <Route path='/list/:id' render={props => lists && <List
lists={lists} {...props} />} />
      </Switch>
    )}
  </ListsContext.Consumer>
</ListsContextProvider>
...
```

2. In the `List` component in the `src/containers/List.js` file, you can retrieve the lists from the props. This array needs to be filtered for the correct `list` and the found object contains `title`, which can be added to the `SubHeader` component so that it will be displayed on the page:

```
- const List = ({ data, loading, error, match, history }) => {
+ const List = ({ data, loading, error, lists, match, history }) =>
{
    const items = data && data.filter(item => item.listId ===
parseInt(match.params.id))
+   const list = lists && lists.find(list => list.id ===
parseInt(match.params.id));

  return (
    <>
```

```
-       {history && <SubHeader goBack={() => history.goBack()}
openForm={() => history.push(`${match.url}/new`)} />}
+       {history && list && <SubHeader goBack={() =>
history.goBack()} title={list.title} openForm={() =>
history.push(`${match.url}/new`)} />}
        <ListItemWrapper>
          {items && items.map(item => <ListItem key={item.id}
data={item} />)}
        </ListItemWrapper>
      </>
    )
};

export default withDataFetching({
  dataSource:
'https://my-json-server.typicode.com/PacktPublishing/React-Projects
/items',
})(List);
```

With these additions, `title` of the current list will now be displayed if you visit the project at `http://localhost:3000/list/1`. In the `SubHeader` component, the title **Daily groceries** is now visible, which looks similar to the following screenshot:

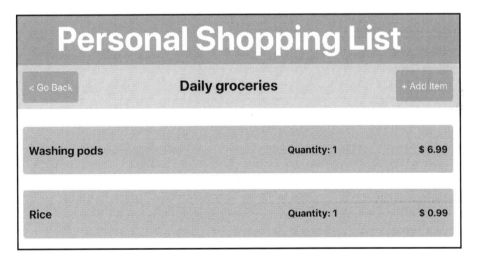

In the next section, you'll also add a Context object for the items, so the items are also available to all of the components within the `Switch` component from `react-router`.

Nesting Context

Just as for the list data, the item data could also be stored in Context and passed to the components that need this data. That way, data is no longer fetched from any of the rendered components but from the ContextProvider components in the src/Providers directory:

1. Again, start by creating a new component where both a Context and Provider are created. This time, it's called ItemsContextProvider, which can also be added to the src/Context directory in a file called ItemsContextProvider.js:

```
import React from 'react';
import withDataFetching from '../withDataFetching';

export const ItemsContext = React.createContext();

const ItemsContextProvider = ({ children, data }) => (
  <ItemsContext.Provider value={{ items: data }}>
    { children }
  </ItemsContext.Provider>
);

export default withDataFetching({
  dataSource:
'https://my-json-server.typicode.com/PacktPublishing/React-Projects
/items',
})(ItemsContextProvider);
```

2. Next, import this new Context and ContextProvider in src/containers/App.js, where you can nest this inside the ListsContextProvider component:

```
import React from 'react';
import styled, { createGlobalStyle } from 'styled-components';
import { Route, Switch } from 'react-router-dom';
import ListsContextProvider, { ListsContext } from
'../Context/ListsContextProvider';
+ import ItemsContextProvider, { ItemsContext } from
'../Context/ItemsContextProvider';

...

const App = () => (
  <>
    <GlobalStyle />
    <AppWrapper>
```

```
      <Header />
      <ListsContextProvider>
+     <ItemsContextProvider>
      <ListsContext.Consumer>
         ...
```

3. `ItemsContextProvider` is now nested below `ListsContextProvider`, which means `Consumer` for `ItemsContext` can also be nested below `Consumer` for `ListsContext`. This makes the value from `ItemsContextProvider` available to the `List` component that uses the `RenderProps` pattern:

```
<ListsContextProvider>
  <ItemsContextProvider>
    <ListsContext.Consumer>
      {({ lists }) => (
+       <ItemsContext.Consumer>
+         {({ items }) => (
            <Switch>
              <Route exact path='/' render={props => lists &&
<Lists lists={lists} {...props} />} />
              <Route path='/new' component={Form} />
              <Route path='/list/:id/new' component={Form} />
-             <Route path='/list/:id' render={props => lists &&
<List lists={lists} {...props} />
+             <Route path='/list/:id' render={props => lists &&
items && <List lists={lists} listItems={items} {...props} />}/>
            </Switch>
+         )}
+       </ItemsContext.Consumer>
      )}
    </ListsContext.Consumer>
  </ItemsContextProvider>
</ListsContextProvider>
```

4. After the item data is passed as a prop to `List`, this can now be used to replace the data fetching that is already in place using the `withDataFetching` HOC. To accomplish this, you need to make the following changes to `src/containers/List.js`:

```
import React from 'react';
import styled from 'styled-components';
- import withDataFetching from '../withDataFetching';
import SubHeader from '../components/SubHeader/SubHeader';
import ListItem from '../components/ListItem/ListItem';

...
```

```
- const List = ({ data, lists, loading, error, match, history }) =>
{
+ const List = ({ lists, listItems, loading = false, error = false,
match, history }) => {
-     const items = data && data.filter(item => item.listId ===
parseInt(match.params.id))
+     const items = listItems && listItems.filter(item => item.listId
=== parseInt(match.params.id))

      const list = lists && lists.find(list => list.id ===
parseInt(match.params.id));

      return (
        <>
          {history && <SubHeader goBack={() => history.goBack()}
title={list.title} openForm={() =>
history.push(`${match.url}/new`)} />}
          <ListItemWrapper>
            {items && items.map(item => <ListItem key={item.id}
data={ item } />) }
          </ListItemWrapper>
        </>
      )
};

- export default withDataFetching({
    dataSource:
'https://my-json-server.typicode.com/PacktPublishing/React-Projects
/items',
  })(List);
+ export default List;
```

All of the data fetching is now no longer by the `List` and `Lists` components. By nesting these Context Providers, the return values can be consumed by multiple components. But this still isn't ideal, as you're now loading all of the lists and all of the items when starting your application.

In the next section, you'll see how to get only the data you need by combining Context with Hooks.

Mutating context with Hooks

There are multiple ways in which you can get data conditionally from the Context; one of these is placing the data from the Context in the local state. That could be a solution for a smaller application but can be inefficient for larger applications, as you'd still need to pass this state down your component tree. Another solution is using React Hooks to create a function that is added to the value of your Context and can be invoked from any of the components that are nested in this Context. Also, this method of getting the data prevents you from efficiently loading only the data that you'd need.

How this can be used together with React life cycles and state management using Hooks is demonstrated in the first part of this section.

Using life cycles in functional components

One of the many great additions that came with Hooks is making life cycles available in functional components. Before Hooks, only class components supported life cycles using to the container components pattern and the `withDataFetching` HOC you've used so far. Follow these steps:

1. The first step in achieving this is by moving the function to do data fetching from the `withDataFetching` HOC to the Provider for the lists, in the `src/Context/ListsContextProvider.js` file. This function will take `dataSource` (which could be a file or an API) and uses `fetch` to retrieve data from this source:

```
import React from 'react';

export const ListsContext = React.createContext();

async function fetchData(dataSource) {
  try {
    const data = await fetch(dataSource);
    const dataJSON = await data.json();

    if (dataJSON) {
      return await ({ data: dataJSON, error: false });
    }
  } catch(error) {
      return ({ data: false, error: error.message });
  }
};

. . . .
```

2. With this function in place, the next step would be to invoke it with `dataSource` and add the data to the Provider. But where should you store the data that is returned by `dataSource`? Before, you've used the `componentDidMount` life cycle method for this and added the results from the source to the local state. With Hooks, you can use local state management inside a function component with the `useState` Hook. You can pass the initial value for the state, which you set in `constructor` before, as an argument to this Hook. The returned value will be an array consisting of the current value for this state and a function to update this state. Also, Hooks should always be created inside the component in which it's used—in this case, inside `ListsContextProvider`:

```
...
async function fetchData(dataSource) {
  try {
    const data = await fetch(dataSource);
    const dataJSON = await data.json();

    if (dataJSON) {
      return await ({ data: dataJSON, error: false });
    }
  } catch(error) {
      return ({ data: false, error: error.message });
  }
};

- const ListsContextProvider = ({ children, data }) => (
+ const ListsContextProvider = ({ children }) => {
+   const [lists, setLists] = React.useState([]);
+   return (
-     <ListsContext.Provider value={{ lists: data }}>
+     <ListsContext.Provider value={{ lists }}>
        {children}
      </ListsContext.Provider>
    )
+ };

- export default withDataFetching({
    dataSource:
'https://my-json-server.typicode.com/PacktPublishing/React-Projects
/items',
  })(ListsContextProvider);
+ export default ListsContextProvider;
```

3. In the preceding code block, you can see the initial value for the state is an empty array, which is passed to the Provider for ListsContext. To fill this state with data from dataSource, you need to actually invoke the fetchData function. Normally, this would be done inside a componentDidMount or componentDidUpdate life cycle method, but as a component is a function component, you're using a Hook instead. This Hook is called useEffect and is used to handle side effects, either when the application mounts or when the state or a prop gets updated. This Hook takes two parameters, where the first one is a callback and the second one is an array containing all of the variables this Hook depends on. When any of these changes, the callback for this Hook will be called. When there are no values in this array, the Hook will only be called on the first mount. After the data is fetched from the source, the state will be updated with the results:

```
...
const ListsContextProvider = ({ children }) => {
  const [lists, setLists] = React.useState([]);
  React.useEffect(() => {
    const asyncFetchData = async dataSource => {
      const result = await fetchData(dataSource);

      setLists([...result.data]);
    };

asyncFetchData('https://my-json-server.typicode.com/PacktPublishing
/React-Projects/lists');

  }, [fetchData, setLists]);

  return (
    <ListsContext.Provider value={{ lists }}>
      {children}
    </ListsContext.Provider>
  )
};

export default ListsContextProvider;
```

You can see the fetchData function isn't invoked directly but is wrapped inside a function called asyncFetchData. As async/await from the fetchData function would return Promise, you'd need another async/await to retrieve the values and resolve Promise. However, you can't use async/await directly with the useEffect Hook. The array block after the callback from the useEffect Hook is called the dependency array, and in here the values that are used in the Hook are defined. The functions fetchData and setLists are created on the first mount of this component, meaning the useEffect Hook mimics a lifecycle that's comparable to componentDidMount. If you want to use this Hook as a componentDidUpdate life cycle method, the array would consist of all of the state variables and props that should be watched for updates.

By using other Hooks, you can also directly pass data to the Provider, without having to use local state management. This will be demonstrated in the next part of this section.

Updating the Provider with a Flux pattern

Another way to use actions to add data to the Provider is by using a pattern similar to Flux, which was introduced by Facebook. The Flux pattern describes a data flow where actions are being dispatched that retrieve data from a store and return it to the view. This would mean that actions need to be described somewhere; there should be a global place where data is stored and this data can be read by the view. To accomplish this pattern with the context API, you can use another Hook that is called useReducer. This Hook can be used to return data not from a local state, but from any data variable:

1. Just as with the useState Hook, the useReducer Hook needs to be added to the component that is using it. useReducer will take an initial value and a function that determines which data should be returned. This initial value needs to be added to the src/Context/ListsContextProvider.js file before adding the Hook:

```
import React from 'react';

export const ListsContext = React.createContext();

const initialValue = {
  lists: [],
  loading: true,
  error: '',
},

...
```

2. Next to `initialValue`, the `useReducer` Hook also takes a function that's called `reducer`. This `reducer` function should also be created and is a function that updates `initialValue`, which was passed and returns the current value, based on the action that was sent to it. If the action that was dispatched doesn't match any of those defined in `reducer`, the reducer will just return the current value without any changes:

```
import React from 'react';

export const ListsContext = React.createContext();

const initialValue = {
  lists: [],
  loading: true,
  error: '',
};

const reducer = (value, action) => {
  switch (action.type) {
    case 'GET_LISTS_SUCCESS':
      return {
        ...value,
        lists: action.payload,
        loading: false,
      };
    case 'GET_LISTS_ERROR':
      return {
        ...value,
        lists: [],
        loading: false,
        error: action.payload,
      };
    default:
      return value;
  }
};

...
```

3. The two parameters for the `useReducer` Hook are now added to the file, so you need to add the actual Hook and pass `initialValue` and `reducer` to it:

```
...

const ListsContextProvider = ({ children }) => {
-     const [lists, setLists] = React.useState([]);
+     const [value, dispatch] = React.useReducer(reducer,
```

```
initialValue);
```

    . . .

4. As you can see, `reducer` changes the value it returns when the
   `GET_LISTS_SUCCESS` or `GET_LISTS_ERROR` action is sent to it. Before it was
   mentioned, you can call this `reducer` by using the `dispatch` function that was
   returned by the `useReducer` Hook. However, as you also have to deal with the
   asynchronous fetching of the data, you can't invoke this function directly.
   Instead, you need to create an `async/await` function that calls the
   `fetchData` function and dispatches the correct action afterward:

   ```
   . . .
   const ListsContextProvider = ({ children }) => {
     const [value, dispatch] = React.useReducer(reducer,
   initialValue);

     const getListsRequest = async () => {
       const result = await
   fetchData('https://my-json-server.typicode.com/PacktPublishing/Reac
   t-Projects/lists');

       if (result.data && result.data.length) {
         dispatch({ type: 'GET_LISTS_SUCCESS', payload: result.data
   });
       } else {
         dispatch({ type: 'GET_LISTS_ERROR', payload: result.error });
       }
     }
   . . .
   ```

With the preceding `getListsRequest` function, an `async/await` call to the
`fetchData` function is made when this function is invoked. If the data that was
returned by `dataSource` is not an empty array, the `GET_LISTS_SUCCESS` action
will be dispatched to the reducer using the `dispatch` function from the
`useReducer` Hook. If not, the `GET_LISTS_ERROR` action will be dispatched,
which returns an error message.

5. This `getListsRequest` function can now be invoked from the `useEffect` Hook when your application mounts, so the application will be filled with the list data. This should be done from the view, so you need to create an action that you can add to `Provider`, so it can be used from any of the components that get this value from `Consumer`:

```
    ...

-   React.useEffect(() => {
-     const asyncFetchData = async (dataSource) => {
-       const result = await fetchData(dataSource);
-
-       setLists([...result.data]);
-     }
-
-
    asyncFetchData('https://my-json-server.typicode.com/PacktPublis
    hing/React-Projects/lists');
-   }, [setLists]);

    return (
-     <ListsContext.Provider value={{ lists: state }}>
+     <ListsContext.Provider value={{ ...value, getListsRequest
    }}>
        {children}
      </ListsContext.Provider>
    );
};

export default ListsContextProvider;
```

6. In the component where the lists are displayed, the `Lists` component, you can retrieve the data for the lists with the `getListsRequest` function. Therefore, you'd need to pass it to this component from `RenderProps` in `Route`, in the `src/containers/App.js` file. Also, you can add a loading indicator that will be displayed when the list data isn't retrieved yet or an error message when some error occurs:

```
  ...
  const App = () => (
    <>
      <GlobalStyle />
        <AppWrapper>
        <Header />
          <ListsContextProvider>
            <ItemsContextProvider>
```

```
                    <ListsContext.Consumer>
-                       {(({ lists }) => (
+                       {(({ lists, loading: listsLoading, error: listsError,
getListsRequest }) => (
                          <ItemsContext.Consumer>
                            {(({ items }) => (
                              <Switch>
-                                <Route exact path='/' render={props => lists
&& <Lists lists={lists} {...props} />} />
+                                <Route exact path='/' render={props => lists
&& <Lists lists={lists} loading={listsLoading} error={listsError}
getListsRequest={getListsRequest} {...props} />} />
...
```

7. And finally, invoke the `getListsRequest` function from the `Lists` component when it mounts, and add the loading indicator or error message. The lists should only be retrieved when there aren't any lists available yet:

```
- const Lists = ({lists, loading = false, error = '', match,
history}) => !loading && !error ? (
+ const Lists = ({lists, loading, error, getListsRequest, match,
history}) => {
+   React.useEffect(() => {
+     if (!lists.length) {
+       getListsRequest();
+     }
+   }, [lists, getListsRequest]);

+   return !loading && !error ? (
    <>
       {history && <SubHeader title='Your Lists' openForm={() =>
history.push('/new')} /> }
       <ListWrapper>
         {lists && lists.map(list => (
           <ListLink key={list.id} to={`list/${list.id}`}>
             <Title>{list.title}</Title>
           </ListLink>
         ))}
       </ListWrapper>
    </>
-   );
+   ) : <Alert>{loading ? 'Loading...' : error}</Alert>;
+ }

export default Lists;
```

If you now visit the project in the browser again, you can see the data from the lists is loaded just as before. The big difference is that the data is fetched using a Flux pattern, meaning this can be extended to fetch the data in other instances as well. The same can be done for `ItemsContextProvider` as well, in the `src/Context/ItemsContextProvider.js` file:

1. First add the initial value for the items, which you'll use with the `useReducer` Hook:

```
import React from 'react';
- import withDataFetching from '../withDataFetching';

+ const initialValue = {
+   items: [],
+   loading: true,
+   error: '',
+ }

export const ItemsContext = React.createContext();

- const ItemsContextProvider = ({ children, data }) => (
+ const ItemsContextProvider = ({ children }) => {
    + const [value, dispatch] = React.useReducer(reducer,
initialValue);

+ return (
  <ItemsContext.Provider value={{ items: data }}>
    {children}
  </ItemsContext.Provider>
);
+ };

...
```

2. After this, you can add the reducer, which has two actions that are quite similar to the ones for the list reducer. The only difference is that they will add information about the items to the Provider. Also, add the same `fetchData` function that as you added to `ListsContextProvider`:

```
import React from 'react';
import withDataFetching from '../withDataFetching';

export const ItemsContext = React.createContext();

const initialValue = {
    items: [],
    loading: true,
```

```
      error: '',
  }

+ const reducer = (value, action) => {
+   switch (action.type) {
+     case 'GET_ITEMS_SUCCESS':
+       return {
+         ...value,
+         items: action.payload,
+         loading: false,
+       };
+     case 'GET_ITEMS_ERROR':
+       return {
+         ...value,
+         items: [],
+         loading: false,
+         error: action.payload,
+       };
+     default:
+       return value;
+   }
+ };

+ async function fetchData(dataSource) {
+   try {
+     const data = await fetch(dataSource);
+     const dataJSON = await data.json();
+
+     if (dataJSON) {
+       return await ({ data: dataJSON, error: false })
+     }
+   } catch(error) {
+       return ({ data: false, error: error.message })
+   }
+ };

  const ItemsContextProvider = ({ children }) => {
      ...
```

3. Now, you can create the `async/await` function that will fetch `dataSource` for the items. This function will also take the `id` variable of the list that is selected, so no over-fetching of data will occur. The `withDataFetching` HOC can be removed, as it's no longer needed to retrieve the data:

```
  ...
  const ItemsContextProvider = ({ children }) => {
      const [value, dispatch] = React.useReducer(reducer,
```

```
initialValue);

+   const getItemsRequest = async (id) => {
+     const result = await fetchData(`
+
https://my-json-server.typicode.com/PacktPublishing/React-Projects/
items/${id}/items
+       `);
+
+     if (result.data && result.data.length) {
+       dispatch({ type: 'GET_ITEMS_SUCCESS', payload: result.data
});
+     } else {
+       dispatch({ type: 'GET_ITEMS_ERROR', payload: result.error
});
+     }
+   }

    return (
-     <ItemsContext.Provider value={{ items: data }}>
+     <ItemsContext.Provider value={{ ...value, getItemsRequest }}>
        {children}
      </ItemsContext.Provider>
    );
}

- export default withDataFetching({
    dataSource:
'https://my-json-server.typicode.com/PacktPublishing/React-Projects
/items',
  })(ItemsContextProvider);
+ export default ItemsContextProvider;
```

4. As the function to retrieve items is now added to the Provider for the items, the Consumer is `src/containers/App.js` and can pass this function to the `List` component that is displaying the items:

```
...
const App = () => (
  <>
    <GlobalStyle />
      <AppWrapper>
      <Header />
        <ListsContextProvider>
          <ItemsContextProvider>
            <ListsContext.Consumer>
              {(({ lists, loading: listsLoading, error: listsError,
getListsRequest }) => (
```

```
                            <ItemsContext.Consumer>
-                             {({ items }) => (
+                             ({ items, loading: itemsLoading, error:
itemsError, getItemsRequest }) => (
                                <Switch>
                                  <Route exact path='/' render={props => lists
&& <Lists lists={lists} loading={listsLoading} error={listsError}
getListsRequest={getListsRequest} {...props} />} />
                                  <Route path='/list/:id/new' component={Form}
/>
-                                 <Route path='list/:id' render={props => lists
&& items && <List lists={lists} listItems={items} {...props} />
+                                 <Route path='/list/:id' render={props =>
lists && items && <List lists={lists} items={items}
loading={itemsLoading} error={itemsError}
getItemsRequest={getItemsRequest} {...props} /> } />
                                </Switch>
                              )}
                            </ItemsContext.Consumer>
                          )}
                      </ListsContext.Consumer>
                    </ItemsContextProvider>
                  </ListsContextProvider>
              </AppWrapper>
          </>
        );

        export default App;
```

5. And finally, call this `getItemsRequest` function from the `List` component in
   `src/containers/List.js`. This function will take the `id` variable for the list
   that you are displaying from the current route, by using the `match` prop. It's
   important to mention that this function should only be called when the value for
   `items` is empty, to prevent unnecessary data fetching:

```
...
- const List = ({ listItems, loading = false, error = '', lists,
match, history }) => {
+ const List = ({ items, loading, error, lists, getItemsRequest,
match, history }) => {
-   const items = listItems && listItems.filter(item => item.listId
=== parseInt(match.params.id));
  const list = lists && lists.find(list => list.id ===
parseInt(match.params.id));

+   React.useEffect(() => {
+     if (!items.length > 0) {
```

```
+       getItemsRequest(match.params.id);
+    };
+ }, [items, match.params.id, getItemsRequest]);

   return !loading && !error ? (
     <>
        {(history && list) && <SubHeader goBack={() =>
history.goBack()} title={list.title} openForm={() =>
history.push(`${match.url}/new`)} />}
        <ListItemWrapper>
           {items && items.map(item => <ListItem key={item.id} data={
item } />)}
        </ListItemWrapper>
     </>
) : <Alert>{loading ? 'Loading... : error}</Alert>
};

export default List;
```

You might notice that the title of the list won't be displayed any longer when you refresh
the page. The information for the lists is only fetched when the Lists component is
mounted, so you'd need to create a new function to always fetch the information for the list
that you're currently displaying in the List component:

1. In the src/Context/ListsContextProvider.js file, you need to
   extend initialValue to also have a field called list:

   ```
   import React from 'react';

   export const ListsContext = React.createContext();

   const initialValue = {
     lists: [],
   + list: {},
     loading: true,
     erorr: '',
   }

   const reducer = (value, action) => {
   ...
   ```

2. In reducer, you now also have to check for two new actions that either add the
   data about a list to the context or add an error message:

   ```
   ...

   const reducer = (value, action) => {
   ```

```
switch (action.type) {
  case 'GET_LISTS_SUCCESS':
    return {
      ...value,
      lists: action.payload,
      loading: false,
    };
  case 'GET_LISTS_ERROR':
    return {
      ...value,
      lists: [],
      loading: false,
      error: action.payload,
    };
+ case 'GET_LIST_SUCCESS':
+   return {
+     ...value,
+     list: action.payload,
+     loading: false,
+   };
+ case 'GET_LIST_ERROR':
+   return {
+     ...value,
+     list: {},
+     loading: false,
+     error: action.payload,
+   };
  default:
    return value;
  }
};

async function fetchData(dataSource) {
...
```

3. These actions will be dispatched from an `async/await` function that
   calls `dataSource` with a specific `id`. If successful, the `GET_LIST_SUCCESS` action
   will be dispatched; otherwise, the `GET_LIST_ERROR` action is dispatched. Also,
   pass the function to the Provider so that it can be used from the `List` component:

```
...
const ListsContextProvider = ({ children }) => {
  const [value, dispatch] = React.useReducer(reducer,
initialValue);

  const getListsRequest = async () => {
    const result = await
```

```
fetchData('https://my-json-server.typicode.com/PacktPublishing/Reac
t-Projects/lists');

    if (result.data && result.data.length) {
      dispatch({ type: 'GET_LISTS_SUCCESS', payload: result.data
});
    } else {
      dispatch({ type: 'GET_LISTS_ERROR', payload: result.error });
    }
  }

+  const getListRequest = async id => {
+    const result = await
fetchData(`https://my-json-server.typicode.com/PacktPublishing/Reac
t-Projects/lists/${id}`);

+    if (result.data && result.data.hasOwnProperty('id')) {
+      dispatch({ type: 'GET_LIST_SUCCESS', payload: result.data
});
+    } else {
+      dispatch({ type: 'GET_LIST_ERROR', payload: result.error });
+    }
+  }

  return (
-    <ListsContext.Provider value={{ ...value, getListsRequest }}>
+    <ListsContext.Provider value={{ ...value, getListsRequest,
getListRequest }}>
        ...
```

4. And pass this to the `List` component, by destructuring it from the `ListsContext` Consumer. Also, take the list data from this Consumer and pass it to the `List` component. The `lists` props can be removed from this component, as filtering the list data is now done by `ListsContextProvider`:

```
<ListsContext.Consumer>
-  {(({ lists, loading: listsLoading, error: listsError,
getListsRequest }) => (
+  {(({ list, lists, loading: listsLoading, error: listsError,
getListsRequest, getListRequest }) => (
    <ItemsContext.Consumer>
      {(({ items, loading: itemsLoading, error: itemsError,
getItemsRequest }) => (
        <Switch>
          <Route exact path='/' render={props => lists && <Lists
lists={lists} loading={listsLoading} error={listsError}
getListsRequest={getListsRequest} {...props} />} />
```

```
                    <Route path='/list/:id/new' component={Form} />
-                   <Route path='/list/:id' render={props => lists && items
&& <List lists={lists} items={items} loading={itemsLoading}
error={itemsError} getItemsRequest={getItemsRequest} {...props} />
} />
+                   <Route path='/list/:id' render={props => list && items
&& <List list={list} items={items} loading={itemsLoading}
error={itemsError} getListRequest={getListRequest}
getItemsRequest={getItemsRequest} {...props} /> } />
              </Switch>
          )}
        </ItemsContext.Consumer>
    )}
</ListsContext.Consumer>

...
```

5. Finally, you can invoke the `getListRequest` function that fetches the list data from the `List` component. You only want to retrieve the list information when this isn't already available; the filtering of the `lists` prop is therefore no longer needed:

```
...
- const List = ({ items, loading, error, lists, getItemsRequest,
match, history }) => {
+ const List = ({ items, loading, error, list, getListRequest,
getItemsRequest, match, history }) => {
-    const list = lists && lists.find(list => list.id ===
parseInt(match.params.id));

  React.useEffect(() => {
+    if (!list.id) {
+      getListRequest(match.params.id);
+    }

    if (!items.length > 0) {
      getItemsRequest(match.params.id);
    }
- }, [items, match.params.id, getItemsRequest]);
+ }, [items, list, match.params.id, getItemsRequest,
getListRequest]);

  return !loading && !error ? (
    ...
```

All of the data in your application is now being loaded using the Providers, which means it's now detached from the views. Also, the `withDataFetching` HOC is completely removed, making your application structure more readable.

Not only can you use the context API with this pattern to make data available to many components, but you can also mutate the data. How to mutate this data will be shown in the next section.

Mutating data in the Provider

Not only can you retrieve data using this Flux pattern, but you can also use it to update data. The pattern would remain the same: you dispatch an action that would trigger the request to the server and, based on the outcome, the reducer will mutate the data with this result. Depending on whether or not it was successful, you could display a success message or an error message.

The code already has a form for adding a new item to a list—something that is not working yet. Let's create the mechanism to add items by updating the Provider for `items`:

1. The first step is to create a new function that can handle POST requests, as this function should also set the method and a body when handling the `fetch` request. You can create this function in the `src/Context/ItemsContextProvider.js` file:

```
...
async function fetchData(dataSource) {
  try {
    const data = await fetch(dataSource);
    const dataJSON = await data.json();

    if (dataJSON) {
      return await ({ data: dataJSON, error: false });
    }
  } catch(error) {
      return ({ data: false, error: error.message });
  }
};

async function postData(dataSource, content) {
  try {
    const data = await fetch(dataSource, {
      method: 'POST',
      body: JSON.stringify(content),
    });
```

```
      const dataJSON = await data.json();

      if (dataJSON) {
        return await ({ data: dataJSON, error: false });
      }
    } catch(error) {
        return ({ data: false, error: error.message });
    }
  };

  const ItemsContextProvider = ({ children }) => {
    ...
```

2. This function takes not only `dataSource` but also information that will be posted to this source. Just as for retrieving the items, a case can be added to the `switch` statement in `reducer`. This time, it will look for an action that is called `ADD_ITEM_REQUEST`, which has a payload consisting of `dataSource` and `content` that should be added to the value. These actions change the value for `loading` and/or `error` and spread the actual current value in its return as well. If you don't do this, all of the information that is already available about the lists will be cleared:

```
...
const reducer = (value, action) => {
  switch (action.type) {
    case 'GET_ITEMS_SUCCESS':
      return {
        ...value,
        items: action.payload,
        loading: false,
      };
    case 'GET_ITEMS_ERROR':
      return {
        ...value,
        items: [],
        loading: action.payload,
      };
+   case 'ADD_ITEM_SUCCESS':
+     return {
+       ...value,
+       items: [
+         ...value.items,
+         action.payload,
+       ],
+       loading: false,
+     };
+   case 'ADD_ITEM_ERROR':
```

```
+        return {
+          ...value,
+          loading: false,
+          error: 'Something went wrong...',
+        };
      default:
        return value;
    }
};

async function fetchData(dataSource) {
...
```

The mock API from **My JSON Server** doesn't persist data once it is added, updated, or deleted with a request. However, you can see whether the request was successful by checking the request in the **Network** tab in the **Developer Tools** of your browser. That's why the input content is spread over the value for items, so this data is available from the Consumer.

3. Also, create an async/await function that handles the POST request. If this request is successful, the data that will be returned has a field called id. So, when this is the case, the ADD_ITEM_SUCCESS action can be dispatched. Otherwise, an ADD_ITEM_ERROR action is dispatched. These actions will change the value for this Provider from reducer:

```
...
const ItemsContextProvider = ({ children }) => {
  const [value, dispatch] = React.useReducer(reducer,
initialValue);

  const getItemsRequest = async (id) => {
    const result = await fetchData(`
https://my-json-server.typicode.com/PacktPublishing/React-Projects/
items/${id}/items
    `);

    if (result.data && result.data.length) {
      dispatch({ type: 'GET_ITEMS_SUCCESS', payload: result.data
});
    } else {
      dispatch({ type: 'GET_ITEMS_ERROR', payload: result.error });
    }
  }

+  const addItemRequest = async (content) => {
+    const result = await
```

```
    postData('https://my-json-server.typicode.com/PacktPublishing/React
    -Projects/items', content);

+     if (result.data && result.data.hasOwnProperty('id')) {
+        dispatch({ type: 'ADD_ITEM_SUCCESS', payload: content });
+     } else {
+        dispatch({ type: 'ADD_ITEM_ERROR' });
+     }
+   }

    return (
-     <ItemsContext.Provider value={{ ...value, getItemsRequest }}>
+     <ItemsContext.Provider value={{ ...value, getItemsRequest,
    addItemRequest }}>
        ...
```

4. Just as for retrieving the list, the `actionDispatch` function for adding a list can be wrapped inside a helper function. This function would take the content that is returned from the form later on. Also, pass this function to the Provider so that it can be used in any of the components that consume this Provider:

```
    ...
    const getListsRequest = () => {
      actionDispatch({
        type: 'GET_LISTS_REQUEST',
        payload:
    'https://my-json-server.typicode.com/PacktPublishing/React-Projects
    /items',
      });
    };

+   const addListRequest = (content) => {
+     actionDispatch({
+       type: 'ADD_LIST_REQUEST',
+       payload: {
+         dataSource:
    'https://my-json-server.typicode.com/PacktPublishing/React-Projects
    /items',
+         content,
+       }
+     });
+   };

    return (
-     <ListsContext.Provider value={{ ...value, getListsRequest }}>
+     <ListsContext.Provider value={{ ...value, getListsRequest,
    addListRequest }}>
        {children}
```

```
        </ListsContext.Provider>
    )
};

export default ListsContextProvider;
```

5. As the function to add a list is now available from the Provider, you can pass it to the `Form` component by using `RenderProps` from its `Route`. This can be done in the `src/containers/App.js` file. Make sure you don't forget to send the `match` and `history` props as well, as these are used by the `Form` component:

```
...
<ListsContext.Consumer>
  {(({ list, lists, loading: listsLoading, error: listsError,
getListsRequest, getListRequest }) => (
    <ItemsContext.Consumer>
-     {(({ items, loading: itemsLoading, error: itemsError,
getItemsRequest }) => (
+     {(({ items, loading: itemsLoading, error: itemsError,
getItemsRequest, addItemRequest }) => (
        <Switch>
          <Route exact path='/' render={props => lists && <Lists
lists={lists} loading={listsLoading} error={listsError}
getListsRequest={getListsRequest} {...props} />} />
-         <Route path='/list/:id/new' component={Form} />
+         <Route path='/list/:id/new' render={props => <Form
addItemRequest={addItemRequest} {...props} />} />
          <Route path='/list/:id' render={props => list && items &&
<List list={list} items={items} loading={itemsLoading}
error={itemsError} getListRequest={getListRequest}
getItemsRequest={getItemsRequest} {...props} /> } />
        </Switch>
      )}
    </ItemsContext.Consumer>
  )}
</ListsContext.Consumer>

...
```

The `Form` component is now able to use the `addListRequest` function that will dispatch the action that triggers the `POST` request that will add an item to `dataSource`. This function needs to be triggered when the user submits the form.

However, the values of the input fields in the form need to be determined first. Therefore, the input fields need to be controlled components, meaning their value is controlled by the local state that encapsulates the value:

1. For this, you can use the `useState` Hook, and call it for every `state` value that you want to create. The Hook will return both the current value of this `state` value and a function to update this value and must be added in `src/containers/Form.js`:

```
...
- const Form = ({ match, history }) => (
+ const Form = ({ addItemRequest, match, history }) => {
+   const [title, setTitle] = React.useState('');
+   const [quantity, setQuantity] = React.useState('');
+   const [price, setPrice] = React.useState('');

+   return (
    <>
      {history && <SubHeader goBack={() => history.goBack()}
title='Add Item' />}
      <FormWrapper>
        <form>
          <FormItem id='title' label='Title' placeholder='Insert
title' />
          <FormItem id='quantity' label='Quantity' type='number'
placeholder='0' />
          <FormItem id='price' label='Price' type='number'
placeholder='0.00' />
          <SubmitButton>Add Item</SubmitButton>
        </form>
      </FormWrapper>
    </>
  );
+ }

export default Form;
```

2. The local state values and the function that triggers an update of the local `state` values must be set as a prop on the `FormItem` components:

```
...
  return (
    <>
      {history && <SubHeader goBack={() => history.goBack()}
title='Add item' /> }
      <FormWrapper>
```

```
          <form>
-           <FormItem id='title' label='Title' placeholder='Insert
title' />
+           <FormItem id='title' label='Title' placeholder='Insert
title' value={title} handleOnChange={setTitle} />
-           <FormItem id='quantity' label='Quantity' type='number'
placeholder='0' />
+           <FormItem id='quantity' label='Quantity' type='number'
placeholder='0' value={quantity} handleOnChange={setQuantity} />
-           <FormItem id='price' label='Price' type='number'
placeholder='0.00' />
+           <FormItem id='price' label='Price' type='number'
placeholder='0.00' value={price} handleOnChange={setPrice} />
          <SubmitButton>Add Item</SubmitButton>
        </form>
      </FormWrapper>
    </>
  )
};

export default Form;
```

3. The `FormItem` component, in the `src/components/FormItem.js` file, can take these props and have the input field invoke the `handleOnChange` function. The element's current `target` value must be used as the parameter for this function:

```
...
- const FormItem = ({ id, label, type = 'text', placeholder = '' })
=> (
+ const FormItem = ({ id, label, type = 'text', placeholder = '',
value, handleOnChange }) => (
  <FormItemWrapper>
    <Label htmlFor={id}>{label}</Label>
-     <Input type={type} name={id} id={id} placeholder={placeholder}
/>
+     <Input type={type} name={id} id={id} placeholder={placeholder}
value={value} onChange={e => handleOnChange(e.target.value)} />
  </FormItemWrapper>
);

export default FormItem;
```

4. The last thing you need to do now is to add a function that will be dispatched when the form is submitted by clicking the submit button. This function takes `value` for the local `state`, adds information about the list and a randomly generated `id` and uses this to call the `addItemRequest` function. After this function is called, the `goBack` function from the `history` prop is called:

```
...
const Form = ({ addItemRequest, match, history }) => {
  ...

+ const handleOnSubmit = e => {
+     e.preventDefault();
+     addItemRequest({
+       title,
+       quantity,
+       price,
+       id: Math.floor(Math.random() * 100),
+       listId: parseInt(match.params.id)
+     });
+     history.goBack();
+   };

  return (
    <>
      {history && <SubHeader goBack={() => history.goBack()}
title={title} />}
        <FormWrapper>
-         <form>
+         <form onSubmit={handleOnSubmit}>

  ...
```

When you now submit the form, a POST request to the mock server will be sent. You'll be sent back to the previous page where you can see the result. If successful, the GET_LIST_SUCCESS action was dispatched and the item you inserted was added to the list.

So far, the information from the Context has been used only separately by using the Providers, but this can also be combined into one global Context, as shown in the next section.

Creating a global Context

If you look at the current structure of the routes in your App component, you can imagine this will get messy if you add more Providers and Consumers to your application. State management packages such as Redux tend to have a global state where all of the data for the application is stored. When using Context, it's possible to create a global Context that can be accessed using the useContext Hook. This Hook acts as a Consumer and can retrieve values from the Provider of the Context that was passed to it. Let's refactor the current application to have a global Context:

1. Start by creating a file called GlobalContext.js in the src/Context directory. This file will import both ListsContextProvider and ItemsContextProvider, nest them, and have them wrap any component that will be passed to it as children prop:

```
import React from 'react';
import ListsContextProvider from './ListsContextProvider';
import ItemsContextProvider from './ItemsContextProvider';

const GlobalContext = ({ children }) => {
  return (
    <ListsContextProvider>
      <ItemsContextProvider>
        {children}
      </ItemsContextProvider>
    </ListsContextProvider>
  );
};

export default GlobalContext;
```

2. In the src/containers/App.js file, you can now import this GlobalContext file in favor of the Providers for the lists and items:

```
import React from 'react';
import styled, { createGlobalStyle } from 'styled-components';
import { Route, Switch } from 'react-router-dom';
- import ListsContextProvider, { ListsContext } from
'../Context/ListsContextProvider';
- import ItemsContextProvider, { ItemsContext } from
'../Context/ItemsContextProvider';
+ import GlobalContext from '../Context/GlobalContext';
...
```

3. You can replace `ListsContextProvider` and `ItemsContextProvider` with `GlobalContext`. The Consumer will still be able to retrieve the data from `ListsContext` and `ItemsContext` if you'd still import them:

```
const App = () => (
  <>
    <GlobalStyle />
      <AppWrapper>
      <Header />
+       <GlobalContext>
-       <ListsContextProvider>
-         <ItemsContextProvider>
          <ListsContext.Consumer>
            {({ list, lists, loading: listsLoading, error:
listsErorr, getListsRequest, getListRequest }) => (
              <ItemsContext.Consumer>
                {({ items, loading: itemsLoading, error:
itemsError, getItemsRequest, addItemRequest }) => (
                  <Switch>
                    <Route exact path='/' render={props => lists &&
<Lists lists={lists} loading={listsLoading} error={listsError}
getListsRequest={getListsRequest} {...props} />} />
                    <Route path='/list/:id/new' render={props =>
<Form addItemRequest={addItemRequest} {...props} />} />
                    <Route path='/list/:id' render={props => list
&& items && <List list={list} items={items} loading={itemsLoading}
error={itemsError} getListRequest={getListRequest}
getItemsRequest={getItemsRequest} {...props} /> } />
                  </Switch>
                )}
              </ItemsContext.Consumer>
            )}
          </ListsContext.Consumer>
-         </ItemsContextProvider>
-       </ListsContextProvider>
+       </GlobalContext>
      </AppWrapper>
  </>
);

export default App;
```

4. Next, you can delete the Consumers and the `RenderProps` pattern from the routes. The value from the Context will no longer be passed from both the Consumers but will be retrieved by using the `useContext` Hooks in each of the routes:

```
...
        <GlobalContext>
-           <ListsContext.Consumer>
-               {(( list, lists, loading: listsLoading, error:
listsError, getListsRequest, getListRequest }) => (
-                   <ItemsContext.Consumer>
-                       {(( items, loading: itemsLoading, error:
itemsError, getItemsRequest, addItemRequest }) => (
                        <Switch>
-                           <Route exact path='/' render={props => lists &&
<Lists lists={lists} loading={listsLoading} error={listsError}
getListsRequest={getListsRequest} {...props} />} />
+                           <Route exact path='/' component={Lists} />
-                           <Route path='/list/:id/new' render={props =>
<Form addItemRequest={addItemRequest} {...props} />} />
+                           <Route path='/list/:id/new' component={Form} />
-                           <Route path='/list/:id' render={props => list
&& items && <List list={list} items={items} loading={itemsLoading}
error={itemsError} getListRequest={getListRequest}
getItemsRequest={getItemsRequest} {...props} /> } />
+                           <Route path='/list/:id' component={List} />
                        </Switch>
-                       )}
-                   </ItemsContext.Consumer>
-               )}
-           </ListsContext.Consumer>
        </GlobalContext>
...
```

5. In each of the components that are being rendered by `Route`, the Context that you want to use should be imported. The `useContext` Hook can then retrieve the value from this Context. You can start by adding this Hook to the `Lists` component in `src/containers/Lists.js`:

```
import React from 'react';
import styled from 'styled-components';
import { Link } from 'react-router-dom';
+ import { ListsContext } from '../Context/ListsContextProvider';
import SubHeader from '../components/Header/SubHeader';

...
```

```
- const Lists = ({lists, loading, error, getListsRequest, match,
history}) => {
+ const Lists = ({ match, history }) => {
+   const { lists, loading, error, getListsRequest } =
React.useContext(ListsContext);
  React.useEffect(() => {
    if (!lists.length) {
      getListsRequest();
    }
  }, [lists, getListsRequest]);

  return !loading && !error ? (
    <>
      {history && <SubHeader title='Your Lists' />}
      <ListWrapper>
        {lists && lists.map((list) => (
          <ListLink key={list.id} to={`list/${list.id}`}>
            <Title>{list.title}</Title>
          </ListLink>
        ))}
      </ListWrapper>
    </>
  ) : <Alert>{loading ? 'Loading...' : error}</Alert>;
}
export default Lists;
```

6. As you can see, `useContext` only takes the Context you want to use as an argument. To implement this in the `List` component, you'd need to import both `ListsContext` and `ItemsContext` in the `src/containers/List.js` file:

```
import React from 'react';
import styled from 'styled-components';
import { ListsContext } from '../Context/ListsContextProvider';
import { ItemsContext } from '../Context/ItemsContextProvider';
import SubHeader from '../components/Header/SubHeader';
import ListItem from '../components/ListItem/ListItem';

...

- const List = ({ items, loading, error, list, getListRequest,
getItemsRequest, match, history }) => {
+ const List = ({ match, history }) => {
+   const { list, getListRequest } = React.useContext(ListsContext);
+   const { loading, error, items, getItemsRequest } =
React.useContext(ItemsContext);

  React.useEffect(() => {
    ...
```

7. And do the same for the `Form` component in the `src/containers/Form.js` file, where you only use `ItemsContext`:

```
import React from 'react';
import styled from 'styled-components';
+ import { ItemsContext } from '../Context/ItemsContextProvider';
import SubHeader from '../components/Header/SubHeader';
import FormItem from '../components/FormItem/FormItem';
import Button from '../components/Button/Button';

...

- const Form = ({ addItemRequest, match, history }) => {
+ const Form = ({ match, history }) => {
+   const { addItemRequest } = React.useContext(ItemsContext);

...
```

You can now see that your application has a much cleaner structure, while the data is still being retrieved by the Providers.

Summary

In this chapter, you've created a shopping list application that uses the context API and Hooks to pass and retrieve data, instead of a HOC. Context is used to store data and Hooks are used to retrieve and mutate data. With the context API, you can create more advanced scenarios for state management using the `useReducer` Hook. Also, you've recreated a situation where all of the data is stored globally and can be accessed from any component by creating a shared Context.

The context API will be used in the next chapter as well, which will show you how to build a hotel review application with automated testing using libraries such as Jest and Enzyme. It will introduce you to the multiple ways you can test your UI components created with React, and also show you how to test state management in your application using the context API.

Further reading

Consuming multiple Context objects: `https://reactjs.org/docs/Context.html#consuming-multiple-Contexts`

6
Build an Application Exploring TDD Using Jest and Enzyme

To keep your application maintainable, it is good practice to have testing set up for your project. Where some developers hate writing tests and therefore try to avoid writing them, other developers like to make testing the core of their development process by implementing a **test-driven development (TDD)** strategy. There are many opinions about testing your applications and how to do this. Luckily, when building an application with React, many great libraries can help you with testing.

In this chapter, you'll use two libraries to unit test React applications. The first one is Jest, which is maintained by Facebook itself and ships with Create React App. The other tool is called Enzyme, which has more functionality than Jest and can be used to test entire life cycles within your components. Together, they are a great fit for testing most React applications if you want to test whether functions or components behave as expected when they're given a certain input.

The following topics will be covered in this chapter:

- Unit testing with Jest
- Rendering React components for testing
- Testing with Enzyme

Project overview

In this chapter, we will create a hotel review application that has unit and integration testing in place with Jest and Enzyme. The application has been prebuilt and uses the same patterns that we've looked at in the previous chapters.

The build time is 2 hours.

Getting started

The application for this chapter builds upon an initial version, which can be found at https://github.com/PacktPublishing/React-Projects/tree/ch6-initial. The complete code for this chapter can be found on GitHub: https://github.com/PacktPublishing/React-Projects/tree/ch6.

Start by downloading the initial project from GitHub and move into the root directory for this project, where you must run the npm install command. Since this project builds upon Create React App, running this command will install react, react-dom, and react-scripts. Also, styled-components and react-router-dom will be installed so that they can handle styling and routing for the application. After finishing the installation process, you can execute the npm start command to run the application so that you can visit the project in the browser at http://localhost:3000. Just like with the applications you've built in the previous chapters, this application functions as a PWA.

The initial application consists of a simple header and a list of hotels. These hotels have a title and meta information, like a thumbnail. This page will look as follows. If you click on any of the hotels in the list, a new page will open with a list of reviews for this hotel. By clicking the button at the top left of this page, you can move back to the previous page, and with the button at the top right, a page with a form where you can add a review will open. If you add a new review, this data will be stored in a global Context and sent to a mock API server:

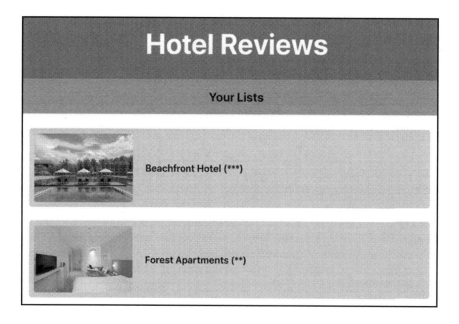

If you look at the project's structure, you'll see that it's using the same structure as the projects we created previously. The entry point of this application is a file called `src/index.js`, which renders a component called App. In this App component, all the routes are declared and wrapped within a router component. Also, the component that holds the global Context and the Providers is declared here. Compared to the applications you created previously, the container component pattern isn't used in this application. Instead, all the data fetching is done by the Context components. Life cycles are accessed using Hooks:

```
hotel-review
|-- node_modules
|-- public
    |-- assets
        |-- beachfront-hotel.jpg
        |-- forest-apartments.jpg
        |-- favicon.ico
        |-- index.html
        |-- manifest.json
|-- src
    |-- components
        |-- Button
            |-- Button.js
        |-- Detail
            |-- Detail.js
            |-- ReviewItem.js
        |-- Form
            |-- Form.js
            |-- FormItem.js
        |-- Header
            |-- Header.js
            |-- SubHeader.js
        |-- Hotels
            |-- Hotels.js
            |-- HotelItem.js
        |-- App.js
    |-- Context
        |-- GlobalContext.js
        |-- HotelsContextProvider.js
        |-- ReviewsContextProvider.js
    |-- api.js
    |-- index.js
    |-- serviceWorker.js
.gitignore
package.json
```

In the preceding project structure, you can see there are also two files in the `public/assets` directory, which are the thumbnails for the hotels. To make them available in the rendered application, you can place them in the `public` directory. Also, there is a file called `api.js` in `src` that exports the functions so that `GET` and `POST` requests can be sent to an API.

Hotel review application

In this section, we will add unit and integration testing to the hotel review application that was created in Create React App. This application lets you add reviews to a list of hotels and controls this data from a global Context. Jest and Enzyme will be used to render React components without a DOM and test assertions on these components.

Unit testing with Jest

Unit testing is an important part of your application since you want to know that your functions and components behave as expected, even when you make code changes. For this, you're going to use Jest, an open source testing package for JavaScript applications that was created by Facebook. With Jest, you can test assertions, for example, if the output of a function matches the value you expected.

To get started with Jest, you don't have to install anything; it's part of Create React App. If you look at the `package.json` file, you will see that a script is already there for running tests.

Let's see what happens if you execute the following command from your Terminal:

```
npm run test
```

This will return a message saying `No tests found related to files changed since last commit.`, which means Jest is running within watch mode and only running tests for files that have been changed. By pressing the `a` key, you can run all the tests, even if you haven't modified any files. If you press this key, the following message will be displayed:

```
No tests found
  26 files checked.
  testMatch: /hotel-review/src/**/__tests__/**/*.{js,jsx,ts,tsx},/hotel-
review/src/**/?(*.)(spec|test).{js,jsx,ts,tsx} - 0 matches
  testPathIgnorePatterns: /node_modules/ - 26 matches
Pattern: - 0 matches
```

This message states that 26 files have been investigated, but no tests have been found. It also states that it's looking for JavaScript or JSX files in directories called __tests__ in your project and files that have the spec or test suffix. The node_modules directory, which is where all the npm packages are installed, is ignored. From this message, you may have noticed that Jest automatically detects files with tests for you.

Creating these tests can be done with Jest, which will be demonstrated in the first part of this section.

Creating a unit test

Since there are multiple ways Jest can detect which file contains a test, let's choose the structure where every component has a separate test file. This test file will have the same name as the file that holds the component, with the .test suffix. If we choose the SubHeader component, we can create a new file called SubHeader.test.js in the src/components/Header directory. Add the following code to this file:

```
describe('the <SubHeader /> component', () => {
  it('should render', () => {
  });
});
```

Two global functions from Jest are used here:

- describe: This is used to define a block of related tests
- it: This is used to define a test

Within the definition of a test, you can add assumptions such as toEqual or toBe, which check whether the value is exactly equal to something or whether just the types match, respectively. The assumptions can be added within the callback of the it function:

```
describe('the <SubHeader /> component', () => {
  it('should render', () => {
+    expect(1+2).toBe(3);
  });
});
```

If you still have the test script running in your Terminal, you will see that Jest has detected your test. The test succeeds since 1+2 is indeed 3. Let's go ahead and change the assumption to the following:

```
describe('the <SubHeader /> component', () => {
  it('should render', () => {
-    expect(1+2).toBe(3);
```

```
+    expect(1+2).toBe('3');
  });
});
```

Now, the test will fail as the second assumption doesn't match. Although 1+2 still equals 3, it's assumed that a string type with a value pf 3 is returned, while in fact a number type is returned. This helps you when you're writing your code as you can make sure that your application doesn't change the types of its values.

However, this assumption has no actual usage as it doesn't test your component. To test your component, you need to render it. Rendering components so that you can test them will be handled in the next part of this section.

Rendering a React component for testing

Jest is based upon Node.js, meaning that it can't use the DOM to render your component and test its functionality. Therefore, you need to add a React core package to your project, which can help you render the component without a DOM. Let's take a look at this here:

1. From your Terminal, execute the following command, which will install `react-test-renderer` in your project. It can be installed as a devDependency as you don't need to run tests on the build version of your application:

   ```
   npm install react-test-renderer --save-dev
   ```

2. With `react-test-renderer` installed, you can now import this package into the `src/components/Header/SubHeader.test.js` file. This package returns a method called `ShallowRenderer` that lets you render the component. With Shallow rendering, you only render a component at its first level, thereby leaving out any possible children components. You also need to import React and the actual component you want to test since these are used by `react-test-renderer`:

   ```
   + import React from 'react';
   + import ShallowRenderer from 'react-test-renderer/shallow';
   + import SubHeader from './SubHeader';

   describe('the <SubHeader /> component', () => {
     ....
   ```

3. In your test, you can now render the component with `ShallowRenderer` and get the output of this component. With the Jest `toMatchSnapshot` assumption, you can test the structure of the component. `ShallowRenderer` will render the component and `toMatchSnapshot` will create a snapshot from this render and compare it to the actual component every time this test is run:

```
import React from 'react';
import ShallowRenderer from 'react-test-renderer/shallow';
import SubHeader from './SubHeader';

describe('the <SubHeader /> component', () => {
  it('should render', () => {
-    expect(1+2).toBe('3');
+    const renderer = new ShallowRenderer();
+    renderer.render(<SubHeader />);
+    const component = renderer.getRenderOutput();

+    expect(component).toMatchSnapshot();
  });
});
```

4. In the `src/components/Header` directory, a new directory called `__snapshots__` has now been created by Jest. Inside this directory is a file called `SubHeader.test.js.snap`, which includes the snapshot. If you open this file, you will see that a rendered version of the `SubHeader` component is stored here:

```
// Jest Snapshot v1, https://goo.gl/fbAQLP

exports[`the <SubHeader /> component should render 1`] = `
<ForwardRef>
  <ForwardRef />
</ForwardRef>
`;
```

The components that have been created with `styled-components` cannot be rendered by `react-test-renderer` because of how they're exported by `styled-components`. If you look at the code for the `SubHeader` component, you will see that the `ForwardRef` components represent `SubHeaderWrapper` and `Title`. Later in this chapter, we will use Enzyme for testing, which handles this test scenario better.

5. No actual values are being rendered by `react-test-renderer` since no props have been passed to the `SubHeader` component. You can inspect how the snapshot works by passing, for instance, a `title` prop to the `SubHeader` component. To do this, create a new test scenario, which should render `SubHeader` with a title. Also, move the creation of the `renderer` constant to the `describe` function, so that it can be used by all the test scenarios:

```
import React from 'react';
import ShallowRenderer from 'react-test-renderer/shallow';
import SubHeader from './SubHeader';

describe('the <SubHeader /> component', () => {
+   const renderer = new ShallowRenderer();

  it('should render', () => {
-     const renderer = new ShallowRenderer();
    renderer.render(<SubHeader />);
    const component = renderer.getRenderOutput();

    expect(component).toMatchSnapshot();
  });

+   it('should render with a dynamic title', () => {
+     renderer.render(<SubHeader title='Test Application' />);
+     const component = renderer.getRenderOutput();

+     expect(component).toMatchSnapshot();
+   });
});
```

6. The next time the tests are run, a new snapshot will be added to the `src/components/Header/__snapshots__/SubHeader.test.js.snap` fil e. This snapshot has a value rendered for the `title` prop. If you change the `title` prop that is displayed by the `SubHeader` component in your test file, the rendered component will no longer match the snapshot. You can try this by changing the value for the `title` prop in the test scenario:

```
import React from 'react';
import ShallowRenderer from 'react-test-renderer/shallow';
import SubHeader from './SubHeader';

describe('the <SubHeader /> component', () => {
  const renderer = new ShallowRenderer();

  ...
```

```
    it('should render with a dynamic title', () => {
-     renderer.render(<SubHeader title='Test Application' />);
+     renderer.render(<SubHeader title='Test Application Test' />);
      const component = renderer.getRenderOutput();

      expect(component).toMatchSnapshot();
    });
  });
```

Jest will return the following message in the Terminal, where it specifies which lines have changed in comparison to the snapshot. In this case, the title that's being displayed is no longer Test Application but Test Application Test, which doesn't match the title in the snapshot:

- **the <SubHeader /> component › should render**

  expect(value).toMatchSnapshot()

  Received value does not match stored snapshot "the <SubHeader /> component should render 1".

  - Snapshot
  + Received

  <ForwardRef>
  <ForwardRef>
  - Test Application
  + Test Application Title
  </ForwardRef>
  </ForwardRef>
  . . .

By pressing the u key, you can update the snapshot to handle this new test scenario. This is an easy way to test the structure of your component and see if the title has been rendered. With the preceding test, the initially created snapshot still matches the rendered component for the first test. Also, another snapshot was created for the second test, where a title prop was added to the SubHeader component.

7. You can do the same for the other props that are passed to the SubHeader component, which renders differently if you do or don't pass certain props to it. Next to title, this component takes goBack and openForm as props, where the openForm prop has a default value of false.

Just like we did for the `title` prop, we can also create test scenarios for the two other props. When there's a value for `goBack`, a button is created that takes us back to the previous page, while when there's a value for `openForm`, a button is created that allows us to proceed to the next page so that we can add a new review. You need to add these two new test scenarios to the `src/components/Header/SubHeader.test.js` file as well:

```
import React from 'react';
import ShallowRenderer from 'react-test-renderer/shallow';
import SubHeader from './SubHeader';

describe('the <SubHeader /> component', () => {
  const renderer = new ShallowRenderer();

    ...

+   it('should render with a goback button', () => {
+     renderer.render(<SubHeader goBack={() => {}} />);
+       const component = renderer.getRenderOutput();
+
+       expect(component).toMatchSnapshot();
+   });

+   it('should render with a form button', () => {
+     renderer.render(<SubHeader openForm={() => {}} />);
+       const result = renderer.getRenderOutput();
+
+       expect(component).toMatchSnapshot();
+   });
});
```

You've now created two more snapshots for the `SubHeader` component, which leads to a total of four snapshots. Something else that Jest does is show you how many lines of code have been covered by your tests. The higher your testing coverage, the more reason to assume your code is stable. You can check the test coverage of your code by executing the `test` script command with the `--coverage` flag, or use the following command in your Terminal:

```
npm run test --coverage
```

This command will run your tests and generate a report with all the test coverage information about your code per file. After adding the tests for `SubHeader`, this report will look as follows:

```
PASS src/components/Header/SubHeader.test.js
----------------------------|----------|----------|----------|----------|--
------------------|
File | % Stmts | % Branch | % Funcs | % Lines | Uncovered Line #s |
----------------------------|----------|----------|----------|----------|--
------------------|
All files | 5 | 6.74 | 4.26 | 5.21 | |
 src | 0 | 0 | 0 | 0 | |
  api.js | 0 | 0 | 0 | 0 |... 20,22,23,26,30 |
  index.js | 0 | 100 | 100 | 0 | 1,2,3,4,5,17 |
  serviceWorker.js | 0 | 0 | 0 | 0 |... 23,130,131,132 |
 src/components | 0 | 100 | 0 | 0 | |
  App.js | 0 | 100 | 0 | 0 |... ,8,10,22,26,27 |
 src/components/Button | 0 | 100 | 0 | 0 | |
  Button.js | 0 | 100 | 0 | 0 | 20 |
 src/components/Detail | 0 | 0 | 0 | 0 | |
  Detail.js | 0 | 0 | 0 | 0 |... 26,27,31,33,35 |
  ReviewItem.js | 0 | 100 | 0 | 0 |... 15,21,26,30,31 |
 src/components/Form | 0 | 0 | 0 | 0 | |
  Form.js | 0 | 0 | 0 | 0 |... 29,30,31,34,36 |
  FormInput.js | 0 | 0 | 0 | 0 |... 17,26,35,40,41 |
 src/components/Header | 100 | 100 | 100 | 100 | |
  Header.js | 100 | 100 | 100 | 100 | |
  SubHeader.js | 100 | 100 | 100 | 100 | |
 . . .
```

Testing coverage only tells us something about the lines and the functions of your code that have been tested and not their actual implementation. Having a test coverage of 100% doesn't mean there aren't any bugs in your code as there will always be edge cases. Also, getting to a testing coverage of 100% means you may end up spending more time on writing tests than on actual code. Usually, a testing coverage above 80% is considered good practice.

As you can see, the test coverage for the component is 100%, meaning that all the lines are covered in your test. However, this method of testing with snapshots will create a lot of new files and lines of code. We'll look at other ways we can test our components in the next part of this section.

Testing components with assertions

In theory, snapshot testing is not necessarily bad practice; however, your files can get quite big over time. Also, since you're not explicitly telling Jest what part of the component you want to test, you might need to update your code regularly.

Luckily, using snapshots isn't the only method we can use to test whether our components are rendering the correct props. Instead, you can also directly compare which props are being rendered by checking the value of the component and making assertions. The big advantage of testing with assertions is that you can test a lot without having to dig deeper into the logic of the component you're testing.

For instance, you can see what the children that are being rendered look like. Let's take a look at how to do this:

1. First, let's create a snapshot test for the `Button` component to compare the impact of test coverage. Create a new file called `src/components/Button/Button.test.js`. In this file, you need to insert a test that creates a snapshot:

```
import React from 'react';
import ShallowRenderer from 'react-test-renderer/shallow';
import Button from './Button';

describe('the <Button /> component', () => {
  const renderer = new ShallowRenderer();

  it('should render', () => {
    const children = 'This is a button';
    renderer.render(<Button>{children</Button>);
    const result = renderer.getRenderOutput();

    expect(result).toMatchSnapshot();
  });
});
```

2. If you run the tests with the `--coverage` flag, a new test coverage report will be created:

```
npm run test --coverage
```

This report generates the following report, which shows the coverage for the
`Button` component, which is 100%:

```
PASS src/components/Header/SubHeader.test.js
PASS src/components/Button/Button.test.js
 › 1 snapshot written.
PASS src/components/Header/Header.test.js
---------------------------|----------|----------|----------|-----
-----|-------------------|
File | % Stmts | % Branch | % Funcs | % Lines | Uncovered Line #s |
---------------------------|----------|----------|----------|-----
-----|-------------------|
All files | 5.45 | 6.74 | 6.38 | 5.69 | |
  src | 0 | 0 | 0 | 0 | |
   api.js | 0 | 0 | 0 | 0 |... 20,22,23,26,30 |
   index.js | 0 | 100 | 100 | 0 | 1,2,3,4,5,17 |
   serviceWorker.js | 0 | 0 | 0 | 0 |... 23,130,131,132 |
  src/components | 0 | 100 | 0 | 0 | |
   App.js | 0 | 100 | 0 | 0 |... ,8,10,22,26,27 |
  src/components/Button | 100 | 100 | 100 | 100 | |
   Button.js | 100 | 100 | 100 | 100 | |
```

If you open the snapshot for the `Button` component, which is in the
`src/components/Button/__snapshots__/Button.test.js.snap` file, you
will see that the only thing that's been rendered within the button (represented by
`ForwardRef`) is the `children` prop:

```
// Jest Snapshot v1, https://goo.gl/fbAQLP

exports[`the <Button /> component should render 1`] = `
<ForwardRef>
  This is a button
</ForwardRef>
`;
```

3. Although the testing coverage is at 100%, there are other ways to test whether the
   correct children have been rendered. For this, we can create a new test that also
   uses `ShallowRenderer` and tries to render the `Button` component with a child.
   This test has the assertion that the rendered `children` prop is equal to the actual
   `children` prop that was rendered by `Button`. You can remove the snapshot test
   since you only want to test the children with assertions:

```
import React from 'react';
import ShallowRenderer from 'react-test-renderer/shallow';
import Button from './Button';
```

```
describe('the <Button /> component', () => {
  const renderer = new ShallowRenderer();

-   it('should render', () => {
-     const children = 'This is a button';
-     renderer.render(<Button>{children}</Button>);
-     const result = renderer.getRenderOutput();

-     expect(result).toMatchSnapshot();
-   })

+   it('should render the correct children', () => {
+     const children = 'This is a button';
+     renderer.render(<Button>{children}</Button>);
+     const component = renderer.getRenderOutput();
+     expect(component.props.children).toEqual(children);
+   });
});
```

4. From your Terminal, run `npm run test --coverage` again to check the impact this testing method has on the test coverage:

```
PASS src/components/Header/Header.test.js
PASS src/components/Header/SubHeader.test.js
PASS src/components/Button/Button.test.js
› 1 snapshot obsolete.
  • the <Button /> component should render 1
----------------------------|----------|----------|----------|-----
-----|-------------------|
File | % Stmts | % Branch | % Funcs | % Lines | Uncovered Line #s |
----------------------------|----------|----------|----------|-----
-----|-------------------|
All files | 5.45 | 6.74 | 6.38 | 5.69 | |
 src | 0 | 0 | 0 | 0 | |
  api.js | 0 | 0 | 0 | 0 |... 20,22,23,26,30 |
  index.js | 0 | 100 | 100 | 0 | 1,2,3,4,5,17 |
  serviceWorker.js | 0 | 0 | 0 | 0 |... 23,130,131,132 |
 src/components | 0 | 100 | 0 | 0 | |
  App.js | 0 | 100 | 0 | 0 |... ,8,10,22,26,27 |
 src/components/Button | 100 | 100 | 100 | 100 | |
  Button.js | 100 | 100 | 100 | 100 | |
...
```

In the preceding report, you can see that the testing coverage is still 100%, meaning that this testing method has the same outcome. But this time, you're specifically testing whether the children are equal to that value. The upside is that you don't have to update snapshots every time you make code changes.

5. Also, a message noting 1 snapshot obsolete is shown. By running npm run test with the -u flag, the snapshot for the Button component is removed by Jest:

    ```
    npm run test -u
    ```

    This provides us with the following output, which shows us that the snapshot has been removed:

    ```
    PASS src/components/Button/Button.test.js
    › snapshot file removed.

    Snapshot Summary
    › 1 snapshot file removed from 1 test suite.
    ```

However, the Button component doesn't just take the children prop – it also takes the onClick prop. If you want to test whether this onClick prop is triggered when you click on the button, you need to render the component differently. This can be done by using react-test-renderer, but the React documentation also notes that you can use Enzyme for this.

In the next section, we'll use the shallow render function from Enzyme, which has more options than ShallowRenderer.

Using Enzyme for testing React

The ShallowRenderer from react-test-renderer allows us to render the structure of a component but doesn't show us how a component interacts in certain scenarios, such as when an onClick event is being triggered. To simulate this, we'll use a more complex tool called Enzyme.

Shallow rendering with Enzyme

Enzyme is an open source JavaScript testing library that was created by Airbnb and works with almost every JavaScript library or framework. With Enzyme, you can also shallow render components to test the first level of the component', as well as render nested components, and simulate life cycles for integration tests. The Enzyme library can be installed with npm, and also needs an adapter to simulate React features. Let's get started:

1. To install Enzyme, you need to run the following command from your Terminal, which installs Enzyme and the specific adapter for the version of React you're using:

   ```
   npm install enzyme enzyme-adapter-react-16 --save-dev
   ```

2. After installing Enzyme, you need to create a setup file that tells Enzyme what adapter should be used to run the tests. Normally, you'd need to specify which file holds this configuration in your package.json file, but, when you're using Create React App, this is already done for you. The filename that's automatically being used as the configuration file for testing libraries is called setupTests.js and should be created in the src directory. Once you've created the file, paste the following code into it:

   ```
   import { configure } from 'enzyme';
   import Adapter from 'enzyme-adapter-react-16';

   configure({ adapter: new Adapter() });
   ```

With the installation of Enzyme, you can no longer use the test scenarios that use react-test-renderer. Therefore, you need to change the tests for the SubHeader and Button components. As we mentioned previously, Enzyme has a method that allows us to shallow render components. Let's try this for the SubHeader component first:

1. Instead of importing react-test-renderer, you need to import shallow from Enzyme. The ShallowRender method should no longer be added to the renderer constant, so you can delete this line:

   ```
   import React from 'react';
   - import ShallowRenderer from 'react-test-renderer/shallow';
   + import { shallow } from 'enzyme';
   import SubHeader from './SubHeader';

   describe('the <SubHeader /> component', () => {
   -   const renderer = new ShallowRenderer();
     it('should render', () => {
       ...
   ```

2. Each test scenario should be changed so that it uses the shallow render function from Enzyme. We can do this by replacing `renderer.render` with `shallow`. The function that we use to get the output of this render can be deleted as well. The `shallow` render from Enzyme will instantly create a result that can be tested by Jest:

```
import React from 'react';
import { shallow } from 'enzyme';
import SubHeader from './SubHeader';

describe('the <SubHeader /> component', () => {
  it('should render', () => {
-     renderer.render(<SubHeader />);
-     const component = renderer.getRenderOutput();
+     const component = shallow(<SubHeader />);

    expect(component).toMatchSnapshot();
  });

  ...
```

3. Just like we did in the first test scenario, we must replace the other test scenarios; otherwise, the tests won't run. This happens because we've already deleted the setup for `react-test-renderer`:

```
import React from 'react';
import { shallow } from 'enzyme';
import SubHeader from './SubHeader';

describe('the <SubHeader /> component', () => {
  ...

  it('should render with a dynamic title', () => {
-     renderer.render(<SubHeader title='Test Application' />);
-     const component = renderer.getRenderOutput();
+     const component = shallow(<SubHeader title='Test Application'
/>);

    expect(component).toMatchSnapshot();
  });

  it('should render with a goback button', () => {
-     renderer.render(<SubHeader goBack={() => {}} />);
-     const component = renderer.getRenderOutput();
+     const component = shallow(<SubHeader goBack={() => {}} />);

    expect(component).toMatchSnapshot();
```

```
    });

    it('should render with a form button', () => {
-       renderer.render(<SubHeader openForm={() => {}} />);
-       const component = renderer.getRenderOutput();
+       const component = shallow(<SubHeader openForm={() => {}} />);

      expect(component).toMatchSnapshot();
    });
  });
```

4. In the Terminal, you can now run the test again by running `npm run test`. Since the tests are running in watch mode, the tests for the `Button` component will probably start running as well. You can specify which tests should be run by pressing the `p` key and then type `SubHeader` in the Terminal. Now, Jest will only run the tests for the `SubHeader` component.

The tests will fail as your snapshots are no longer the snapshots that were created by `react-test-renderer`. Enzyme's shallow render has a better understanding of the exports from `styled-components` and no longer renders those components as a `ForwardRef` component. Instead, it returns, for instance, a component called `styled.div` or `styled.h2`:

```
FAIL src/components/Header/SubHeader.test.js
  the <SubHeader /> component
    X should render (27ms)
    X should render with a dynamic title (4ms)
    X should render with a goback button (4ms)
    X should render with a form button (4ms)

  • the <SubHeader /> component › should render

    expect(value).toMatchSnapshot()

    Received value does not match stored snapshot "the <SubHeader />
component should render 1".

    - Snapshot
    + Received

    - <ForwardRef>
    - <ForwardRef />
    - </ForwardRef>
    + <styled.div>
    + <styled.h2 />
    + </styled.div>
```

By pressing the u key, all the snapshots that were created by `react-test-renderer` will be replaced by the new snapshots from Enzyme.

The same can be done for the `Button` component, where no snapshot is used for testing. Instead, an assertion is used. In your test scenario, in the `src/components/Button/Button.test.js` file, replace `ShallowRenderer` with the shallow render from Enzyme. Also, the value for `component.props.children` is no longer present due to how Enzyme renders the component. Instead, you need to use the `props` method, which is available on the shallow rendered component, to get the `children` prop:

```
  import React from 'react';
- import ShallowRenderer from 'react-test-renderer/shallow';
+ import { shallow } from 'enzyme';
  import Button from './Button';

  describe('the <Button /> component', () => {
-   const renderer = new ShallowRenderer();

    it('should render the correct children', () => {
      const children = 'This is a button';
-     renderer.render(<Button>{children}</Button>);
-     const component = renderer.getRenderOutput();
+     const component = shallow(<Button>{children}</Button>)

-     expect(component.props.children).toEqual(children)
+     expect(component.props().children).toEqual(children)
    })
  })
```

All the tests should now succeed when you run the tests, and the testing coverage should be unaffected as you're still testing whether the props are rendered on your components. However, with the snapshots from Enzyme, you've got more information about the structure of the component that's being rendered. Now, you can test even more and find out how, for example, `onClick` events are being handled.

However, snapshots aren't the only way of testing your React components, as we'll see in the next part of this section.

Testing assertions with shallow rendering

Other than `react-test-renderer`, Enzyme can handle `onClick` events on the shallow rendered component. To test this, you have to create a mocked version of the function, which should be fired once the component is clicked. After this, Jest can check whether or not the function was executed.

The `Button` component that you tested previously doesn't just take `children` as a prop – it also takes the `onClick` function. Let's try and see if this can be tested using Jest and Enzyme by creating a new test scenario in the file for the `Button` component:

```
import React from 'react';
import { shallow } from 'enzyme';
import Button from './Button';

describe('the <Button /> component', () => {
  ...

+  it('should handle the onClick event', () => {
+    const mockOnClick = jest.fn();
+    const component = shallow(<Button onClick={mockOnClick} />);

+    component.simulate('click');

+    expect(mockOnClick).toHaveBeenCalled();
+  });
});
```

In the preceding test scenario, a mocked `onClick` function was created with Jest, which is passed as a prop to the shallow rendered `Button` component. Then, a `simulate` method with a click event handler is invoked on that component. Simulating a click on the `Button` component should execute the mocked `onClick` function, which you can confirm by checking the test results for this test scenario.

The tests for the `SubHeader` component can also be updated since two buttons with an `onClick` event are rendered by it. Let's get started:

1. First, you need to make some changes to the file for the `SubHeader` component in `src/components/Header/SubHeader.js` since you need to export the components that have been created with `styled-components`. By doing this, they can be used for testing in your test scenario for `SubHeader`:

   ```
   import React from 'react';
   import styled from 'styled-components';
   import Button from '../Button/Button';
   ```

```
const SubHeaderWrapper = styled.div`
  width: 100%;
  display: flex;
  justify-content: space-between;
  background: cornflowerBlue;
`;

- const Title = styled.h2`
+ export const Title = styled.h2`
  text-align: center;
  flex-basis: 60%;

  &:first-child {
    margin-left: 20%;
  }

  &:last-child {
    margin-right: 20%;
  }
`;

- const SubHeaderButton = styled(Button)`
+ export const SubHeaderButton = styled(Button)`
  margin: 10px 5%;
`;

...
```

2. Once they've been exported, we can import these components into our test file for SubHeader:

```
import React from 'react';
import { shallow } from 'enzyme';
- import SubHeader from './SubHeader';
+ import SubHeader, { Title, SubHeaderButton } from './SubHeader';

describe('the <SubHeader /> component', () => {
    ...
```

3. This makes it possible to find these components from any of our tests. In this scenario, the rendering of the title prop is tested with a snapshot, but you can also directly test whether the title prop is being rendered by the Title component in SubHeader. To test this, change the following lines of code:

```
import React from 'react';
import { shallow } from 'enzyme';
import SubHeader, { Title, SubHeaderButton } from './SubHeader';
```

```
   describe('the <SubHeader /> component', () => {
     it('should render with a dynamic title', () => {
+      const title = 'Test Application';
-      const component = shallow(<SubHeader title='Test Application'
/>);
+      const component = shallow(<SubHeader title={title} />);

-      expect(component).toMatchSnapshot();

+      expect(component.find(Title).text()).toEqual(title);
     });

     ...
```

A new constant for the `title` prop is created here and passed to the `SubHeader` component. Instead of using a snapshot as an assertion, a new one is created that tries to find the `Title` component and checks whether the text inside this component is equal to the `title` prop.

4. Next to the `title` prop, you can also test for the `goBack` (or `openForm`) prop. If this prop is present, a button will be rendered that has the `goBack` prop as an `onClick` event. This button is rendered as a `SubHeaderButton` component. Here, we need to change the second test scenario so that it has a mocked function for the `goBack` prop and then create an assertion to check for the existence of `SubHeaderButton` in the rendered component:

```
import React from 'react';
import { shallow } from 'enzyme';
import SubHeader, { Title, SubHeaderButton } from './SubHeader';

describe('the <SubHeader /> component', () => {
  ...

  it('should render with a goback button and handle the onClick
event', () => {
+    const mockGoBack = jest.fn();
-    const component = shallow(<SubHeader goBack={() => {}} />);
+    const component = shallow(<SubHeader goBack={mockGoBack} />);

-    expect(component).toMatchSnapshot();

+    const goBackButton = component.find(SubHeaderButton);
+    expect(goBackButton.exists()).toBe(true);
  });
  ...
```

5. Not only do we want to test whether the button with the `goBack` prop is being rendered, but we also want to test whether this function is being called once we click on the button. Just like we did for the `Button` component test, we can simulate a click event and check whether the mocked `goBack` function was called:

```
import React from 'react';
import { shallow } from 'enzyme';
import SubHeader, { Title, SubHeaderButton } from './SubHeader';

describe('the <SubHeader /> component', () => {
  ...

  it('should render with a goback button and handle the onClick
event', () => {
    const mockGoBack = jest.fn();
    const component = shallow(<SubHeader goBack={mockGoBack} />);

    const goBackButton = component.find(SubHeaderButton);
    expect(goBackButton.exists()).toBe(true);

+    goBackButton.simulate('click');
+    expect(mockGoBack).toHaveBeenCalled();
  })
  ...
```

6. The same can be done for the `openForm` prop if we replace the assertion that's testing the snapshot with two assertions that test for the existence of the button and if it fired the mocked `openForm` function. Instead of adding this to the existing test scenario, we can extend the test scenario for the `goBack` button:

```
import React from 'react';
import { shallow } from 'enzyme';
import SubHeader, { Title, SubHeaderButton } from './SubHeader';

describe('the <SubHeader /> component', () => {
  ...

-    it('should render with a goback button and handle the onClick
event', () => {
+    it('should render with a buttons and handle the onClick
events', () => {
    const mockGoBack = jest.fn();
+    const mockOpenForm = jest.fn();
-    //const component = shallow(<SubHeader goBack={mockGoBack}
/>);
+    const component = shallow(<SubHeader goBack={mockGoBack}
```

```
    openForm={mockOpenForm} />);

        ...
    });

-   it('should render with a form button', () => {
-       const component = shallow(<SubHeader openForm={() => {}} />);

-       expect(component).toMatchSnapshot();
-   });
});
```

7. The component that is now being rendered for the SubHeader should have both a button to go back to the previous page and a button to open the form. However, they're both using the SubHeaderButton component to render. The button to go back is rendered in the component tree first since it's placed on the left-hand side of SubHeader. Therefore, we need to specify which rendered SubHeaderButton is which button:

```
import React from 'react';
import { shallow } from 'enzyme';
import SubHeader, { Title, SubHeaderButton } from './SubHeader';

describe('the <SubHeader /> component', () => {
    ...

   it('should render with buttons and handle the onClick events', ()
=> {
        const mockGoBack = jest.fn();
        const mockOpenForm = jest.fn();
        const component = shallow(<SubHeader goBack={mockGoBack}
openForm={mockOpenForm} />);

-       const goBackButton = component.find(SubHeaderButton);
+       const goBackButton = component.find(SubHeaderButton).at(0);
        expect(goBackButton.exists()).toBe(true);

+       const openFormButton = component.find(SubHeaderButton).at(1);
+       expect(openFormButton.exists()).toBe(true)

        goBackButton.simulate('click');
        expect(mockGoBack).toHaveBeenCalled();

+       openFormButton.simulate('click');
+       expect(mockOpenForm).toHaveBeenCalled();
    });
    ...
```

After these changes, all the test scenarios that use snapshots are removed and replaced with more concrete tests that are less vulnerable once we change any of the code. Apart from snapshots, these tests will keep working if we change any props that make refactoring easier.

In this section, we've created unit tests that will test a specific part of our code. However, it can be interesting to test how different parts of our code work together. For this, we'll add integration tests to our project.

Integration testing with Enzyme

The tests that we've created all use shallow rendering to render components, but, with Enzyme, we also have the option to mount components. When using this, we can enable lifecycles and test larger components deeper than just the first level. When we want to test multiple components at once, this is called integration testing. In our application, the components that are rendered directly by the routes are rendering other components as well. A good example of this is the `Hotels` component, which renders the list of hotels that were returned by the Context. Let's get started:

1. As always, the starting point is to create a new file with the `.test` suffix in the same directory that the component we want to test is located. Here, we need to create the `Hotels.test.js` file in the `src/components/Hotels` directory. In this file, we need to import `mount` from Enzyme, import the component that we want to test, and create a new test scenario:

   ```
   import React from 'react';
   import { mount } from 'enzyme';
   import Hotels from './Hotels';

   describe('the <Hotels /> component', () => {

   });
   ```

2. The `Hotels` component is using the `useContext` Hook to get the data it needs to display the hotels. However, since this is a test for this specific component, that data needs to be mocked. Before we can mock this data, we need to create a mock function for the `useContext` Hook. If we have multiple test scenarios that use this mock, we also need to use the `beforeEach` and `afterEach` methods to create and reset this mock function for every scenario:

   ```
   import React from 'react';
   import { mount } from 'enzyme';
   import Hotels from './Hotels';
   ```

```
+ let useContextMock;

+ beforeEach(() => {
+   useContextMock = React.useContext = jest.fn();
+ });

+ afterEach(() => {
+   useContextMock.mockReset();
+ });

describe('the <Hotels /> component', () => {
    ...
```

3. We can now use the mocked `useContextMock` function to generate the data that will be used as a mock for the Context by the `Hotels` component. The data that will be returned should also be mocked, which can be done by invoking the `mockReturnValue` function, which is available on the mocked function. If we take a look at the actual code for the `Hotels` component, we will see that it takes four values from the Context: `loading`, `error`, `hotels`, and `getHotelsRequest`. These values should be mocked and returned by `mockReturnValue` in the first test scenario that we will create to check the behavior when the Context is loading the hotels' data:

```
import React from 'react';
import { mount } from 'enzyme';
import Hotels from './Hotels';

...

describe('the <Hotels /> component', () => {
  it('should handle the first mount', () => {
+       const mockContext = {
+         loading: true,
+         error: '',
+         hotels: [],
+         getHotelsRequest: jest.fn(),
+       }
+     useContextMock.mockReturnValue(mockContext);
+     const wrapper = mount(<Hotels />);
+
+     expect(mockContext.getHotelsRequest).toHaveBeenCalled();
  });
});
```

This first test scenario checks whether the `Hotels` component will call the `getHotelsRequest` function from the Context when it first mounts. This means that the `useEffect` Hook that's used in `Hotels` has been tested.

4. Since the data is still loading here, we can also test whether the `Alert` component is rendering the `loading` value from the Context and displaying a loading message. Here, we need to export this component from `Hotels` in `src/components/Hotels/Hotels.js`:

```
...

- const Alert = styled.span`
+ export const Alert = styled.span`
  width: 100%;
  text-align: center;
`;

const Hotels = ({ match, history }) => {
    ...
```

Now, we can import this component in the test file and write the assertion to check whether it's displaying the value from the Context:

```
import React from 'react';
import { mount } from 'enzyme';
- import Hotels from './Hotels';
+ import Hotels, { Alert } from './Hotels';

...

describe('the <Hotels /> component', () => {
  it('should handle the first mount', () => {
    const mockContext = {
       loading: true,
       error: '',
       hotels: [],
       getHotelsRequest: jest.fn(),
    }
    useContextMock.mockReturnValue(mockContext);
    const wrapper = mount(<Hotels />);

    expect(mockContext.getHotelsRequest).toHaveBeenCalled();
+   expect(wrapper.find(Alert).text()).toBe('Loading...');
  });
```

5. After the `Hotels` component has mounted and the data has been fetched, the values for `loading`, `error`, and `hotels` in the Context will be updated. When the values for `loading` and `error` are `false`, the `HotelItemsWrapper` component will be rendered by `Hotels`. To test this, we need to export `HotelItemsWrapper` from `Hotels`:

```
import React from 'react';
import styled from 'styled-components';
import { Link } from 'react-router-dom';
import { HotelsContext } from
'../../Context/HotelsContextProvider';
import SubHeader from '../Header/SubHeader';
import HotelItem from './HotelItem';

- const HotelItemsWrapper = styled.div`
+ export const HotelItemsWrapper = styled.div`
  display: flex;
  justify-content: space-between;
  flex-direction: column;
  margin: 2% 5%;
`;

...
```

In the testing file, this component can now be imported, which means we can add the new test scenario that checks whether this component is being rendered:

```
import React from 'react';
import { mount } from 'enzyme';
- import Hotels, { Alert } from './Hotels';
+ import Hotels, { Alert, HotelItemsWrapper } from './Hotels';

describe('the <Hotels /> component', () => {
  ...

+  it('should render the list of hotels', () => {
+    const mockContext = {
+      loading: false,
+      error: '',
+      hotels: [{
+        id: 123,
+        title: 'Test Hotel',
+        thumbnail: 'test.jpg',
+      }],
+      getHotelsRequest: jest.fn(),
+    }
+    useContextMock.mockReturnValue(mockContext);
```

```
+    const wrapper = mount(<Hotels />);

+    expect(wrapper.find(HotelItemsWrapper).exists()).toBe(true);
+  });
});
```

Now, when we run the test, we'll get an error saying `Invariant failed: You should not use <Link> outside a <Router>` since Enzyme can't render the `Link` component, which is used to navigate when we click on a hotel. Due to this, we need to wrap the `Hotels` component within a router component from `react-router`:

```
import React from 'react';
import { mount } from 'enzyme';
+ import { BrowserRouter as Router } from 'react-router-dom';
import Hotels, { Alert, HotelItemsWrapper } from './Hotels';

...

describe('the <Hotels /> component', () => {
  ...

  it('should render the list of hotels', () => {
    const mockContext = {
      loading: false,
      alert: '',
      hotels: [{
        id: 123,
        title: 'Test Hotel',
        thumbnail: 'test.jpg',
      }],
      getHotelsRequest: jest.fn(),
    }
    useContextMock.mockReturnValue(mockContext);
-    const wrapper = mount(<Hotels />);
+    const wrapper = mount(<Router><Hotels /></Router>);

    expect(wrapper.find(HotelItemsWrapper).exists()).toBe(true);
  });
});
```

This test will now pass, as Enzyme can render the component, including the `Link` to navigate to a hotel.

6. Inside the `HotelItemsWrapper` component is a `map` function that iterates over the hotel data from the Context. For every iteration, a `HotelItem` component will be rendered. In these `HotelItem` components, the data will be displayed in, for instance, a `Title` component. We can test whether the data that will be displayed in these components is equal to the mocked Context data. The component that displays the title of the hotel should be exported from `src/components/Hotels/HotelItem.js`:

```
- const Title = styled.h3`
+ export const Title = styled.h3`
  margin-left: 2%;
`
```

Along with the `HotelItem` component, this should be imported into the test for `Hotels`. In the test scenario, we can now check for the existence of the `<HotelItem` component and check whether this component has a `Title` component. The value that's displayed by this component should be equal to the mocked Context value for the title of the first row in the array of `hotels`:

```
import React from 'react';
import { mount } from 'enzyme';
import { BrowserRouter as Router } from 'react-router-dom';
import Hotels, { Alert, HotelItemsWrapper } from './Hotels';
+ import HotelItem, { Title } from './HotelItem';

...

describe('the <Hotels /> component', () => {
  ...

  it('should render the list of hotels', () => {
    const mockContext = {
      loading: false,
      alert: '',
      hotels: [{
        id: 123,
        title: 'Test Hotel',
        thumbnail: 'test.jpg',
      }],
      getHotelsRequest: jest.fn(),
    }
    useContextMock.mockReturnValue(mockContext);
    const wrapper = mount(<Router><Hotels /></Router>);

    expect(wrapper.find(HotelItemsWrapper).exists()).toBe(true);
+   expect(wrapper.find(HotelItem).exists()).toBe(true);
```

```
+
expect(wrapper.find(HotelItem).at(0).find(Title).text()).toBe(mockC
ontext.hotels[0].title);
  });
});
```

After running the tests again with the `--coverage` flag, we will be able to see what impact writing this integration test has on our coverage. Since an integration test not only tests one specific component but multiple at once, the testing coverage for `Hotels` will be updated. This test also covers the `HotelItem` component, which we will be able to see in the coverage report after running `npm run test --coverage`:

```
PASS src/components/Button/Button.test.js
PASS src/components/Header/SubHeader.test.js
PASS src/components/Hotels/Hotels.test.js
---------------------------|----------|----------|--------'--|-----
-----|-------------------|
File | % Stmts | % Branch | % Funcs | % Lines | Uncovered Line #s |
---------------------------|----------|----------|----------|-----
-----|-------------------|
All files | 13.27 | 11.24 | 12.77 | 13.73 | |
 ...
 src/components/Hotels | 100 | 83.33 | 100 | 100 | |
   HotelItem.js | 100 | 100 | 100 | 100 | |
   Hotels.js | 100 | 83.33 | 100 | 100 | 33 |
```

The coverage for `Hotels` is close to 100%. The test coverage for `HotelItems` has also got to 100%. This means that we can skip writing unit tests for `HotelItem`, assuming that we only use this component within the `Hotels` component.

The only downside of having integration tests over unit tests is that they're harder to write as they usually contain more complex logic. Also, these integration tests will run slower than unit tests because of them having more logic and bringing together multiple components.

Summary

In this chapter, we covered testing for React applications using Jest in combination with either `react-test-renderer` or Enzyme. Both packages are a great resource to every developer that wants to add test scripts to their application, and they also work well with React. The advantages of having tests for your application were discussed in this chapter, and hopefully, you now know how to add test scripts to any project. Also, the differences between unit tests and integration tests were shown.

Since the application that was tested in this chapter has the same structure as the applications from the previous chapters, the same testing principles can be applied to any of the applications we've built in this book.

The next chapter will combine a lot of the patterns and libraries we've already used in this book as we'll be creating a full-stack e-commerce store with React, GraphQL, and Apollo.

Further reading

- **Enzyme shallow rendering:** `https://airbnb.io/enzyme/docs/api/shallow.html`
- **Enzyme mount:** `https://airbnb.io/enzyme/docs/api/mount.html`

7
Build a Full Stack E-Commerce Application with React Native and GraphQL

If you're reading this, this means you've reached the final part of this book, which uses React to build web applications. In the preceding chapters, you've already used the core features of React, such as rendering components, state management with Context, and Hooks. You've learned how to create a PWA and an SSR application and how to add routing to your React application. Also, you know how to add testing to a React application with Jest and Enzyme. Let's add GraphQL to the list of things you've learned about so far.

In this chapter, you will not only build the frontend of an application, but also the backend. For this, GraphQL will be used, which can best be defined as a query language for APIs. Using mock data and Apollo Server, you'll extend a GraphQL server that exposes a single endpoint for your React application. On the frontend side, this endpoint will be consumed using Apollo Client, which helps you handle sending requests to the server and state management for this data.

In this chapter, the following topics will be covered:

- Querying and mutating data with GraphQL
- Consuming GraphQL with Apollo Client
- Handling state management with GraphQL

Project overview

In this chapter, we will create a full stack e-commerce application that has a GraphQL server as a backend and consumes this server in React using Apollo Client. For both the backend and frontend, an initial application is available to get you started quickly.

The build time is 3 hours.

Getting started

The project that we'll create in this chapter builds upon an initial version that you can find on GitHub: `https://github.com/PacktPublishing/React-Projects/tree/ch7-initial`. The complete source code can also be found on GitHub: `https://github.com/PacktPublishing/React-Projects/tree/ch7`.

The initial project consists of both a boilerplate application based on Create React App to get you started quickly and a GraphQL server that you can run locally. You can find the application in the `client` directory and the GraphQL server can be found in the `server` directory. Both the initial application and the GraphQL server need dependencies installed and need to be running at all times during development, which you can do by running the following commands in both the `client` and `server` directories:

```
npm install && npm start
```

This command will install all of the dependencies that are needed to run both the React application and the GraphQL server, including `react`, `react-scripts`, `graphql`, and `apollo-server`. If you'd like to know about all of the dependencies that were installed, please have a look at the `package.json` files in both the `client` and `server` directories.

After the installation process has finished, both the GraphQL server and the React application will be started.

Getting started with the initial React application

Since the React application is created by Create React App, it will automatically launch in your browser at `http://localhost:3000/`. This initial application doesn't show any data as it still needs to be connected to the GraphQL server, which you'll do later on in this chapter. At this point, the application will, therefore, render only a header with the title **Ecommerce Store** and a subheader as well, which looks something like this:

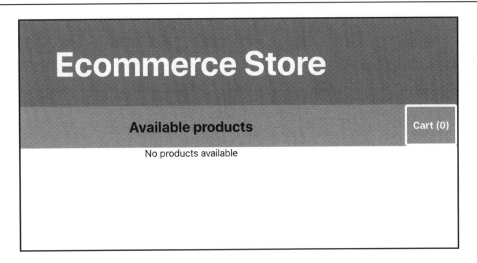

The structure of this initial React application is as follows:

```
ecommerce-store
|-- client
    |-- node_modules
    |-- public
        |-- favicon.ico
        |-- index.html
        |-- manifest.json
    |-- src
        |-- components
            |-- Button
                |-- Button.js
            |-- Cart
                |-- Cart.js
                |-- CartButton.js
                |-- Totals.js
            |-- Header
                |-- Header.js
                |-- SubHeader.js
            |-- Products
                |-- ProductItem.js
                |-- Products.js
            |-- App.js
        |-- index.js
        |-- serviceWorker.js
    |-- package.json
```

In the `client/src` directory, you'll find the entry point to the application, which is `index.js`. This file will refer to the `App` component in `App.js`. The `App` component has a `Router` component that either renders the `Products` or `Cart` component, dependent on which URL the user is visiting. When no specific route is specified, the `Products` component will be rendered which consists of a `SubHeader` component, with `Button` to the `Cart` component, and a `map` function that returns a list of `ProductItem` components that display product information. The `/cart` route will render the `Cart` component that also has `SubHeader`, this time with `Button` to go back to the previous page. Also, again return a list of products will be returned and the `Totals` component will show the total number of products in the cart.

Getting started with the GraphQL server

Although you won't be making any code changes to the GraphQL server, it's important to know how the server is functioning and what the basic concepts of GraphQL are.

GraphQL is best described as a query language for APIs and is defined as a convention for retrieving data from an API. Often, GraphQL APIs are compared to RESTful APIs, which is a well-known convention for sending HTTP requests that are dependant on multiple endpoints that will all return a separate data collection. As opposed to the well-known RESTful APIs, a GraphQL API will provide a single endpoint that lets you query and/or mutate data sources such as a database. You can query or mutate data by sending a document containing either a query or mutation operation to the GraphQL server. Whatever data is available can be found in the schema of the GraphQL server, which consists of types that define what data can be queried or mutated.

The GraphQL server can be found in the `server` directory and provides a backend for the frontend React application that you'll build in this chapter. This server is created using Express and Apollo Server, where Express is a framework to create APIs using JavaScript and Apollo Server is an open source package that helps you create GraphQL servers with a limited amount of code. After making sure you've run the `npm install` and `npm start` commands in the `server` directory, the GraphQL API becomes available on `http://localhost:4000/graphql` Apollo Server will run your GraphQL server on port `4000` by default. On this page in the browser, the GraphQL Playground will be displayed, and is where you can use and explore the GraphQL server. An example of this playground can be seen in the following screenshot:

With this playground, you can send queries and mutations to the GraphQL server, which you can type on the left-hand side of this page. The queries and mutations that you're able to send can be found in **SCHEMA** for this GraphQL server, which you can find by clicking on the green button labeled **SCHEMA**. This button will open an overview of **SCHEMA**, which shows you all of the possible return values of the GraphQL server:

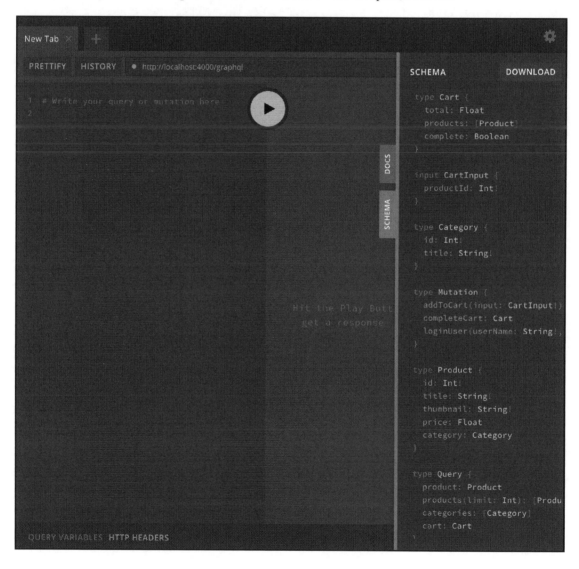

Whenever you describe a query or mutation on the left-hand side of this page, the output that is returned by the server will be displayed on the right-hand side of the playground. The way a GraphQL query is constructed will determine the structure of the returned data since GraphQL follows the principle of *ask for what you need, get exactly that*. Since GraphQL queries always return predictable results, this means we can have a query that looks like this:

```
query {
  products {
    id
    title
    thumbnail
  }
}
```

This will return an output that will follow the same structure of the query that's defined in the document that you sent to the GraphQL server and has the following format:

```
{
  "data": {
    "products": [
      {
        "id": 16608,
        "title": "Awesome Rubber Shoes",
        "thumbnail": "http://lorempixel.com/400/400/technics"
      },
      {
        "id": 20684,
        "title": "Refined Soft Table",
        "thumbnail": "http://lorempixel.com/400/400/fashion"
      }
    ]
  }
}
```

Applications that are using GraphQL are often fast and stable because they control the data they get, not the server.

In the next section, you'll connect the GraphQL server to the React web application using Apollo, and send documents to the server from your application.

Building a full stack e-commerce application with React, Apollo, and GraphQL

In this section, you'll connect the React web application to the GraphQL server. Apollo Server is used to create a single GraphQL endpoint that uses dynamic mock data as a source. Apollo Client is used by React to consume this endpoint and handle state management for your application.

Adding GraphQL to a React application

With the GraphQL server in place, let's move on to the part where you make requests to this server from a React application. For this, you'll use Apollo packages that help you add an abstraction layer between your application and the server. That way, you don't have to worry about sending documents to the GraphQL endpoint yourself by using, for example, `fetch`, and can send documents directly from a component.

As we mentioned previously, you can use Apollo to connect to the GraphQL server; for this, Apollo Client will be used. With Apollo Client, you can set up the connection with the server, handle queries and mutations, and enable caching for data that's been retrieved from the GraphQL server, among other things. Apollo Client is added to your application by following these steps:

1. To install Apollo Client and its related packages, you need in order to run the following command from the `client` directory where the React application is initialized:

   ```
   npm install apollo-client apollo-link-http react-apollo graphql
   graphql-tag
   ```

   This will install not only Apollo Client but also the other dependencies you need to use Apollo Client and GraphQL in your React application:

   - `apollo-link-http` will connect with the GraphQL server
   - `react-apollo` will provide the components you need to send queries to and mutations and handle the data flow
   - `graphql` and `graphql-tag` will handle GraphQL and write in the query language

2. These packages should be imported into the file where you want to create the Apollo Client, which, in this case, would be `client/src/App.js`:

```
import React from 'react';
import styled, { createGlobalStyle } from 'styled-components';
import { Route, Switch } from 'react-router-dom';
import Header from './Header/Header';
import Products from './Products/Products';
import Cart from './Cart/Cart';

import ApolloClient from 'apollo-client';
import { HttpLink } from 'apollo-link-http';
import { ApolloProvider } from 'react-apollo';

const GlobalStyle = createGlobalStyle`
    ...
```

3. Now you can define the `client` constant using the `ApolloClient` class and use `HttpLink` to make the connection with the GraphQL server; therefore, create a `client` constant like this:

```
import React from 'react';
import styled, { createGlobalStyle } from 'styled-components';
import { Route, Switch } from 'react-router-dom';
import Header from './Header/Header';
import Products from './Products/Products';
import Cart from './Cart/Cart';

import ApolloClient from 'apollo-client';
import { InMemoryCache } from 'apollo-cache-inmemory';
import { HttpLink } from 'apollo-link-http';
import { ApolloProvider } from 'react-apollo';

const client = () => new ApolloClient({
  link: new HttpLink({
    uri: 'http://localhost:6000',
  }),
});

const GlobalStyle = createGlobalStyle`
    ...
```

4. Within the `return` function for the `App` component, you need to add `ApolloProvider` and pass `client` you've just created as a prop:

```
...
const App = () => (
-    <>
+    <ApolloProvider client={client}>
      <GlobalStyle />
        <AppWrapper>
        <Header />
        <Switch>
          <Route exact path='/' component={Products} />
          <Route path='/cart' component={Cart} />
        </Switch>
        </AppWrapper>
-    </>
+    </ApolloProvider>
);

export default App;
```

After these steps, all of the components that are nested within `ApolloProvider` can access this `client` and send documents with queries and/or mutations to the GraphQL server. The method for getting data from `ApolloProvider` is similar to how the context API interacts with the Context value and will be demonstrated in the next part of this section.

Sending GraphQL queries with React

The `react-apollo` package doesn't only export a Provider but also methods to consume the value from this Provider. That way, you can easily get any value using the client that was added to the Provider. One of those methods is `Query`, which helps you to send a document containing a query to the GraphQL server, without having to use a `fetch` function, for example.

Since a `Query` component should always be nested inside an `ApolloProvider` component, they can be placed in any component that's been rendered within `App`. One of those is the `Products` component in `client/src/components/Product/Products.js`. This component is being rendered for the `/` route and should display products that are available in the e-commerce store.

To send a document from the `Products` component, follow these steps, which will guide you in the process of sending documents using `react-apollo`:

1. The query to get products from the GraphQL server can be found using the introspection methods in the playground or from the `server/typeDefs.js` file, and looks as follows:

```
query {
  products {
    id
    title
    thumbnail
  }
}
```

Sending this document with a query to the GraphQL server will return an array consisting of objects with product information, which has a limit of 10 products by default. The result will be returned in JSON format and will consist of different products every time you send the requests, since the data is mocked by the GraphQL server.

2. In the `Products` component, you can import the `Query` component from `react-apollo` and define a constant for the named `getProducts` query. Also, you need to import `gql` from `graphql-tag` to use the GraphQL query language inside your React file, which is given as follows:

```
import React from 'react';
import styled from 'styled-components';
import { Query } from 'react-apollo';
import gql from 'graphql-tag';
import SubHeader from '../Header/SubHeader';
import ProductItem from './ProductItem';

const GET_PRODUCTS = gql`
  query getProducts {
    products {
      id
      title
      thumbnail
    }
  }
`;

export const ProductItemsWrapper = styled.div`
    ...
```

3. The imported `Query` component can be returned from `Products` and handle the data fetching process based on the query that you pass to it as a prop. In the same way as the context API, `Query` can consume the data from the Provider by returning a `data` variable. You can iterate over the `products` field from this object and return a list of `ProductItem` components by adding the `Query` component:

```
...
const Products = ({ match, history, loading, error, products })
=> {
-   const isEmpty = products.length === 0 ? 'No products
available' : false;

  return (
    <>
      {history && (
        <SubHeader title='Available products' goToCart={() =>
history.push('/cart')} />
      )}

-       {!loading && !error && !isEmpty ? (
+       <Query query={GET_PRODUCTS}>
+         {(({ data }) => {
+           return (
            <ProductItemsWrapper>
              {data.products && data.products.map(product => (
                <ProductItem key={product.id} data={product}
/>
              ))}
            </ProductItemsWrapper>
+           );
+         }}
+       </Query>
-       ) : (
-         <Alert>{loading ? 'Loading...' : error ||
isEmpty}</Alert>
-       )}
    </>
  );
};
...
```

4. Not only will the `Query` component return a `data` object, but it will also return the `loading` and `error` variables. So, instead of setting a default value for the `loading` prop, you can use this value and return a loading message if its value is `true`. For the `error` variable, you apply the same approach. Also, the default value for the `Products` prop is hereby no longer used and can be deleted:

```
- const Products = ({ match, history, loading, error, products })
=> {
-   return (
+ const Products = ({ match, history }) => (
    <>
      {history && (
        <SubHeader title='Available products' goToCart={() =>
history.push('/cart')} />
      )}
      <Query query={GET_PRODUCTS}>
-       {({ data }) => {
+       {({ loading, error, data }) => {
+         if (loading || error) {
+           return <Alert>{loading ? 'Loading...' : error}</Alert>;
+         }
          return (
            <ProductItemsWrapper>
              {data.products && data.products.map(product => (
                <ProductItem key={product.id} data={product} />
              ))}
            </ProductItemsWrapper>
          );
        }}
      </Query>
    </>
);
- };

- Products.defaultProps = {
-   loading: false,
-   error: '',
-   products: [],
- }
```

This will send a document with the GET_PRODUCTS query to the GraphQL server when your application mounts and subsequently display the product information in the list of the ProductItem components. After adding the logic to retrieve the product information from the GraphQL server, your application will look similar to the following:

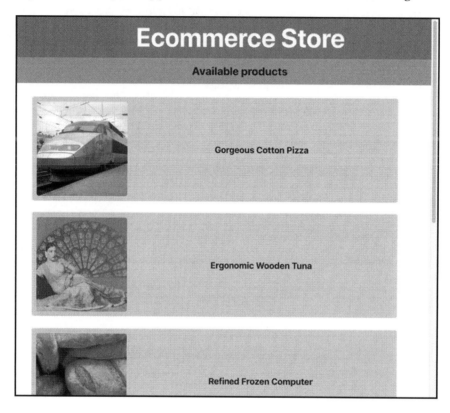

Since the Cart component on the /cart route also needs to query data from the GraphQL server, changes to the src/components/Cart/Cart.js file should be made as well. Just like we did for Products, a Query component should be added to retrieve data from the server and can be done by following these steps:

1. Start by importing the dependencies that are needed to send queries to the GraphQL server, which are react-apollo to get the Query component and graphql-tag to use the GraphQL query language to define the query you want to send to GraphQL:

```
import React from 'react';
import styled from 'styled-components';
+ import { Query } from 'react-apollo';
```

```
+ import gql from 'graphql-tag';
import SubHeader from '../Header/SubHeader';
import ProductItem from '../Products/ProductItem';
import Totals from './Totals';

const CartWrapper = styled.div`
    ...
```

2. After this, you can define `query`, which should be sent in the document. This will retrieve the information for `cart`, including any `products` that might be in `cart`:

```
import React from 'react';
import styled from 'styled-components';
import { Query } from 'react-apollo';
import gql from 'graphql-tag';
import SubHeader from '../Header/SubHeader';
import ProductItem from '../Products/ProductItem';
import Totals from './Totals';

+ const GET_CART = gql`
+   query getCart {
+     cart {
+       total
+       products {
+         id
+         title
+         thumbnail
+       }
+     }
+   }
+ `;

const CartWrapper = styled.div`
    ...
```

3. Replace the existing code for the `Cart` component with the following, where the `Query` component is implemented and the `Cart` component only receives the `match` and `history` props. Therefore, you'd need to replace the code for this component with the following:

```
    ...

- const Cart = ...

+ const Cart = ({ match, history }) => (
+   <>
```

```
+        {history && (
+          <SubHeader goBack={() => history.goBack()} title='Cart' />
+        )}
+        <Query query={GET_CART}>
+          {({ loading, error, data }) => {
+            if (loading || error) {
+              return <Alert>{loading ? 'Loading...' : error}</Alert>;
+            }
+            return (
+              <CartWrapper>
+                <CartItemsWrapper>
+                  {data.cart && data.cart.products.map(product => (
+                    <ProductItem key={product.id} data={product} />
+                  ))}
+                </CartItemsWrapper>
+                <Totals count={data.cart.total} />
+              </CartWrapper>
+            );
+          }}
+        </Query>
+    </>
+  );

export default Cart;

...
```

4. This won't show any products yet as the cart is empty; the cart will be filled with products in the next section. However, let's proceed by adding a Query component to the button to the cart with a placeholder counter in SubHeader for the / route. Therefore, a new file called CartButton.js can be created in the client/src/components/Cart directory. In this file, a Query component will return data from a query that requests the total number of products in the cart. Also, we can add a value to the Button component by adding the following code to this file:

```
import React from 'react'
import { Query } from 'react-apollo';
import gql from 'graphql-tag';
import Button from '../Button/Button';

const GET_CART_TOTAL = gql`
  query getCartTotal {
    cart {
      total
    }
  }
```

```
`;

const CartButton = ({ onClick }) => (
  <Query query={GET_CART_TOTAL}>
    {(({ data, loading, error }) => (
      <Button onClick={onClick}>
        {`Cart (${(loading || error) ? 0 : data &&
data.cart.total})`}
      </Button>
    )}
  </Query>
);

export default CartButton
```

5. This `CartButton` component replaces `Button`, which is now being displayed with a placeholder count for the number of products in the cart, in the `client/src/components/Header/SubHeader.js` file:

```
import React from 'react';
import styled from 'styled-components';
import Button from '../Button/Button';
+ import CartButton from '../Cart/CartButton';

...

const SubHeader = ({ goBack, title, goToCart = false }) => (
  <SubHeaderWrapper>
    {goBack && <SubHeaderButton onClick={goBack}>{`< Go
Back`}</SubHeaderButton>}
    <Title>{ title }</Title>
-    {goToCart && <SubHeaderButton onClick={goToCart}>{`Cart
(0)`}</SubHeaderButton>}
+    {goToCart && <CartButton onClick={goToCart} />}
  </SubHeaderWrapper>
);

export default SubHeader;
```

With all of the components that show either a product or cart information connected to the GraphQL Client, you can proceed by adding mutations that add products to the cart. How to add mutations to the application and send document container mutations to the GraphQL server will be shown in the final part of this section.

Handling mutations with Apollo Client

Mutating data makes using GraphQL more interesting because when data is mutated, some side effects should be executed. For example, when a user adds a product to their cart, the data for the cart should be updated throughout the component as well. This is quite easy when you're using Apollo Client since the Provider handles this in the same way the context API.

Before writing your first mutation, the definitions of the executable queries for the cart should be moved to a constants file. That way, you can easily import them into other components to reuse and execute them as a side effect. Creating the new constants file and moving all the GraphQL queries and mutations to it requires that we make the following changes:

1. In the `client/src` directory, you should create a new file called `constants.js` and place the two already defined queries here, which can be found in the `Cart` and `CartButton` components. Also, you will need to import `graphql-tag` to use the GraphQL query language by adding the following code block to that newly created file:

    ```javascript
    import gql from 'graphql-tag';

    export const GET_CART_TOTAL = gql`
      query getCartTotal {
        cart {
          total
        }
      }
    `;

    const GET_CART = gql`
      query getCart {
        cart {
          total
          products {
            id
            title
            thumbnail
          }
        }
      }
    `;

    export default GET_CART
    ```

2. In the `Cart` component, you can remove the definition to `GET_CART`, and import that definition from `client/src/constants.js` in the `client/src/components/Cart/Cart.js` file:

```
import React from 'react';
import styled from 'styled-components';
import { Query } from 'react-apollo';
- import gql from 'graphql-tag';
import SubHeader from '../Header/SubHeader';
import ProductItem from '../Products/ProductItem';
import Totals from './Totals';
+ import { GET_CART } from '../../constants';

- const GET_CART = gql`
-   query getCart {
-     cart {
-       total
-       products {
-         id
-         title
-         thumbnail
-       }
-     }
-   }
- `;

const CartWrapper = styled.div`
  ...
```

3. For the `CartButton` component in `CartButton.js`, you should apply the same changes, but this time for the `GET_CART_TOTAL` query, which can also be imported from the `constants` file and deleted from the `CartButton.js` file:

```
import React from 'react'
import { Query } from 'react-apollo';
- import gql from 'graphql-tag';
import Button from '../Button/Button';
+ import { GET_CART_TOTAL } from '../../constants';

- const GET_CART_TOTAL = gql`
-   query getCartTotal {
-     cart {
-       total
-     }
-   }
- `;
```

```
const CartButton = ({ onClick }) => (
    ...
```

Any new definition of a query or mutation that relates to the components in the directory should be placed in this file from now on.

Since you want your users to be able to add products to the cart, a definition of a mutation can be added to this file. The mutation to add products to the cart looks as follows, which takes the `productId` parameter to add a product to the cart. The following mutation can return the fields for the cart in return, just like a query can:

```
mutation addToCart($productId: Int!) {
    addToCart(input: { productId: $productId }) {
        total
    }
}
```

You can already test this mutation by trying it out on the GraphQL Playground that's available at `http://localhost:4000/graphql`. Here, you'd need to add the mutation in the upper-left box of this page. The variable that you want to include in this mutation for `productId` must be placed in the bottom-left box of this page, called **QUERY VARIABLES**. This would result in the following output:

To be able to use this mutation from your React application, you will need to make the following changes to some files:

1. Create a new exported constant in the `client/src/constants.js` file and add the mutation to it:

```
import gql from 'graphql-tag';

+ export const ADD_TO_CART = gql`
+  mutation addToCart($productId: Int!) {
+    addToCart(input: { productId: $productId }) {
+       total
+    }
+  }
+ `;

export const GET_CART_TOTAL = gql`
    ...
```

2. Currently, there's no button to add a product to the cart yet, so you can create a new file in the `Cart` directory and call this `AddToCartButton.js`. In this file, you can add the following code:

```
import React from 'react'
import { Mutation } from 'react-apollo';
import Button from '../Button/Button';
import { ADD_TO_CART } from '../../constants';

const AddToCartButton = ({ productId }) => (
  <Mutation mutation={ADD_TO_CART}>
    {addToCart => (
      <Button onClick={() => addToCart({ variables: { productId
}})}>
        {`+ Add to cart`}
      </Button>
    )}
  </Mutation>
);

export default AddToCartButton;
```

This new `AddToCartButton` takes `productId` as a prop and has a `Mutation` component from `react-apollo`, which uses the `Mutation` you created in `client/src/constants.js`. The output of `Mutation` is the actual function to call this mutation, which takes an object containing the inputs as a parameter. Clicking on the `Button` component will execute the mutation.

3. This button should be displayed next to the products in the list in the
   Products component, where each product is displayed in a
   ProductItem component. This means, you will need to import
   AddCartButton in 'src/components/Products/ProductItem.js' and pass
   a productId prop to it by using the following code:

```
import React from 'react';
import styled from 'styled-components';
+ import AddToCartButton from '../Cart/AddToCartButton';

...

const ProductItem = ({ data }) => (
  <ProductItemWrapper>
    <Thumbnail src={data.thumbnail} width={200} />
    <Title>{data.title}</Title>
+   <AddToCartButton productId={data.id} />
  </ProductItemWrapper>
);

export default ProductItem;
```

Now, when you open the React application in the browser, a button will be
displayed next to the product titles. If you click this button, the mutation will be
sent to the GraphQL server and the product will be added to the cart. However,
you won't see any changes to the button that displays **Cart (0)** in the
SubHeader component.

4. To update CartButton, you will need to specify that, when the mutation to the
   cart takes place, other queries should be executed again. This can be done by
   setting the refetchQueries prop on the Mutation component in
   client/src/components/Cart/AddToCartButton.js. This prop takes an
   array of objects with information about the queries that should be requested.
   These queries are the GET_CART_TOTAL query, which is executed by
   CartButton, and the GET_CART query from the Cart component. To do this,
   make the following changes:

```
import React from 'react'
import { Mutation } from 'react-apollo';
import Button from '../Button/Button';
- import { ADD_TO_CART, GET_CART_TOTAL } from '../../constants';
+ import { GET_CART, ADD_TO_CART, GET_CART_TOTAL } from
'../../constants';

const AddToCartButton = ({ productId }) => (
```

```
-    <Mutation mutation={ADD_TO_CART}>
+    <Mutation mutation={ADD_TO_CART} refetchQueries={[{ query:
GET_CART }, { query: GET_CART_TOTAL }]}>
      {addToCart => (
        <Button onClick={() => addToCart({ variables: { productId
}})}>
          {`+ Add to cart`}
        </Button>
      )}
   </Mutation>
);

export default AddToCartButton;
```

Now, every time you send a mutation in a document to the GraphQL server from this component, both the GET_CART and GET_CART_TOTAL queries will be sent as well. If the results have changed, the CartButton and Cart components will be rendered with this new output.

In this section, you've added some logic to send queries and mutations to the GraphQL server, by using the GraphQL client from Apollo. This client has other features as well, such as local state management, which you'll learn about in the next section.

Managing local state

Not only can you use Apollo Client to manage the data that is fetched from the GraphQL server, but you can also use it for managing the local state. With Apollo, it becomes easy to combine local state with data from the GraphQL server since you can also use queries and mutations to deal with the local state.

A good example of information you might want to put in your local state for this e-commerce store is the number of products that should be requested from the GraphQL server. In the first part of this chapter, you already created a query that takes a parameter called limit, which defines how many products will be returned.

To add local state to your application, some changes need to made to the setup of Apollo Client, after which you need to make the following changes as well:

1. In the `client/src/App.js` file, you need to detach the `cache` constant; that way, you can use the `writeData` method to add new values to `cache`. Also, you will need to add local `resolvers` and `typeDefs` to `client`, which will be used next to `resolvers` and `typeDefs` from the GraphQL server. To do this, change the following code:

    ```
    + const cache = new InMemoryCache();

    const client = new ApolloClient({
        link: new HttpLink({
          uri: 'http://localhost:4000/',
        }),
    -   cache,
    +   resolvers: {},
    +   typeDefs: `
    +     extend type Query {
    +         limit: Int!
    +     }
    +   `,
    });

    + cache.writeData({
    +   data: {
    +       limit: 5,
    +   },
    + });
    ```

    In the preceding code block, the schema is extended with a `Query` type that has a field for `limit`, meaning you can query `client` for this value. Also, an initial value for `limit` is written to `cache`. This means the value for `limit` will always be 5 when the application first mounts.

2. Let's also add all of the queries related to products to the `client/src/constants.js` file. This can be added to the `client/src/components/Products` directory by adding the following code to the file:

    ```
    import gql from 'graphql-tag';

    ...

    + export const GET_LIMIT = gql`
    +   query getLimit {
    ```

```
+        limit @client
+    }
+    `;

+ export const GET_PRODUCTS = gql`
+    query getProducts {
+        products {
+            id
+            title
+            thumbnail
+        }
+    }
+    `;
```

3. For the query for `products` to use `limit` from the local state, a small change has to be made to the `GET_PRODUCTS` query:

```
    . . .

    const GET_PRODUCTS = gql`
-    query getProducts {
+    query getProducts($limit: Int) {
-        products {
+        products(limit: $limit) {
            id
            title
            thumbnail
        }
    }
    `;

    export default GET_PRODUCTS;
```

This `query` will now use the `limit` variable to request the number of products, instead of the predefined value of `10` in your GraphQL server. By adding `@client`, the Apollo Client will know to get this value from `cache`, meaning the local state.

4. In the `Products` component, these queries should be imported from the
   `constants.js` file, and the value for `limit` should be requested with a
   `Query` component from `react-apollo`. Also, the value for `limit` that is
   returned by `Query` should be sent in the `variables` prop when requesting the
   `GET_PRODUCTS` query. Therefore, make the following changes to use the updated
   query and pass the variables to it:

```
import React from 'react';
import styled from 'styled-components';
import {Query} from 'react-apollo';
- import gql from 'graphql-tag';
import SubHeader from '../Header/SubHeader';
import ProductItem from './ProductItem';
+ import { GET_PRODUCTS, GET_LIMIT } from '../../constants';

- const GET_PRODUCTS = gql`
- query getProducts {
-     products {
-         id
-         title
-         thumbnail
-     }
- }
- `;

...

const Products = ({ match, history }) => (
  <>
    {history && (
      <SubHeader title='Available products' goToCart={() =>
history.push('/cart')} />
    )}
    <Query query={GET_LIMIT}>
      {({ loading, error, data }) => (
-         <Query query={GET_PRODUCTS}>
+         <Query query={GET_PRODUCTS} variables={{ limit:
parseInt(data.limit) }}>
          {({ loading, error, data }) => {
            if (loading || error) {
              return <Alert>{loading ? 'Loading...' :
error}</Alert>;
            }
            return (
              <ProductItemsWrapper>
                {data.products && data.products.map(product => (
                  <ProductItem key={product.id} data={product} />
```

```
              )) }
          </ProductItemsWrapper>
        );
      }}
    </Query>
  )}
 </Query>
</>
);

export default Products;
```

With the previous changes, the returned value from the GET_LIMIT query will be sent as a variable to the GET_PRODUCTS query, where you need to make sure this value is an integer by using parseInt. If you look at the application in the browser now, 5 products will be displayed.

5. Next, to have an initial value for limit, this value can also be set dynamically. Therefore, you can use the writeData method again to update the cache. This should be done from a different component that can access the client. To accomplish this, you need to create a component in the client/src/components/Products directory in the new Filter.js file. In this file, you can place the following code:

```
import React from 'react';
import { ApolloConsumer } from 'react-apollo';

const Filters = ({ limit }) => (
  <ApolloConsumer>
    {client => (
      <>
      <label for='limit'>Number of products: </label>
      <select id='limit' value={limit} onChange={e =>
client.writeData({ data: { limit: e.target.value } })}>
          <option value={5}>5</option>
          <option value={10}>10</option>
          <option value={20}>20</option>
      </select>
      </>
    )}
  </ApolloConsumer>
);

export default Filters;
```

This `Filter` component uses `ApolloConsumer` to get the value for the client from `ApolloProvider`, which is similar to how the React context API works. From any component that is nested in `ApolloProvider`, you will be able to get the client value by using the Consumer from `react-apollo`. The client will be used to write data to the cache, and this data is retrieved from the value of the select drop-down menu.

6. The `Filter` component should also be added to the `Products` component so that it can actually be used to change the value for `limit`:

```
import React from 'react';
import styled from 'styled-components';
import { Query } from 'react-apollo';
import SubHeader from '../Header/SubHeader';
import ProductItem from './ProductItem';
+ import Filters from './Filters';
import { GET_PRODUCTS, GET_LIMIT } from '../../constants';

...

const Products = ({ match, history }) => (
  <>
    {history && (
      <SubHeader title='Available products' goToCart={() =>
history.push('/cart')} />
    )}
    <Query query={GET_LIMIT}>
      {({ loading, error, data }) => (
+       <>
+         <Filters limit={parseInt(data.limit)} />
          <Query query={GET_PRODUCTS} variables={{ limit:
parseInt(data.limit) }}>
            {({ loading, error, data }) => {
              if (loading || error) {
                return <Alert>{loading ? 'Loading...' :
error}</Alert>;
              }
              return (
                <ProductItemsWrapper>
                  {data.products && data.products.map(product => (
                    <ProductItem key={product.id} data={product} />
                  ))}
                </ProductItemsWrapper>
              );
            }}
          </Query>
+       </>
```

```
    )}
  </Query>
</>
);

export default Products;
```

Since the `Query` component for `GET_PRODUCTS` is nested in the `Query` component for `GET_LIMIT`, whenever the `GET_LIMIT` query is sent, this query will also be sent. So, when you use the select drop-down menu to change `limit`, the `GET_PRODUCTS` query will be sent and the number of products that are displayed will have changed.

With these changes, your application uses the Apollo Client for getting data from the GraphQL server and for handling local state management. Also, users can now filter the number of products that they'll see in your application, which will make your application look similar to the following:

The buttons to add a product to the cart were added in the previous section, while the functionality of the cart will be handled in the next section, when you add authentication to the project.

Using authentication with React and GraphQL

When the users have added products to the cart, you want them to be able to checkout, but before that, the users should be authenticated as you want to know who's buying the product. Handling authentication in React will also require an interaction with the backend, since you need to store the user's information somewhere or check whether the user exists.

For authentication in frontend applications, most of the time, **JSON Web Tokens (JWTs)** are used, which are encrypted tokens that can easily be used to share user information with a backend. The JWT will be returned by the backend when the user is successfully authenticated and often, this token will have an expiration date. With every request that the user should be authenticated for, the token should be sent so that the backend server can determine whether the user is authenticated and allowed to take this action. Although JWTs can be used for authentication since they're encrypted, no private information should be added to them since the tokens should only be used to authenticate the user. Private information can only be sent from the server when a document with the correct JWT has been sent.

React Router and authentication

The GraphQL server for this project has already been set up to handle authentication and will return a JWT token when the correct user information has been sent to it. When the user wants to check out the cart, the application will look for a JWT token in the local or session storage and redirect the user either to the checkout page or the login page. For this, private routes should be added to `react-router`, which are only available when the user is authenticated.

Adding a private route requires that we make the following changes:

1. New routes for the checkout and the login pages must be added to the `Router` component in the `client/src/components/App.js` file, where the user can either checkout or log in. For this, you must import the `Checkout` and `Login` components that have already been created and a `Redirect` component from `react-router-dom`:

   ```
   import React from 'react';
   import styled, { createGlobalStyle } from 'styled-components';
   ```

```
- import { Route, Switch } from 'react-router-dom';
+ import { Route, Switch, Redirect } from 'react-router-dom';
import Header from './Header/Header';
import Products from './Products/Products';
import Cart from './Cart/Cart';
+ import Login from './Checkout/Login';
+ import Checkout from './Checkout/Checkout';

...
```

2. After importing these, routes must be added to `Switch` in `Router`, making them available to the user:

```
const App = () => (
  <ApolloProvider client={client}>
    <GlobalStyle />
    <AppWrapper>
      <Header />
      <Switch>
        <Route exact path='/' component={Products} />
        <Route path='/cart' component={Cart} />
+       <Route path='/checkout' component={Checkout} />
+       <Route path='/login/ component={Login} />
      </Switch>
    </AppWrapper>
  </ApolloProvider>
);

export default App;
```

3. In the current situation, the user can navigate to the `login` and `checkout` pages without being authenticated. To check whether the user is authenticated, the render props method for the `Route` component can be used. In this method, you must check whether or not a JWT is stored in the session storage for this user. Currently, no token is stored in the session storage since this will be added later on. But you can still create the function to check for it by adding the following function:

```
...

+ const isAuthenticated = sessionStorage.getItem('token');

const cache = new InMemoryCache();

const client = new ApolloClient({
  ...
```

There are many ways to store a JWT, such as using the local storage, session storage, cookies, or a local state in the form of the `apollo-link-state` package. As long as you follow the protocol of JWT, encrypt no private information in the token, and add an expiration date to it, all of these places can be considered as a safe place to store the token.

4. After this, the render props method is used for the checkout route to check whether the user is authenticated or not. If not, the user will be redirected to the login page using the `Redirect` component. Otherwise, the user will see the `Checkout` component, which will receive the router props that are returned by the render props method. To make this happen, make the following changes:

```
const App = () => (
  <ApolloProvider client={client}>
    <GlobalStyle />
    <AppWrapper>
      <Header />
      <Switch>
        <Route exact path='/' component={Products} />
        <Route path='/cart' component={Cart} />
-       <Route path='/checkout' component={Checkout} />
+       <Route
+         path='/checkout'
+         render={props =>
+           isAuthenticated()
+             ? <Checkout />
+             : <Redirect to='/login' />
+         }
+       />
        <Route path='/login' component={Login} />
      </Switch>
    <AppWrapper>
  </ApolloProvider>
);

export default App;
```

When you try to visit the `http://localhost:3000/checkout` route in your browser, you'll always be redirected to the `/login` route since no JWT has been stored in the session storage yet. In the next part of this section, you'll add the logic to retrieve the JWT from the GraphQL server by sending a mutation with login information.

Receiving JWT from the GraphQL server

The GraphQL server has already been set up to handle authentication since we sent a document containing a mutation with our login information to it. When you send the correct username and password, the server will return a JWT containing your username and expiration date. Sending a query to the GraphQL server can be done by using a `Mutation` component from `react-apollo` or by using the React Apollo Hooks, which offer you more flexibility. Logging in can be done from the `Login` component, which you can find in the `client/src/components/Checkout/Login.js` file, where the following changes need to be made to authenticate the user:

1. The React Apollo Hook for the mutation will need a document that will be sent to the GraphQL server. This mutation can also be defined in the `client/src/constants.js` file, which is where you've defined all of the other queries and mutations as well:

   ```
   import gql from 'graphql-tag';

   ...

   + export const LOGIN_USER = gql`
   +   mutation loginUser($userName: String!, $password: String!) {
   +     loginUser(userName: $userName, password: $password) {
   +       userName
   +       token
   +     }
   +   }
   + `;
   ```

2. The `Login` component in `client/src/components/Checkout/Login.js` is already using `useState` Hooks to control the value of the input fields for `userName` and `password`. The `useMutation` Hook can be imported from `react-apollo` and you can use this Hook to replace a `Mutation` component and still have the same functionalities. This Hook can also be used from anywhere within `ApolloProvider` and returns a login function that will send the document to the GraphQL server. Adding this is done by importing the Hook and passing the `LOGIN_USER` mutation from `client/src/constants.js` to it:

   ```
   import React from 'react';
   import styled from 'styled-components';
   + import { useMutation } from 'react-apollo';
   import Button from '../Button/Button';
   + import { LOGIN_USER } from '../../constants';

   ...
   ```

```
  const Login = () => {
+ const [loginUser] = useMutation(LOGIN_USER);
  const [userName, setUserName] = React.useState('');
  const [password, setPassword] = React.useState('');
  return (
    ...
```

React Apollo Hooks can be used from the `react-apollo` package, but if you only want to use the Hooks, you can install `@apollo/react-hooks` instead by executing `npm install @apollo/react-hooks`. GraphQL components such as `Query` or `Mutation` are available in both the `react-apollo` and `@apollo/react-components` packages. Using these packages will decrease the size of your bundle as you're only importing the features you need.

3. After creating the `loginUser` function, this can be added to the `onClick` event from `Button`, and the values for `userName` and `password` should be passed to this function as variables:

```
return (
  <LoginWrapper>
    <TextInput
      onChange={e => setUserName(e.target.value)}
      value={userName}
      placeholder='Your username'
    />
    <TextInput
      onChange={e => setPassword(e.target.value)}
      value={password}
      placeholder='Your password'
    />
-   <Button color='royalBlue'>
+   <Button
+     color='royalBlue'
+     onClick={() => loginUser({ variables: { userName, password }
})}
+   >
      Login
    </Button>
  </LoginWrapper>
);
```

4. Clicking `Button` will send the document containing the `userName` and `password` values to the GraphQL server and if successful, it returns the JWT for this user. However, this token should also be stored in the session storage and as the `loginUser` function returns a promise, the `onClick` event should become an asynchronous function. That way, you can wait for the `loginUser` function to resolve and store the token afterward or send an error message if no token was returned:

```
. . .

<Button
  color='royalBlue'
- onClick={() => loginUser({ variables: { userName, password } })}
+ onClick={async () => {
+   const { data } = await loginUser({
+     variables: { userName, password }
+   });
+
+   if (data.loginUser && data.loginUser.token) {
+     sessionStorage.setItem('token', data.loginUser.token);
+   } else {
+     alert('Please provide (valid) authentication details');
+   }
+ }}
>
  Login
</Button>

. . .
```

5. Finally, the user should be redirected to the `checkout` page if the authentication succeeded. SInce the `Login` component is rendered by the checkout route using the render props method, it received the props from `react-router`. To redirect the user back, you can use the `history` prop from `react-router` to push the user to the `checkout` page:

```
. . .

- const Login = () => {
+ const Login = ({ history }) => {

  . . .

  return (
    . . .
```

```
        <Button
          color='royalBlue'
          onClick={async () => {

          ...

          if (data.loginUser && data.loginUser.token) {
            sessionStorage.setItem('token', data.loginUser.token);
+           return history.push('/checkout');
          } else {
            alert('Please provide (valid) authentication details');
          }

        ...
```

Every user that has a token stored in their session storage is now able to visit the checkout page for as long as the token is stored there. You can delete the token from the session storage by going to the **Application** tab in the **Developer tools** of your browser; there, you'll find another tab called **Session Storage**.

Since you want your users to be able to navigate from the cart page to the checkout page, you should add Button in the Cart component that lets the user navigate using a Link component from react-router-dom. If the user isn't authenticated yet, this will redirect the user to the login page; otherwise, it will redirect them to the checkout page. Also, the button should only be displayed when there are products in the cart. To add this Button, the following changes need to be made in client/src/components/Cart/Cart.js:

```
import React from 'react';
import styled from 'styled-components';
import { Query } from 'react-apollo';
+ import { Link } from 'react-router-dom';
import SubHeader from '../Header/SubHeader';
import ProductItem from '../Products/ProductItem';
+ import Button from '../Button/Button';
import Totals from './Totals';
import { GET_CART } from '../../constants';

...

const Cart = ({ history }) => (

  ...

  return (
    <CartWrapper>
      <CartItemsWrapper>
        {data.cart && data.cart.products.map(product => (
```

```
            <ProductItem key={product.id} data={product} />
        ))}
      </CartItemsWrapper>
      <Totals count={data.cart.total} />
+     {data.cart && data.cart.products.length > 0 && (
+       <Link to='/checkout'>
+         <Button color='royalBlue'>Checkout</Button>
+       </Link>
+     )}
    </CartWrapper>
  );

  ...
```

You've now added the functionality to proceed to the final checkout page of your application, which makes the /cart route look like this in your application after adding a product to it:

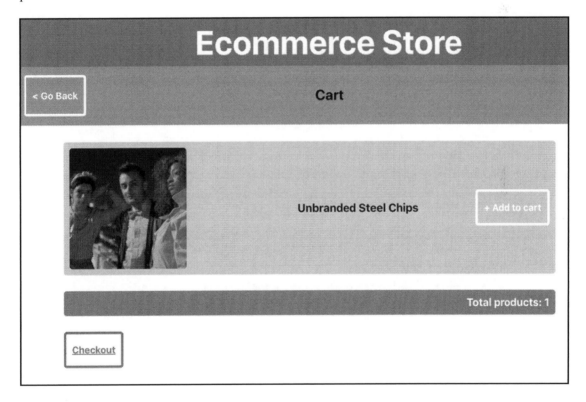

In the final part of this section, you'll add this token to the document that you send to the GraphQL server, where the token is validated to make sure the user is authenticated for a certain action.

Passing JWT to the GraphQL server

The user's authentication details in the form of the JWT are now stored in the session storage, and the route to the checkout page is now private. But for the user to check out, this token should also be sent to the GraphQL server, along with every document for the server, to validate whether the user is actually authenticated or whether the token has expired. Therefore, you need to extend the setup of the Apollo Client to also send the token when you make a request to the server and prefix it with `Bearer`, since this is how a JWT is recognized.

Follow these steps to pass the JWT to the GraphQL server:

1. You need to install an Apollo package to deal with adding values to the Context since you need the `setContext` method to do this. This method is available from the `apollo-link-Context` package, which you can install from npm:

   ```
   npm install apollo-link-Context
   ```

2. The Apollo Client is created in the `client/src/components/App.js` file, where you import the `setContext` method from `apollo-link-Context`. Also, the creation of the link to the GraphQL server must be decoupled as this should also take the authentication details, that is, `token`:

   ```
   . . .

   import { ApolloClient } from 'apollo-client';
   import { InMemoryCache } from 'apollo-cache-inmemory';
   import { HttpLink } from 'apollo-link-http';
   import { ApolloProvider } from 'react-apollo';
   + import { setContext } from 'apollo-link-Context';

   const isAuthenticated = sessionStorage.getItem('token');

   + const httpLink = new HttpLink({
   +   uri: 'http://localhost:4000/graphql',
   + });

   const cache = new InMemoryCache();

   const client = new ApolloClient({
   ```

```
link: new HttpLink({
  uri: 'http://localhost:4000/graphql',
}),
cache,
resolvers: {

  . . .
```

3. Now, you can use the `setContext` method to extend the request headers that are being sent to the GraphQL server so that it also include the token that can be retrieved from the session storage. The token that you retrieve from the session storage must be prefixed with `Bearer` since the GraphQL server expects the JWT token in that format:

```
. . .

const httpLink = new HttpLink({
  uri: 'http://localhost:4000/graphql',
})

+ const authLink = setContext((_, { headers }) => {
+   const token = isAuthenticated;
+
+   return {
+     headers: {
+       ...headers,
+       authorization: token ? `Bearer ${token}` : '',
+     },
+   };
+ });

const cache = new InMemoryCache();

const client = new ApolloClient({
  . . .
```

4. Together with the `HttpLink` method, the `authLink` constant must be used in the setup of Apollo Client; this will make sure the Context value from `authLink` is being added to the headers being sent by `httpLink`:

```
...

const client = new ApolloClient({
- link: new HttpLink({
-   uri: 'http://localhost:4000/graphql',
- }),
+ link: authLink.concat(httpLink),
  cache,
  resolvers: {

...
```

If you visit the application in the browser again and make sure you are logged in by either going to the `checkout` or `login` page, you will see that the requests are still sent to the GraphQL server. The difference can be seen when you open the **Developer tools** of your browser and go to the **Network** tab. The requests to the server now have different header information since a field called `authorization` is also sent, which has a value that looks like **Bearer eyAABBB...**.

When the user goes to the checkout page, there should be a button to finalize the order. This button will call a function that completes the cart. As the user must be authenticated to create an order, the token must be sent with this request that sends the `completeCart` mutation. This mutation completes the cart and clears its content, after which the contents of the checkout page change.

Adding this feature to the `checkout` page requires making the following changes:

1. The `completeCart` mutation has the following shape and can be found in `client/constants.js`:

```
export const COMPLETE_CART = gql`
  mutation completeCart {
    completeCart {
      complete
    }
  }
`;
```

It must be imported into
the `client/src/components/Checkout/Checkout.js` file:

```
import React from 'react';
import styled from 'styled-components';
import Button from '../Button/Button';
+ import { COMPLETE_CART } from '../../constants';

...

const Checkout = () => {
  ...
```

2. The mutation can be sent to the GraphQL server by using a `useMutation` Hook, which can be imported from `react-apollo`. At the beginning of the `Checkout` component, the Hook can be added with the `COMPLETE_CART` mutation as a parameter. The Hook returns the function to send the mutation and the data that was returned from the mutation:

```
import React from 'react';
import styled from 'styled-components';
+ import { useMutation } from 'react-apollo';
import Button from '../Button/Button';
import { COMPLETE_CART } from '../../constants';

...

const Checkout = () => {
+ [completeCart, { data }] = useMutation(COMPLETE_CART);

  ...
```

3. The `completeCart` function must be added to the `Button` component as an `onClick` prop so that when the button is clicked, that function will be called. Also, you must check whether the `COMPLETE_CART` mutation returns a value for the `complete` field, which indicates whether the cart was completed or not. If it was, the checkout is complete and a different message can be displayed to the user:

```
...

const Checkout = () => {
  const [completeCart, { data }] = useMutation(COMPLETE_CART);
  return (
    <CheckoutWrapper>
```

```
+        {data && data.completeCart.complete ? (
+          <p>Completed checkout!</p>
+        ) : (
+          <>
             <p>This is the checkout, press the button below to
complete:</p>
-            <Button color='royalBlue'>
+            <Button color='royalBlue' onClick={completeCart}>
               Complete checkout
             </Button>
+          </>
+        )}
      </CheckoutWrapper>
    );
  };


  ...
```

This concludes the checkout process for the user and this chapter, where you've used React and GraphQL to create an e-commerce application.

Summary

In this chapter, you've created a full stack React application that uses GraphQL as its backend. Using Apollo Server and mock data, the GraphQL server was created, which takes queries and mutations to provide you with data. This GraphQL server is used by a React application that uses Apollo Client to send and receive data from the server and to handle local state management. Authentication is handled by the GraphQL server using JWT and in the frontend by React and `react-router`.

That's it! You've completed the seventh chapter of this book and have already created seven web applications with React. By now, you should feel comfortable with React and its features and be ready to learn some more. In the next chapter, you'll be introduced to React Native and learn how you can use your React skills to build a mobile application by creating a house listing application with React Native and Expo.

Further reading

- Creating an Apollo Server from scratch: `https://www.apollographql.com/docs/apollo-server/essentials/server`
- GraphQL: `https://graphql.org/learn/`
- JWT tokens: `https://jwt.io/introduction/`

8

Build a House Listing Application with React Native and Expo

One of the taglines for development with React is *learn once, write anywhere,* which is due to the existence of React Native. With React Native, you can write native mobile applications using JavaScript and React while using the same features as React for things such as state management. Building on the React knowledge that you've already gathered from this book, you'll start exploring React Native from this chapter on. As React and React Native share a lot of similarities, it's advised that you have another look at some of the previous chapters whenever you feel insecure about your React knowledge.

In this chapter, you'll create a mobile application using React Native, which uses the same syntax and patterns that you've seen in the previous chapters. You'll set up basic routing, explore the differences between development for iOS and Android, and learn about styling React Native components with `styled-components`. Also, a toolchain called **Expo** will be used to run and deploy your React Native application.

In this chapter, the following topics will be covered:

- Creating a React Native project
- Routing for mobile applications
- Life cycles in React Native
- Styling components in React Native

Project overview

In this chapter, we will create a house listing application that shows an overview of the available houses with a detail page of every listing, with `styled-components` for styling and **React Navigation** for routing. The data is fetched from a mock API.

The build time is 1.5 hours.

Getting started

Make sure you have the Expo Client application installed on your iOS or Android device to be able to run the application that you'll create in this chapter. Expo Client is available in both the Apple App Store and the Google Play Store.

Once you've downloaded the application, you need to create an Expo account to make the development process smoother. Make sure you store your account details somewhere safe, as you'll need these later on in this chapter. **Don't forget to verify your email address by clicking the link that was sent to you by email.**

The complete code for this chapter can be found on GitHub: `https://github.com/ PacktPublishing/React-Projects/tree/ch8`.

This application was created using **Expo SDK version 33.0.0** and so you need to make sure the version of Expo you're using on your local machine is similar. Since React Native and Expo are updated frequently, make sure that you're working with this version to ensure the patterns described in this chapter behave as expected. In case your application won't start or you're receiving errors, make sure to check the Expo documentation to learn more about updating the Expo SDK.

Building a house listing application with React Native and Expo

In this section, you'll build a house listing application with React Native and Expo, which allows you to use the same syntax and patterns you already know from React, as it's using the React library. Also, Expo makes it possible to prevent having to install and configure Xcode (for iOS) or Android Studio to start creating native applications on your machine. Therefore, you can write applications for both the iOS and Android platforms from any machine.

 You can also run a React Native application in the browser using Expo web to create **Progressive Web Applications (PWAs)**. However, developing for iOS, Android, and the web at the same time is still experimental and might need a lot of performance and architectural fixes. Also, not all the packages that work in React Native on mobile devices will work on Expo web as well.

Expo combines React APIs and JavaScript APIs with the React Native development process in order to allow features such as JSX components, Hooks, and native features such as camera access. Roughly, the Expo toolchain consists of multiple tools that help you with React Native, such as the Expo CLI, which allows you to create React Native projects from your Terminal, with all of the dependencies that you need to run React Native. With the Expo Client, you can open these projects from iOS and Android mobile devices that are connected to your local network. Expo SDK is the package that contains all of the libraries that make it possible to run your application on multiple devices and platforms.

Create a React Native project

Previously, the starting point of every new React project in this book was using Create React App to create a boilerplate for your application. For React Native, a similar boilerplate is available, which is part of the Expo CLI, and it can be set up just as easily:

You need to globally install the Expo CLI with the following command using npm:

```
npm install -g expo-cli
```

This will start the installation process, which can take some time as it will install the Expo CLI with all of its dependencies that help you develop mobile applications. After this, you're able to create a new project using the init command from the Expo CLI:

```
expo init house-listing
```

Expo will now create the project for you but, first, it will ask you to answer the following questions:

1. It will ask you whether to create just a blank template, a blank template with TypeScript configuration, or a sample template with some example screens set up. For this chapter, you'll need to choose the first option: blank (`expo-template-blank`).

2. After selecting a template, you need to type in the name of your application, which is house listing in this case. This name will be added to the `app.json` file with configuration information about your application.

3. Expo automatically detects whether you have Yarn installed on your machine. If so, it will ask you to use Yarn to install other dependencies that are needed to set up your computer. If you have Yarn installed, select `yes`; otherwise, `npm` will be used by default. For this chapter, it's advised to use `npm` instead of Yarn so that you're consistent with the previous chapters.

Now, your application will be created using the settings you've selected. This application can now be started by moving into the directory that was just created by Expo using the following commands:

```
cd house-listing
npm start
```

This will start Expo and give you the ability to start your project both from the Terminal or from your browser, making it possible to either run the application on your mobile device or by using the iOS or Android Emulator. In your Terminal, there are multiple ways to open the application:

- Sign in using the username from your Expo Client on Android or iOS. Your projects will automatically appear in the **Projects** tab on your mobile device.

- Scan the displayed QR Code from your mobile device that runs on Android or iOS. If you're using an Android device, you can scan the QR Code directly from the Expo Client application. On iOS, you need to use your camera to scan the code that will ask you to open Expo Client.

- Press a to open the Android Emulator or i for the iOS Emulator. Keep in mind that you need to have Xcode and/or Android Studio installed to use either one of the emulators.

- By pressing e to send a link to you by email, this link can be opened from a mobile device that has the Expo Client application installed on it.

Alternatively, running the `npm start` command will open your browser on the `http://localhost:19002/` URL, showing the Expo Developer Tools. This page will look like this, assuming you have the version of the Expo SDK installed that was mentioned in the *Getting started* section:

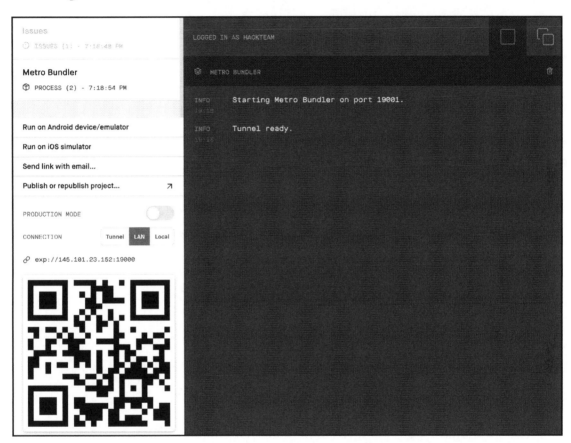

On this page, you can see a sidebar on the left and the logs from your React Native application on the right. This sidebar contains buttons so that you can start the iOS or Android Emulator, for which you need to have either Xcode or Android Studio installed. Otherwise, you can also find a button to send a link to open the application by email or a QR Code on your mobile device using the Expo application you've previously installed.

At this point, your application should look as follows. This screenshot was taken from an iOS device. It shouldn't matter if you've opened the application using the emulator for iOS or Android or from an iOS or Android device:

Open up App.js to start working on your app!

This application was created using **Expo SDK version 33.0.0** and so you need to make sure the version of Expo you're using on your local machine is similar. Since React Native and Expo are updated frequently, make sure that you're working with this version to ensure the patterns described in this chapter behave as expected. In case your application won't start or you're receiving errors, make sure to check the Expo documentation to learn more about updating the Expo SDK.

The project structure from this React Native application, which we created with Expo, is quite similar to the React projects you've created in the previous chapters. It looks as follows:

```
house-listing
|-- .expo
|-- assets
    |-- icon.png
    |-- splash.png
|-- node_modules
.gitignore
App.js
app.json
babel.config.js
package.json
```

In the `assets` directory, you can find the images that are used for the application icon on the home screen once you've installed this application on your mobile device, as well as the image that will serve as the splash screen, which is displayed when you start the application. The `App.js` file is the actual entry point of your application, where you'll return the component that will be rendered when the application mounts. Configurations for your application, for example, for the App Store are placed in `app.json`, while `babel.config.js` holds specific Babel configurations.

Setting up routing in React Native

As we mentioned previously, the `App.js` file is the entry point of your application, which is defined by Expo. If you open this file, you will see it consists of components and that `StyleSheet` has been imported directly from `react-native`. The syntax of writing styles in React Native is different from React being used in a browser, so you'll have to install `styled-components` later on in this chapter.

Creating routes with React Navigation

Let's proceed by installing React Navigation. There are many packages available to help you handle routing in React Native, but this is one of the most popular and advised to use by Expo. Besides React Navigation, you must also install the related packages, called `react-navigation-stack` and `react-navigation-tabs`, which are needed to create the navigators for your application. React Navigation and its dependencies can be installed by running the following command:

```
npm install react-navigation react-navigation-stack react-navigation-tabs
```

To add routing to your React Native application, you will need to understand the difference between routing in a browser and a mobile application. History in React Native doesn't behave the same way as it does in a browser, where users can navigate to different pages by changing the URL in the browser and the previously visited URLs will be added to the browser history. Instead, you will need to keep track of transitions between pages yourself and store a local history in your application.

With React Navigation, you can use multiple different navigators to help you do this, including a stack navigator and a tab navigator. The stack navigator behaves in a way that is very similar to the browser as it stacks pages after transitioning between them and lets you navigate using native gestures and animations for iOS and Android:

1. You can set up a stack navigator by passing an object containing routing configuration to the `createStackNavigator` method, which can be imported from `react-navigation-stack` in the `App.js` file. Also, you will need to import `createAppContainer` from `react-navigation`, which helps you return a component that wraps all of the routes:

   ```
   import React from 'react';
   import { StyleSheet, Text, View } from 'react-native';
   + import { createAppContainer } from 'react-navigation';
   + import { createStackNavigator } from 'react-navigation-stack';

   export default function App() {
       ...
   ```

2. Instead of returning a component called `App`, you need to return the component that was created with `createStackNavigator`, which holds all of the routes for your application. This `StackNavigator` component needs to be exported using `createAppContainer`, as follows:

   ```
   import React from 'react';
   import { StyleSheet, Text, View } from 'react-native';
   ```

```
import { createAppContainer } from 'react-navigation';
import { createStackNavigator } from 'react-navigation-stack';

- export default function App() {
- return (
+ const Home = () => (
    <View style={styles.container}>
        <Text>Open up App.js to start working on your app!</Text>
    </View>
  );
- }

const styles = StyleSheet.create({
  container: {
    flex: 1,
    backgroundColor: '#fff',
    alignItems: 'center',
    justifyContent: 'center',
  },
});

+ const StackNavigator = createStackNavigator({
+   Home: {
+     screen: Home,
+   },
+ });

+ export default createAppContainer(StackNavigator);
```

3. Your application now has one route, which is `Home`, and renders the
   `Home` component. You can also add `title` for this screen by setting the
   `navigationOptions` field in the object that's passed to
   `createStackNavigator` using the following code:

```
...

const AppNavigator = createStackNavigator({
  Home: {
    screen: Home,
+   navigationOptions: { title: 'Home' },
  },
});

export default createAppContainer(AppNavigator);
```

4. To create another route, you can copy this process by adding a
`Detail` component and add a route that renders this component as well:

```
import React from 'react';
import { StyleSheet, Text, View } from 'react-native';
import { createAppContainer } from 'react-navigation';
import { createStackNavigator } from 'react-navigation-stack';

const Home = () => (
  <View style={styles.container}>
    <Text>Open up App.js to start working on your app!</Text>
  </View>
);

+ const Detail = () => (
+   <View style={styles.container}>
+     <Text>Open up App.js to start working on your app!</Text>
+   </View>
+ );

...

const AppNavigator = createStackNavigator({
  Home: {
    screen: Home,
    navigationOptions: { title: 'Home' },
  },
+ Detail: {
+   screen: Detail,
+   navigationOptions: { title: 'Detail' },
+ },
});

export default createAppContainer(AppNavigator);
```

5. Now that you have two screens in your application, you will also need to set a default route that will be rendered when the application first mounts. You can do this by extending the routing configuration object passed to `createStackNavigator` using the following code:

```
...

const AppNavigator = createStackNavigator({
  Home: {
    screen: Home,
    navigationOptions: { title: 'Home' },
  },
```

```
    Detail: {
      screen: Detail,
      navigationOptions: { title: 'Detail' },
    },
+ }, { initialRouteName: 'Home' });
- });

  export default createAppContainer(AppNavigator);
```

You can see that the Detail route is also rendering by changing the value for initialRouteName to Detail, and checking whether the screen that is rendered in your application has the title Detail.

In the next part of this section, you'll learn how to transition between the different screens that are created by this navigator.

Transitioning between screens

Transitioning between screens in React Native also works a bit differently than in the browser because again, there are no URLs. Instead, you need to use the navigation prop, which is available from components that are rendered by the stack navigator. The navigation prop can be used to handle routing by making the following changes:

1. You can access the navigation prop in this example from the Home and Detail components:

```
import React from 'react';
import { StyleSheet, Text, View } from 'react-native';
import { createAppContainer } from 'react-navigation';
import { createStackNavigator } from 'react-navigation-stack';

- const Home = () => (
+ const Home = ({ navigation }) => (
  <View style={styles.container}>
    <Text>Open up App.js to start working on your app!</Text>
  </View>
);

...
```

2. The `navigation` prop holds multiple values, including the `navigate` function, which takes a route name as a parameter. You can use this function as an event on, for example, a `Button` component that you can import from `react-native`. Compared to what you're used to with React, you can click a button by calling an `onPress` event handler instead of `onClick`. Also, the `Button` component doesn't take any children as a prop but a `title` prop instead. To do this, change the following code:

```
import React from 'react';
- import { StyleSheet, Text, View } from 'react-native';
+ import { Button, StyleSheet, Text, View } from 'react-native';
import { createAppContainer } from 'react-navigation';
import { createStackNavigator } from 'react-navigation-stack';

const Home = ({ navigation }) => (
  <View style={styles.container}>
    <Text>Open up App.js to start working on your app!</Text>
+   <Button onPress={() => navigation.navigate('Detail')} title='Go
to Detail' />
  </View>
);

. . .
```

3. When you press the button with the `Go to Detail` title, you'll transition to the `Detail` screen. The header of this screen will also render a `Return` button, which will send you back to the `Home` screen when you press it. You can also create a custom return button by using the `goBack` function from the `navigation` prop, like this:

```
. . .

- const Detail = () => (
+ const Detail = ({ navigation }) => (
  <View style={styles.container}>
    <Text>Open up App.js to start working on your app!</Text>
+   <Button onPress={() => navigation.goBack()} title='Go to back
to Home' />
  </View>
);

. . .
```

Usually, it's good practice to store these components in a different directory and only use the App.js file to make your application more readable. To achieve this, you need to create a new directory called Screens in the root directory of your application, where you need to add a file for each of the two screens you've just created. Let's learn how we can do that:

1. Create a file called Home.js in the Screens directory and add the Home component to this file, including the imports of the used modules. The code for the Home component is as follows:

```
import React from 'react';
import { Button, StyleSheet, Text, View } from 'react-native';

const Home = ({ navigation }) => (
  <View style={styles.container}>
    <Text>Open up App.js to start working on your app!</Text>
    <Button onPress={() => navigation.navigate('Detail')} title='Go
to Detail' />
  </View>
);

const styles = StyleSheet.create({
  container: {
    flex: 1,
    backgroundColor: '#fff',
    alignItems: 'center',
    justifyContent: 'center',
  },
});

export default Home;
```

2. You need to do the same for the Detail screen by creating the Screens/Detail.js file and adding the code for the Detail component and the used modules to this file. You can do this by adding the following code block to that new file:

```
import React from 'react';
import { Button, StyleSheet, Text, View } from 'react-native';

const Detail = ({ navigation }) => (
  <View style={styles.container}>
    <Text>Open up App.js to start working on your app!</Text>
    <Button onPress={() => navigation.goBack()} title='Go to back
to Home' />
  </View>
);
```

```
const styles = StyleSheet.create({
  container: {
    flex: 1,
    backgroundColor: '#fff',
    alignItems: 'center',
    justifyContent: 'center',
  },
});

export default Detail;
```

3. In the `App.js` file, you need to import the `Home` and `Detail` components and remove the code blocks that created these two components previously, as follows:

```
import React from 'react';
- import { Button, StyleSheet, Text, View } from 'react-native';
import { createAppContainer } from 'react-navigation';
import { createStackNavigator } from 'react-navigation-stack';
+ import Home from './Screens/Home';
+ import Detail from './Screens/Detail';

- const Home = ({ navigation }) => (
-   <View style={styles.container}>
-     <Text>Open up App.js to start working on your app!</Text>
-     <Button onPress={() => navigation.navigate('Detail')}
title='Go to Detail' />
-   </View>
- );

- const Detail = ({ navigation }) => (
-   <View style={styles.container}>
-     <Text>Open up App.js to start working on your app!</Text>
-     <Button onPress={() => navigation.goBack()} title='Go to back
to Home' />
-   </View>
- );

- const styles = StyleSheet.create({
-   container: {
-     flex: 1,
-     backgroundColor: '#fff',
-     alignItems: 'center',
-     justifyContent: 'center',
-   },
- });

const AppNavigator = createStackNavigator({
```

```
    Home: {
      screen: Home,
      navigationOptions: { title: 'Home' },
    },
    Detail: {
      screen: Detail,
      navigationOptions: { title: 'Detail' },
    },
}, { initialRouteName: 'Home' });

export default createAppContainer(AppNavigator);
```

Your application only uses the `App.js` file to create the routes and set up the stack navigator. Many applications use multiple types of navigators next to each other, which is something that will be shown in the next part of this section.

Using multiple navigators together

For more complex applications, you don't want all of your routes to be stacked on top of each other; you only want these stacks to be created for routes that are related to each other. Luckily, you can use different types of navigators next to each other with React Navigation. Using multiple navigators for the application can be done as follows:

1. One of the most common ways of navigation in mobile applications is by using tabs; React Navigation can also create a tab navigator for you. Therefore, you'd need to pass a routing object to the `createBottomTabNavigator` method, which you can import from `react-navigation-tabs` using the following code:

```
import React from 'react';
import { Button, StyleSheet, Text, View } from 'react-native';
import { createAppContainer } from 'react-navigation';
import { createStackNavigator } from 'react-navigation-stack';
+ import { createBottomTabNavigator } from 'react-navigation-tabs';

import Home from './Screens/Home';
import Detail from './Screens/Detail';


...
```

2. Suppose you want the Home screen and the adjoining Detail screen to be available on the same tab—you'd need to rename the stack navigator for these screens. This stack navigator should be added to the routing object that is passed to createBottomTabNavigator, which creates the tab navigator. The declaration of the initial route that is loaded is now also linked to the tab navigator:

```
import React from 'react';
import { Button, StyleSheet, Text, View } from 'react-native';
import { createAppContainer } from 'react-navigation';
import { createStackNavigator } from 'react-navigation-stack';
import { createBottomTabNavigator } from 'react-navigation-tabs';
import Home from './Screens/Home';
import Detail from './Screens/Detail';

- const AppNavigator = createStackNavigator({
+ const HomeStack = createStackNavigator({
    Home: {
      screen: Home,
      navigationOptions: { title: 'Home' },
    },
    Detail: {
      screen: Detail,
      navigationOptions: { title: 'Detail' },
    },
-   }, { initialRouteName: 'Home' });
+ });

+ const AppNavigator = createBottomTabNavigator({
+   Home: HomeStack
+ }, { initialRouteName: 'Home' });

export default createAppContainer(AppNavigator);
```

The main navigation for your application is now the tab navigator, which has only one tab, called Home. This tab will render the stack navigator that contains the Home and Detail routes, meaning you can still navigate to the Detail screen without having to leave the Home tab.

3. You can easily add another tab to the tab navigator that renders either a component or another stack navigator. Let's create a new screen called Settings, for which you'll first need to create a new component in the Screens/Settings.js file:

```
import React from 'react';
import { StyleSheet, Text, View } from 'react-native';

const Settings = ({ navigation }) => (
  <View style={styles.container}>
    <Text>Open up App.js to start working on your app!</Text>
  </View>
);

const styles = StyleSheet.create({
  container: {
    flex: 1,
    backgroundColor: '#fff',
    alignItems: 'center',
    justifyContent: 'center',
  },
});

export default Settings;
```

4. Import this component in App.js to add the new Screens route to the tab navigator. This screen renders the Settings component after you make these changes:

```
import React from 'react';
import { Button, StyleSheet, Text, View } from 'react-native';
import { createAppContainer } from 'react-navigation';
import { createStackNavigator } from 'react-navigation-stack';
import { createBottomTabNavigator } from 'react-navigation-tabs';
import Home from './Screens/Home';
import Detail from './Screens/Detail';
+ import Settings from './Screens/Settings';

...

const AppNavigator = createBottomTabNavigator({
    Home: HomeStack,
+   Settings,
}, { initialRouteName: 'Home' });

export default createAppContainer(AppNavigator);
```

5. Your application now has a tab called `Settings`, which will render the `Settings` component. However, it isn't possible to customize, for example, `title` of this screen. Therefore, you will need to create another stack navigator that only has the `Settings` route by using the following code:

```
. . .

+ const SettingsStack = createStackNavigator({
+   Settings: {
+     screen: Settings,
+     navigationOptions: { title: 'Settings' },
+   },
+ });

const AppNavigator = createBottomTabNavigator({
    Home: HomeStack,
-   Settings,
+   Settings: SettingsStack,
}, { initialRouteName: 'Home' });

export default createAppContainer(AppNavigator);
```

You've now added both a stack navigator and a tab navigator to your application, which allows you to navigate between screens and tabs at the same time. If you're running your application using the iOS Emulator or on a device that runs iOS, it will look exactly like the following screenshot. For Android, the application should look very similar at this point:

In the next section, you'll load data from the mock API and use React life cycles to load this data in the different screens.

Using life cycles in React Native

Before you start adding styling to your React Native components, you need to fetch some data in your application that will be displayed by these components. Therefore, you will need to use life cycles to retrieve this data and add it to the local state of your application.

To fetch data, you'll use the `fetch` API again and combine this with the `useState` and `useEffect` Hooks to retrieve this data within the life cycles. Once the data has been fetched from the mock API, it can be displayed in a React Native `FlatList` component. Life cycle methods can be added to your React Native application using Hooks by making the following additions:

1. You'll use the `useState` Hook to set the constants for the loading indicator, error message, and displaying the data, where the `loading` constant should initially be true, the `error` constant should be empty, and the `data` constant should be an empty array:

```
    ...
-   const Home = ({ navigation }) => (
+   const Home = ({ navigation }) => {
+     const [loading, setLoading] = React.useState(true);
+     const [error, setError] = React.useState('');
+     const [data, setData] = React.useState([]);

+     return (
        <View style={styles.container}>
          <Text>Open up App.js to start working on your app!</Text>
          <Button onPress={() => navigation.navigate('Detail')}
title='Go to Detail' />
        </View>
      )
+   };
```

2. Next, you need to create an asynchronous function to retrieve the data from the mock API and call this function from a `useEffect` Hook that is invoked when the application mounts. The `fetchAPI` function will change both of the constants for `loading`, `error`, and `data` when the API request is successful. If not, the error message will be added to the `error` constant:

```
      ...
    const Home = ({ navigation }) => {
      const [loading, setLoading] = React.useState(true);
      const [error, setError] = React.useState('');
      const [data, setData] = React.useState([]);
```

```
+   const fetchAPI = async () => {
+     try {
+       const data = await
fetch('https://my-json-server.typicode.com/PacktPublishing/React-Pr
ojects/listings');
+       const dataJSON = await data.json();

+       if (dataJSON) {
+         setData(dataJSON);
+         setLoading(false);
+       }
+     } catch(error) {
+       setLoading(false);
+       setError(error.message);
+     }
+   };

+   React.useEffect(() => {
+     fetchAPI();
+   }, []);

    return (
      ...
```

3. This data constant can now be added as a prop to a `FlatList` component, which iterates over the data and renders components that display this data.
   `FlatList` returns an object that contains a field called `item`, which contains the data of each iteration, as follows:

```
import React from 'react';
- import { Button, StyleSheet, Text, View } from 'react-native';
+ import { FlatList, StyleSheet, Text, View } from 'react-native';

const Home = ({ navigation }) => {

  ...

    return (
      <View style={styles.container}>
-       <Text>Open up App.js to start working on your app!</Text>
-       <Button onPress={() => navigation.navigate('Detail')}
title='Go to Detail' />
+       {!loading && !error && <FlatList
+         data={data}
+         renderItem={({item}) => <Text>{item.title}</Text>}
+       />}
      </View>
    )
```

```
};

. . .
```

4. Just like we can with React, when using a `map` or `forEach` function, you need to specify a `key` prop on each iterated component. `FlatList` automatically looks for a `key` field in your `data` object, but if you don't have a specific `key` field, you need to set this using the `keyExtractor` prop. It's important to know that the value that's used for the key should be a string, so you need to transform the `id` field that's returned by the mock API into a string:

```
      . . .

      return (
        <View style={styles.container}>
          {!loading && !error && <FlatList
            data={data}
+           keyExtractor={item => String(item.id)}
            renderItem={({item}) => <Text>{item.title}</Text>}
          />}
        </View>
      );
    };

    . . .
```

Now, your application will display a list with titles of house listings from the mock API, without any routing to a specific listing or styling. This will make your application look as follows, where the differences between Android and iOS should be limited since we haven't added any significant styling to the application yet:

Home

Canalside house
Old center townhouse
Centrally located appartment
Downtown apartment
Fairytale castle

Home   Settings

To add the navigation to the `Detail` route again, you need to return a component from `FlatList`, which supports `onPress` events. These are, for example, the `Button` component you used previously and the `TouchableOpacity` component. This last component can be used as a replacement for a `View` component, which doesn't support `onPress` events. Creating navigation here is done by making the following changes:

1. You need to import the `TouchableOpacity` component from `react-native` and wrap the `Text` component returned by `FlatList` with this component. The `onPress` event will call the `navigate` function from the `navigation` prop and navigate to the `Detail` route if we change the following code:

```
import React from 'react';
- import { FlatList, View, Text } from 'react-native';
+ import { FlatList, View, Text, TouchableOpacity } from 'react-native';

const Home = ({ navigation }) => {
  ...

  return (
    <View style={styles.container>
      {!loading && !error && <FlatList
        data={data}
        keyExtractor={item => String(item.id)}
-       renderItem={({item}) => <Text>{item.text}</Text>}
+       renderItem={({item}) => (
+         <TouchableOpacity onPress={() =>
navigation.navigate('Detail')}>
+           <Text>{item.title}</Text>
+         </TouchableOpacity>
+       )}
      />}
    </View>
  );
};

...
```

2. When you click on any of the titles that are displayed in your application, you'll navigate to the `Detail` route. However, you want this screen to display the item you've just pressed. Therefore, you will need to pass parameters to this route once the `TouchableOpacity` components are pressed. To do this, you will need to pass these parameters inside an object to the `navigate` function:

```
. . .

    return (
      <View style={styles.container}>
        {!loading && !error && <FlatList
          data={data}
          keyExtractor={item => String(item.id)}
          renderItem={({item}) => (
-           <TouchableOpacity onPress={() =>
  navigation.navigate('Detail')}>
+           <TouchableOpacity onPress={() =>
  navigation.navigate('Detail', { item })}>
              <Text>{item.title}</Text>
            </TouchableOpacity>
          )}
        />}
      </View>
    );
  };

. . .
```

3. From the component that is rendered by the `Detail` route, you can take this parameter object from the `navigation` prop and use this to display the item. To get the parameters from the `navigation` prop, you can use the `getParam` function, where you need to specify the name of the parameter you want to get and a fallback value for this parameter. Just like we did for the `Home` route, you can display `title` of the listing, which in this case should be `title` from the `item` parameter:

```
import React from 'react';
- import { Button, StyleSheet, Text, View } from 'react-native';
+ import { StyleSheet, Text, View } from 'react-native';

- const Detail = ({ navigation }) => (
+ const Detail = ({ navigation }) => {
+   const item = navigation.getParam('item', {})

+   return (
      <View style={styles.container}>
```

```
-         <Text>Open up - App.js to start working on your app!</Text>
-         <Button onPress={() => navigation.goBack()} title='Go to
back to Home' />
+         <Text>{item.title}</Text>
      </View>
    );
+ };


...


export default Detail;
```

 Instead of passing the entire object containing the data from the item you've clicked, you could just send the ID of the item. That way, you could fetch the mock API to get the data for this listing and display it on the Detail route as well. To get an individual listing, you need to send a request to the 'listings/:id' route.

You're now able to view both a list of all of the listings from the mock API and a specific listing from this API. Styling will be added in the next section using styled-components.

Styling React Native applications

The syntax you've used so far to style React Native components in this application looks a bit different from what you've used already. Therefore, you can install styled-components to use the syntax for writing styles you're already familiar with. To install this, you need to run the following command:

```
npm install styled-components
```

This will install the styled-components package, after which you can proceed by creating styling for the components that are already present in your application:

1. Let's start by transforming the View and FlatList components in the Screens/Home.js file into styled-components. To do this, you need to import styled from styled-components/native as you only want to import the specific native parts of the package:

```
import React from 'react';
- import { FlatList, StyleSheet, Text, View, TouchableOpacity }
from 'react-native';
+ import { FlatList, Text, View, TouchableOpacity } from 'react-
native';
+ import styled from 'styled-components/native';
```

```
const Home = ({ navigation }) => {
  ...
```

2. StyleSheet at the bottom of the file creates the styling for the View component, which should be transformed into a component styled with styled-components. As we saw in the previous chapters, you can extend the style of existing components as well. Most of the styling rules can be copied and changed to the styled-components syntax, as seen in the following code block:

```
...

+ const ListingsWrapper = styled(View)`
+   flex: 1;
+   background-color: #fff;
+   align-items: center;
+   justify-content: center;
+ `

- const styles = StyleSheet.create({
-   container: {
-     flex: 1,
-     backgroundColor: '#fff',
-     alignItems: 'center',
-     justifyContent: 'center',
-   },
- });

const Home = ({ navigation }) => {
  ...
  return (
-     <View style={styles.container}>
+     <ListingsWrapper>
      {!loading && !error && <FlatList
        data={data}
        keyExtractor={item => String(item.id)}
        renderItem={({item}) => (
          <TouchableOpacity onPress={() =>
navigation.navigate('Detail', { item })}>
            <Text>{item.title}</Text>
          </TouchableOpacity>
        )}
      />}
+     </ListingsWrapper>
-     </View>
  );
};
```

```
export default Home;
```

3. The same can be done for the `FlatList` component, that is, by extending the style for this component with `styled` from `styled-components` and setting custom styling rules like this:

```
...

const ListingsWrapper = styled(View)`
  flex: 1;
  background-color: #fff;
  align-items: center;
  justify-content: center;
`

+ const Listings = styled(FlatList)`
+   width: 100%;
+   padding: 5%;
+ `;

const Home = ({ navigation }) => {
  ...
  return (
    <ListingsWrapper>
-       {!loading && !error && <FlatList
+       {!loading && !error && <Listings
        data={data}
        keyExtractor={item => String(item.id)}
        renderItem={({item}) => (
          <TouchableOpacity onPress={() =>
navigation.navigate('Detail', { item })}>
            <Text>{item.title}</Text>
          </TouchableOpacity>
        )}
      />}
    </ListingsWrapper>
  );
};

export default Home;
```

4. `FlatList` is currently only returning a `Text` component with `title`, while more data can be displayed. To do this, you need to create a new component that returns multiple components containing the listings data from the mock API. You can do this in a new directory called `Components`, which contains another directory called `Listing`. In this directory, you need to create the `ListingItem.js` file and place the following code block in there:

```js
import React from 'react';
import styled from 'styled-components/native';
import { Image, Text, View, TouchableOpacity } from 'react-native';

const ListingItemWrapper = styled(TouchableOpacity)`
 display: flex;
 flex-direction: row;
 padding: 2%;
 background-color: #eee;
 border-radius: 5px;
 margin-bottom: 5%;
`;

export const Title = styled(Text)`
 flex-wrap: wrap;
 width: 99%;
 font-size: 20px;
`

export const Price = styled(Text)`
 font-weight: bold;
 font-size: 20px;
 color: blue;
`

const Thumbnail = styled(Image)`
 border-radius: 5px;
 margin-right: 4%;
 height: 200px;
 width: 200px;
`

const ListingItem = ({ item, navigation }) => (
 <ListingItemWrapper onPress={() => navigation.navigate('Detail', {
item })}>
   <Thumbnail
     source={{uri: item.thumbnail}}
   />
   <View>
     <Title>{item.title}</Title>
```

```
        <Price>{item.price}</Price>
      </View>
  </ListingItemWrapper>
);

export default ListingItem;
```

In this code block, you import `styled` from `styled-components/native` and the components from React Native that you want to style. The `ListingItem` component that is exported at the bottom of the file takes an `item` and a `navigation` prop to display this data within the created components and handle navigation. As we saw with the styled `Image` component, a `source` prop is been given an object to display the thumbnail from the mock API.

5. This `ListingItem` component should now be imported into `Screens/Home.js`, where it will be used by `FlatList` to display the listings. This component takes both `item` and `navigation` as props, which is done in the following code block:

```
import React from 'react';
- import { FlatList, View, Text, TouchableOpacity } from 'react-native';
+ import { FlatList, View } from 'react-native';
import styled from 'styled-components/native';
+ import ListingItem from '../Components/Listing/ListingItem'

...
const Home = ({ navigation }) => {
  ...

  return (
    <ListingsWrapper>
      {!loading && !error && <Listings
        data={data}
        keyExtractor={item => String(item.id)}
-       renderItem={({item}) => (
-         <TouchableOpacity onPress={() =>
navigation.navigate('Detail', { item })}>
-           <Text>{item.title}</Text>
-         </TouchableOpacity>
-       )}
+       renderItem={({item}) => <ListingItem item={item} />}
      />}
    </ListingsWrapper>
  );
};

export default Home;
```

In React Native, styling rules are scoped to components, meaning a `Text` component can only take styling rules that are specified for this component by React Native. When you try to add a styling rule that isn't supported, you'll receive an error and a list of all the possible styling rules for this component. Note that `styled-components` automatically renames styling rules for you to match the syntax for styling in React Native.

After these changes, you'll have added the first `styled-components` to your application. Your application should look as follows when you're using either the iOS Emulator or a device that runs on iOS:

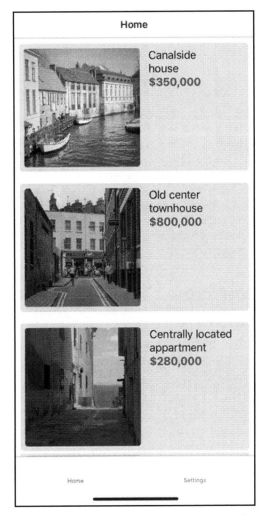

So far, the styling should look similar on both iOS and Android since we haven't added any platform-specific styling to the application yet. This will be done in the next part of this section, where you'll explore multiple ways to add styling that differs based on the platform that your application is running on.

Differences in styling for iOS and Android

When styling your application, you might want to have different styling rules for iOS and Android, for example, to match the styling of the Android operating system better. There are multiple ways to apply different styling rules to different platforms; one of them is by using the `Platform` module, which can be imported from React Native.

Let's try this by adding icons to the tabs in the `navigator` tab and have different icons for iOS and Android:

1. First, import the icons from Expo into the `App.js` file. There are a lot of icon sets available from Expo. For this application, you'll import the `Ionicons` icon set:

    ```
    import React from 'react';
    + import { Ionicons } from '@expo/vector-icons';
    import { createAppContainer } from 'react-navigation';
    import { createStackNavigator } from 'react-navigation-stack';
    import { createBottomTabNavigator } from 'react-navigation-tabs';
    import Home from './Screens/Home';
    import Detail from './Screens/Detail';
    import Settings from './Screens/Settings';

    const HomeStack = createStackNavigator({
      ...
    ```

2. When creating the tab navigator, you can define which icons should be added to the tabs for each route. Therefore, you need to create a `defaultNavigationOptions` field in the routing object that should contain a `tabBarIcon` field. In this field, you need to take the current route from the `navigation` prop and return the icon for this route:

    ```
    ...

    const AppNavigator = createBottomTabNavigator({
      Home: HomeStack,
      Settings: SettingsStack,
    - }, { initialRouteName: 'Home' });
    + }, {
    +   initialRouteName: 'Home',
    ```

```
+   defaultNavigationOptions: ({ navigation }) => ({
+     tabBarIcon: () => {
+       const { routeName } = navigation.state;

+       let iconName;
+       if (routeName === 'Home') {
+         iconName = `ios-home`;
+       } else if (routeName === 'Settings') {
+         iconName = `ios-settings`;
+       }

+       return <Ionicons name={iconName} size={20} />;
+     }
+   })
});

export default createAppContainer(AppNavigator);
```

3. To make a distinction between iOS and Android, you need to import the
Platform module from react-native. With this module, you can check
whether your mobile device is running iOS or Android by checking whether the
value of Platform.OS is either ios or android. The module must be imported
into the following code block:

```
import React from 'react';
+ import { Platform } from 'react-native';
import { Ionicons } from '@expo/vector-icons';
import { createAppContainer } from 'react-navigation';
import { createStackNavigator } from 'react-navigation-stack';
import { createBottomTabNavigator } from 'react-navigation-tabs';
import Home from './Screens/Home';
import Detail from './Screens/Detail';
import Settings from './Screens/Settings';

const HomeStack = createStackNavigator({
   ...
```

4. Using the Platform module, you can change the icon that is being rendered for
   each of the tabs in the navigator. Besides icons designed for iOS, Ionicons also
   has icons designed for Android based on Material Design and can be used like
   this:

```
   ...

const AppNavigator = createBottomTabNavigator({
   Home: HomeStack,
   Settings: SettingsStack,
```

```
  }, {
    initialRouteName: 'Home',
    defaultNavigationOptions: ({ navigation }) => ({
      tabBarIcon: () => {
        const { routeName } = navigation.state;

        let iconName;
        if (routeName === 'Home') {
-         iconName = `ios-home`;
+         iconName = `${Platform.OS === 'ios' ? 'ios' : 'md'}-home`;
        } else if (routeName === 'Settings') {
-         iconName = `ios-settings`;
+         iconName = `${Platform.OS === 'ios' ? 'ios' : 'md'}-
settings`;
        }

        return <Ionicons name={iconName} size={20} />;
      }
    }),
  });

export default createAppContainer(AppNavigator);
```

When you're running the application on a mobile device with Android, the
`navigator` tab will display the icons based on Material Design. If you're using an
Apple device, it will display different icons; you can change the `Platform.OS`
`=== 'ios'` condition to `Platform.OS === 'android'` to add the Material
Design icons to iOS instead.

5. The displayed icons are colored black, while the labels for the active and inactive
   tabs have a different color. You can specify the colors of the icons and the labels
   in the active and inactive state by changing the configuration object. After the
   `tabBarIcon` field, you can create a new field called `tabBarOptions` and add
   the `activeTintColor` and `inActiveTintColor` fields to them as follows:

```
...
const AppNavigator = createBottomTabNavigator({
  Home: HomeStack,
  Settings: SettingsStack,
}, {
  initialRouteName: 'Home',
  defaultNavigationOptions: ({ navigation }) => ({
    tabBarIcon: () => {
      const { routeName } = navigation.state;

      let iconName;
      if (routeName === 'Home') {
```

```
            iconName = `${Platform.OS === 'ios' ? 'ios' : 'md'}-home`;
          } else if (routeName === 'Settings') {
            iconName = `${Platform.OS === 'ios' ? 'ios' : 'md'}-
settings`;
          }

          return <Ionicons name={iconName} size={20} />;
        },
+       tabBarOptions: {
+         activeTintColor: 'blue',
+         inactiveTintColor: '#556',
+       },
      })
});

export default createAppContainer(AppNavigator);
```

6. This only changes the value for the label, but the values for the active and inactive tint color are also available on the `tabBarIcon` field it will take the `tintColor` prop. This value can be passed to `Ionicons` to change the color of the icon as well:

```
...

const AppNavigator = createBottomTabNavigator({
  Home: HomeStack,
  Settings: SettingsStack,
}, {
  initialRouteName: 'Home',
  defaultNavigationOptions: ({ navigation }) => ({
-   tabBarIcon: () => {
+   tabBarIcon: ({ tintColor }) => {
      const { routeName } = navigation.state;

      let iconName;
      if (routeName === 'Home') {
        iconName = `${Platform.OS === 'ios' ? 'ios' : 'md'}-home`;
      } else if (routeName === 'Settings') {
        iconName = `${Platform.OS === 'ios' ? 'ios' : 'md'}-
settings`;
      }

-     return <Ionicons name={iconName} size={20} />;
+     return <Ionicons name={iconName} size={20} color={tintColor}
/>;
    },
    tabBarOptions: {
```

```
        activeTintColor: 'blue',
        inactiveTintColor: '#556',
      },
    }),
  });

  export default createAppContainer(AppNavigator);
```

Now, when you view the **Home** screen, both the tab icon and label are colored blue, while the **Settings** tab will be colored gray. Also, there will be a difference in the icons that are displayed on either iOS or Android no matter whether you're running the application on the emulator or a mobile device. If you're using iOS, the application should look like this:

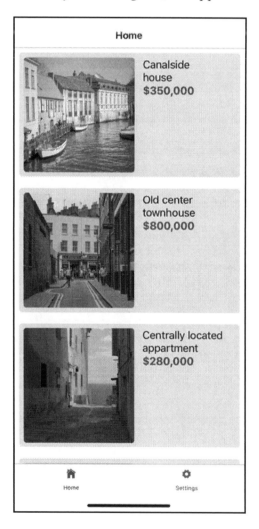

Another page that can be styled is the `Detail` screen. For this screen, you can also choose to have differences in styling between iOS and Android. As mentioned before, there are multiple ways to do this; besides using the `Platform` module, you can also use platform-specific file extensions. Any file that has the `*.ios.js` or `*.android.js` extension will only be rendered on the platform specified in the extension. Not only can you apply different styling rules, but also have changes in functionality on different platforms:

1. To create a specific `Detail` screen for mobile devices running Android, you need to create a new file called `Components/Listing/ListingDetail.android.js`. This file will have the following code inside:

```
import React from 'react';
import styled from 'styled-components/native';
import { Image, Text, View, Dimensions } from 'react-native';

const ListingDetailWrapper = styled(View)`
  display: flex;
`;

const Details = styled(View)`
  padding: 5%;
`

export const Title = styled(Text)`
  flex-wrap: wrap;
  width: 99%;
  font-size: 30px;
`

export const Price = styled(Text)`
  font-weight: bold;
  font-size: 20px;
  color: blue;
`

const Thumbnail = styled(Image)`
  width: 100%;
  height: ${Dimensions.get('window').width};
`

const ListingDetail = ({ item }) => (
  <ListingDetailWrapper>
    <Thumbnail
      source={{uri: item.thumbnail}}
    />
```

```
      <Details>
        <Title>{item.title}</Title>
        <Price>{item.price}</Price>
      </Details>
    </ListingDetailWrapper>
  );

  export default ListingDetail;
```

As you can see, some components will be rendered by the
ListingDetail component. Also, the Dimensions module is imported from
react-native. This module can help you get the screen size of the device that
which the application is running on. By getting the width, you can display an
image over the entire width of the user's screen.

2. For devices running iOS, you can do the same, but this time you need to create a
   new file called Components/Listing/ListingDetail.ios.js. This file will
   contain a variant of the code that's running on Android, where the image will be
   displayed over the entire height of the screen using the Dimensions module.
   The ListingDetail component for iOS can be created by pasting the following
   code block into that file:

```
import React from 'react';
import styled from 'styled-components/native';
import { Image, Text, View, Dimensions } from 'react-native';

const ListingDetailWrapper = styled(View)`
  display: flex;
`;

const Details = styled(View)`
  position: absolute;
  top: 0;
  padding: 5%;
  width: 100%;
  background: rgba(0, 0, 255, 0.1);
`

export const Title = styled(Text)`
  flex-wrap: wrap;
  width: 99%;
  font-size: 30px;
`

export const Price = styled(Text)`
  font-weight: bold;
```

```
    font-size: 20px;
    color: blue;


const Thumbnail = styled(Image)`
  width: 100%;
  height: ${Dimensions.get('window').height};


const ListingDetail = ({ item }) => (
  <ListingDetailWrapper>
    <Thumbnail
      source={{uri: item.thumbnail}}
    />
    <Details>
      <Title>{item.title}</Title>
      <Price>{item.price}</Price>
    </Details>
  </ListingDetailWrapper>
);

export default ListingDetail;
```

3. To display one of these components in your application, some changes need to made to the `Screens/Detail.js` file. The `ListingDetail` component should be imported into this file and returned with the `item` prop:

```
import React from 'react';
import { StyleSheet, Text, View } from 'react-native';
+ import ListingDetail from '../Components/Listing/ListingDetail';

const Detail = ({ navigation }) => {
  const item = navigation.getParam('item', {});

  return (
-   <View style={styles.container}>
+   <ListingDetail item={item} />
-   </View>
  )
};

- const styles = StyleSheet.create({
-   container: {
-     flex: 1,
-     backgroundColor: '#fff',
-     alignItems: 'center',
-     justifyContent: 'center',
-   },
```

```
-   });

export default Detail;
```

Your application now has two different versions of the **Detail** screen for iOS and Android, and React Native will make sure that the file with the right extension will run on that operating system. You can check this by comparing the application that runs on your Android Emulator or mobile device with the following screenshot, which was taken from an iOS device:

With these last changes, you've created your first React Native application that will run on both Android and iOS devices and has basic routing and styling implemented.

Summary

In this chapter, you created a house listing application with React Native for both iOS and Android mobile devices. Expo was used to create the first version of the application and provides a lot of functionality to smoothen the developer experience. The `react-navigation` package is used to handle different kinds of routing for mobile applications, while `styled-components` is utilized to handle styling for this React Native application.

Since this was probably your first introduction to React Native, you shouldn't feel bad if not everything was clear from the start. The basics you learned about in this chapter should provide a proper baseline so that we can continue your journey into the world of mobile app development. The project you'll create in the next chapter will build upon these principles further and handle features such as animations while we create a *Tic-Tac-Toe* game.

Further reading

- To find out more about custom headers in React Navigation, check out this link: `https://reactnavigation.org/docs/en/headers.html`.
- You can find a list of Expo icons here: `https://expo.github.io/vector-icons/`.

Build an Animated Game Using React Native and Expo

9

Most of the projects that you've created in this book focused on displaying data and making it possible to navigate between pages. In the previous chapter, you explored some of the differences between creating a web and a mobile application. One other difference when building a mobile application is that your users expect animations and gestures since they make using the application easy and familiar. This is something that you'll focus on in this chapter.

In this chapter, you'll add animations and gestures to a React Native application using the Animated API from React Native, a package called Lottie, and Expo's `GestureHandler`. Together, they make it possible for us to create applications that make the best use of a mobile's interaction methods, which is perfect for a game such as *Tic-Tac-Toe*. Also, the application will show a leaderboard with the high scores for this game next to the game interface.

To create this game, the following topics will be covered:

- Using the React Native Animated API
- Advanced animations with Lottie
- Handling native gestures with Expo

Project overview

In this chapter, we will be creating an animated *Tic-Tac-Toe* game build with React Native and Expo, which uses the Animated API to add basic animations, Lottie for advanced animations, and Gesture Handler from Expo to handle native gestures. The starting point will be creating an application with the Expo CLI that has basic routing implemented in it, so that our users can switch between the game interface and an overview of the high scores for this game.

The build time is 1.5 hours.

Getting started

The project that we'll create in this chapter builds upon an initial version that you can find on GitHub: `https://github.com/PacktPublishing/React-Projects/tree/ch9-initial`. The complete source code can also be found on GitHub: `https://github.com/PacktPublishing/React-Projects/tree/ch9`.

You need to have the application Expo Client installed on a mobile iOS or Android device to run the project on a physical device. Alternatively, you can install either Xcode or Android Studio on your computer to run the application on a virtual device:

- **For iOS**: Information on how to set up your local machine to run the iOS simulator can be found here: `https://docs.expo.io/versions/v36.0.0/workflow/ios-simulator/`.
- **For Android**: Information on how to set up your local machine to run the emulator from Android Studio can be found here: `https://docs.expo.io/versions/v36.0.0/workflow/android-studio-emulator/`. There's a known issue when running the emulator, which can be prevented by ensuring that the following lines are present in your `~/.bash_profile` or `~/.bash_rc` file:

    ```
    export ANDROID_SDK=ANDROID_SDK_LOCATION
    export PATH=ANDROID_SDK_LOCATION/platform-tools:$PATH
    export PATH=ANDROID_SDK_LOCATION/tools:$PATH
    ```

    The value for `ANDROID_SDK_LOCATION` is the path to the Android SDK on your local machine and can be found by opening Android Studio and going to **Preferences | Appearance & Behavior | System Settings | Android SDK**. The path is listed in the box that states the Android SDK location and looks like this: `/Users/myuser/Library/Android/sdk`.

This application was created using **Expo SDK version 33.0.0,** and so, you need to ensure that the version of Expo you're using on your local machine is similar. As React Native and Expo are frequently updated, make sure that you're working with this version so that the patterns described in this chapter behave as expected. In case your application doesn't start or if you encounter errors, refer to the Expo documentation to learn more about updating the Expo SDK.

Checking out the initial project

The application that you'll be working on in this chapter has already been built for you, but we will need to complete it by adding features such as animations and transitions. After downloading or cloning the project, you'll need to move into the root directory of the project, where you can run the following command to install the dependencies and start the application:

```
npm install && npm start
```

This will start Expo and give you the ability to start your project from the Terminal or from your browser. In the Terminal, you can either use the QR Code to open the application on your mobile device or select to open the application in a simulator.

No matter whether you've opened the application on a virtual or physical device, at this point, the application should look something like this:

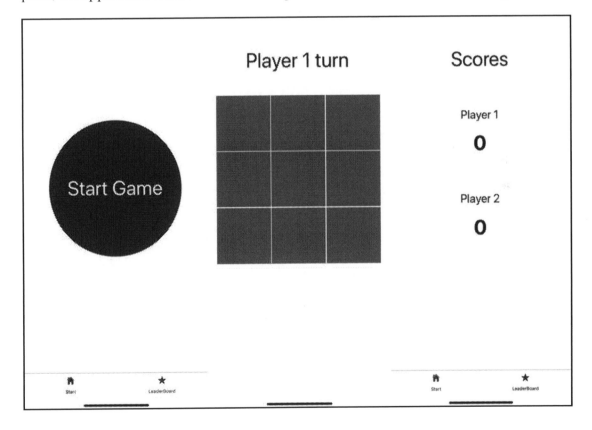

The application consists of three screens: Start, Game, and LeaderBoard. The first screen is Start, where the game can be started by clicking the green button. This will lead to the Game screen, which is set up as a modal. The Start screen uses tab navigation, from which you can also visit the LeaderBoard screen, which is where the scores of the players will be displayed.

The project structure for this React Native application is as follows. This structure is similar to the projects we've created already in this book:

```
tic-tac-toe
|-- .expo
|-- assets
    |-- icon.png
    |-- splash.png
    |-- winner.json
|-- Components
    |-- // ...
|-- context
    |-- AppContext.js
|-- node_modules
|-- Screens
    |-- Game.js
    |-- LeaderBoard.js
    |-- Start.js
|-- utils
    |-- arrayContainsArray.js
    |-- checkSlots.js
.gitignore
App.js
AppContainer.js
app.json
babel.config.js
package.json
```

In the assets directory, you'll find the two images: one that will be used as the application's icon on the **Home** screen once you've installed this application on your mobile device, and one that will serve as the splash screen that is displayed when you start the application. A Lottie animation file has also been placed here, which you'll use later on in this chapter. The configurations for your application, for example, the App Store, are placed in app.json, while babel.config.js holds specific Babel configurations.

The App.js file is the actual entry point of your application, where the AppContainer.js file is being imported and returned within a Context Provider that was created in the context/AppContext.js file. In AppContainer, all the routes for this application are defined and AppContext will contain information that should be available in the entire application. In the utils directory, you can find the logic for the game, that is, the functions that will fill the slots of the *Tic-Tac-Toe* board and determine which player won the game.

All the components for this game are located in the Screens and Components directories, where the former holds the components that are rendered by the Start, Game, and LeaderBoard routes. The child components for these screens can be found in the Components directory, which has the following structure:

```
|-- Components
    |-- Actions
        |-- Actions.js
    |-- Board
        |-- Board.js
    |-- Button
        |-- Button.js
    |-- Player
        |-- Player.js
    |-- Slot
        |-- Slot.js
        |-- Filled.js
```

The most important components in the preceding structure are Board, Slot, and Filled, since they construct most of the game. Board is rendered by the Game screen and holds some logic for the game, while Slot and Filled are components that are rendered on this board. The Actions component returns two Button components so that we can either navigate away from the Game screen or restart the game. Player displays the name of the player whose turn it is, or the player that has won the game.

Creating an animated Tic-Tac-Toe game application with React Native and Expo

Mobile games often have flashy animations that make the user want to keep playing and make the game more interactive. The *Tic-Tac-Toe* game that is already functioning uses no animations so far and just has some transitions that have been built in with React Navigation. In this section, you'll be adding animations and gestures to the application, which will improve the game interface and make the user feel more comfortable while playing the game.

Using the React Native Animated API

There are multiple ways to use animations in React Native and one of those is to use the Animated API, which can be found in the core of React Native. With the Animated API, you can create animations for `View`, `Text`, `Image`, and `ScrollView` components from `react-native` by default. Alternatively, you can use the `createAnimatedComponent` method to create your own.

Creating a basic animation

One of the simplest animations you can add is fading an element in or out by changing the value for the opacity of that element. In the *Tic-Tac-Toe* game you created previously, the slots were filled with either a green or blue color, depending on which player filled that slot. These colors already show a small transition since you're using the `TouchableOpacity` element to create the slot. However, it's possible to add a custom transition to this by using the Animated API. To add an animation, the following code blocks must be changed:

1. Start by creating a new file in the `src/Components/Slot` directory and calling it `Filled.js`. This file will contain the following code, which will be used to construct the `Filled` component. Inside this file, add the following code:

```
import React from 'react';
import { View } from 'react-native';

const Filled = ({ filled }) => {
  return (
    <View
        style={{
            position: 'absolute',
```

```
                    display: filled ? 'block' : 'none',
                    width: '100%',
                    height: '100%',
                    backgroundColor: filled === 1 ? 'blue' : 'green',
              }}
          />
        );
    }

export default Filled;
```

This component displays a `View` element and is styled using a styling object that's using the JSS syntax, which is the default for React Native. This element can be used to fill in another element since its position is absolute with 100% width and 100% height. It also takes the `filled` prop so that we can set the `backgroundColor` and determine whether the component is displayed or not.

2. You can import this component into the `Slot` component and display it once the slot has been filled by any of the players. Instead of setting the background color for the `SlotWrapper` component, you can pass the color that belongs to player one or two to the `Filled` component:

```
import React from 'react';
import { TouchableOpacity, Dimensions } from 'react-native';
import styled from 'styled-components/native';
+ import Filled from './Filled';

const SlotWrapper = styled(TouchableOpacity)`
    width: ${Dimensions.get('window').width * 0.3};
    height: ${Dimensions.get('window').width * 0.3};
-   background-color: ${({ filled }) => filled ? (filled === 1 ?
'blue' : 'green') : 'grey'};
+   background-color: grey;
    border: 1px solid #fff;
`;

const Slot = ({ index, filled, handleOnPress }) => (
- <SlotWrapper filled={filled} onPress={() => !filled &&
handleOnPress(index)} />
+ <SlotWrapper onPress={() => !filled && handleOnPress(index)}>
+    <Filled filled={filled} />
+ </SlotWrapper>
);

export default Slot;
```

3. Now, whenever you click on a slot, nothing visible will change since you'll need to change the clickable element from a `TouchableOpacity` element to a `TouchableWithoutFeedback` element first. That way, the default transition with the opacity will be gone, so you can replace this with your own. The `TouchableWithoutFeedback` element can be imported from `react-native` and should be placed around a `View` element, which will hold the default styling for the slot:

```
import React from 'react';
- import { TouchableOpacity, Dimensions } from 'react-native';
+ import { TouchableWithoutFeedback, View, Dimensions } from
'react-native';
import styled from 'styled-components/native';
import Filled from './Filled';

- const SlotWrapper = styled(TouchableOpacity)`
+ const SlotWrapper = styled(View)`
    width: ${Dimensions.get('window').width * 0.3};
    height: ${Dimensions.get('window').width * 0.3};
    background-color: grey;
    border: 1px solid #fff;
`;

const Slot = ({ index, filled, handleOnPress }) => (
- <SlotWrapper onPress={() => !filled && handleOnPress(index)}>
+ <TouchableWithoutFeedback onPress={() => !filled &&
handleOnPress(index)}>
+    <SlotWrapper>
      <Filled filled={filled} />
    </SlotWrapper>
+ <TouchableWithoutFeedback>
);

export default Slot;
```

Now, the slot that you've just pressed on will be immediately filled in with the color you've specified in the `backgroundColor` field for the `Filled` component, without any transition whatsoever.

4. To recreate this transition, you can use the Animated API, which you'll use to change the opacity of the `Filled` component from the moment it's rendered by a slot. Therefore, you need to import `Animated` from `react-native` in `src/Components/Slot/Filled.js`:

```
import React from 'react';
- import { View } from 'react-native';
```

```
+ import { Animated, View } from 'react-native';

const Filled = ({ filled }) => {
  return (
    ...
```

5. A new instance of the Animated API starts by specifying a value that should be changed during the animation that we created with the Animated API. This value should be changeable by the Animated API in your entire component, so you can add this value to the top of the component. This value should be created with a useState Hook since you want this value to be changeable later on:

```
import React from 'react';
import { Animated, View } from 'react-native';

const Filled = ({ filled }) => {
+ const [opacityValue] = React.useState(new Animated.Value(0));

  return (
    ...
```

6. This value can now be changed by the Animated API using any of the three animations types that are built-in. These are decay, spring, and timing, where you'll be using the timing method from the Animated API to change the animated value within a specified time frame. The Animated API can be triggered from any function that is, for example, linked to an onPress event or from a life cycle method. Since the Filled component should only be displayed when the slot is filled, you can use a life cycle method that is triggered when the filled prop component is changed, that is, a useEffect Hook with the filled prop as a dependency. The styling rule for the display can be removed since the component will have an opacity of 0 when the filled prop is false:

```
import React from 'react';
import { Animated, View } from 'react-native';

const Filled = ({ filled }) => {
  const [opacityValue] = React.useState(new Animated.Value(0));

+   React.useEffect(() => {
+     filled && Animated.timing(
+       opacityValue,
+       {
+           toValue: 1,
+           duration: 500,
+       }
+     ).start();
```

```
+   }, [filled]);

    return (
        <View
            style={{
                position: 'absolute',
-               display: filled ? 'block' : 'none',
                width: '100%',
                height: '100%',
                backgroundColor: filled === 1 ? 'blue' : 'green',
            }}
        />
    );
}

export default Filled;
```

The `timing` method takes the `opacityValue` that you've specified at the top of your component and an object with the configuration for the Animated API. One of the fields is `toValue`, which will become the value for `opacityValue` when the animation has ended. The other field is for the field's duration, which specifies how long the animation should last.

The other built-in animation types next to `timing` are `decay` and `spring`. Where the `timing` method changes gradually over time, the `decay` type has animations that change fast in the beginning and gradually slow down until the end of the animation. With `spring`, you can create animations that move a little outside of its edges at the end of the animations.

7. Finally, you only need to change the `View` element into an `Animated.View` element and add the `opacity` field and the `opacityValue` value to the `style` object:

```
import React from 'react';
-   import { Animated, View } from 'react-native';
+   import { Animated } from 'react-native';

const Filled = ({ filled }) => {

...

    return (
-       <View
+       <Animated.View
            style={{
```

```
                         position: 'absolute',
                         width: '100%',
                         height: '100%',
                         backgroundColor: filled === 1 ? 'blue' : 'green',
+                        opacity: opacityValue,
                }}
         />
       );
  }

  export default Filled;
```

Now, when you press any of the slots, the `Filled` component will fade in, since the opacity value transitions for 500 ms. This will make a filled slot look as follows for both players when you run the application in either the iOS simulator or a device that runs on iOS. On Android, the application should look similar, since no platform-specific styling has been added:

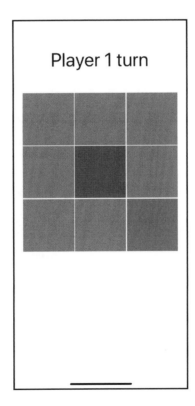

Something else you can do to make the animation appear smoother is add an easing field to the Animated object. The value for this field comes from the Easing module, which can be imported from react-native. The Easing module has three standard functions: linear, quad, and cubic Here, the linear function can be used for smoother timing animations:

```
import React from 'react';
- import { Animated } from 'react-native';
+ import { Animated, Easing } from 'react-native';

const Filled = ({ filled }) => {
  const [opacityValue] = React.useState(new Animated.Value(0));

  React.useEffect(() => {
    filled && Animated.timing(
      opacityValue,
      {
          toValue: 1,
          duration: 1000,
+         easing: Easing.linear(),
      }
    ).start();
  }, [filled]);

  return (
    ...
```

With this last change, the animation is complete and the game interface already feels smoother since the slots are being filled using your own custom animation. In the next part of this section, we will combine some of these animations to make the user experience for this game even more advanced.

Combining animations with the Animated API

Having the transition by changing the opacity of the Filled component is already an improvement to the game interface. But there are more animations we can create to make the game's interaction even more appealing.

One of the things we can do is add a fade-in animation to the size of the
Filled component. To make this animation work well with the fading in animation we've
just created, we can use the parallel method from the Animated API. This method will
start the animations that are specified within the same moment. To create this effect, we
need to make the following changes:

1. For this second animation, you want the Filled component to not only have a
   color that fades in, but also a size that is fading in. To set an initial value for the
   opacity, you have to set an initial value for the size of this component:

```
import React from 'react';
import { Animated, Easing } from 'react-native';

const Filled = ({ filled }) => {
  const [opacityValue] = React.useState(new Animated.Value(0));
+ const [scaleValue] = React.useState(new Animated.Value(0));

  React.useEffect(() => {
    ...
```

2. The Animated.timing method that you created in the useEffect Hook needs
   to be wrapped inside an Animated.parallel function. That way, you can add
   another animation that changes the size of the Filled component later on. The
   Animated.parallel function takes an array of the Animated method as a
   parameter and must be added like this:

```
import React from 'react';
import { Animated, Easing } from 'react-native';

const Filled = ({ filled }) => {
  const [opacityValue] = React.useState(new Animated.Value(0));
  const [scaleValue] = React.useState(new Animated.Value(0));

  React.useEffect(() => {
+   filled && Animated.parallel([
-   filled && Animated.timing(
+     Animated.timing(
        opacityValue,
        {
          toValue: 1,
          duration: 1000,
          easing: Easing.linear(),
        }
-     ).start();
+     ),
+   ]).start();
```

```
}, [filled]);

return (
...
```

Next to the `parallel` function, three other functions help you with animation composition. These functions are `delay`, `sequence`, and `stagger`, and can also be used in combination with each other. The `delay` function starts any animation after a predefined delay, the `sequence` function starts animations in the order you've specified and waits until an animation is resolved before starting another one, and the `stagger` function can start animations both in order and parallel with specified delays in-between.

3. Within the `parallel` function, you need to add the Animated API's `spring` method, which animates the size of the `Filled` component. This time, you won't be using a `timing` method, but a `spring` method, which adds a little bounce effect to the end of the animation. An `Easing` function is also added to make the animation look a little smoother:

```
...
const Filled = ({ filled }) => {
    const [opacityValue] = React.useState(new Animated.Value(0));
    const [scaleValue] = React.useState(new Animated.Value(0));

    React.useEffect(() => {
      filled && Animated.parallel([
        Animated.timing(
          opacityValue,
          {
            toValue: 1,
            duration: 1000,
            easing: Easing.linear(),
          }
        ),
+       Animated.spring(
+         scaleValue,
+         {
+           toValue: 1,
+           easing: Easing.cubic(),
+         },
+       ),
      ]).start();
    }, [filled]);
```

```
        return (
            ...
```

4. This `spring` animation will change the value of `scaleValue` from 0 to 1 and create a little bounce effect at the end of the animation. `scaleValue` must also be added to the `style` object for the `Animated.View` component for the animation to become effective. `scaleValue` will be added to the `scale` field within the `transform` field, which will change the size of the `Filled` component:

```
    ...

    return (
        <Animated.View
            style={{
                position: 'absolute',
                width: '100%',
                height: '100%',
                backgroundColor: filled === 1 ? 'blue' : 'green',
                opacity: opacityValue,
+               transform: [
+                   {
+                       scale: scaleValue,
+                   }
+               ],
            }}
        />
    );
}

export default Filled
```

When you click on any of the slots, the `Filled` component won't only fade in by changing the opacity but also by changing its size. The bounce effect at the end of the animation adds a nice touch to the fading effect.

5. However, when you click on the slot that depicts the winner of the game, the animation doesn't have enough time to end while the winning state is rendered by the component. Therefore, you will also need to add a timeout to the function that sets the winner of the game. This function can be found in `src/Screens/Game.js`, where you can add a constant that sets the number of ms the animation should last for:

```
import React from 'react';
import { View } from 'react-native';
import styled from 'styled-components/native';
import Board from '../Components/Board/Board';
```

```
import Actions from '../Components/Actions/Actions';
import Player from '../Components/Player/Player';
import checkSlots from '../utils/checkSlots';
import { AppContext } from '../context/AppContext';

+ export const ANIMATION_DURATION = 1000;

. . .
```

This will also wrap the functions that set the winner in a `setTimeout` function, which delays the execution of these functions by the same amount of time the animation lasts for:

```
. . .
const checkWinner = (player) => {
  const slots = state[`player${player}`];

  if (slots.length >= 3) {
    if (checkSlots(slots)) {
+     setTimeout(() => {
        setWinner(player);
        setPlayerWins(player);
+     }, ANIMATION_DURATION);
    }
  }

  return false;
}

. . .
```

6. Since the `ANIMATION_DURATION` constant is exported, you can import this constant in the `src/Components/Slot/Filled.js` file and use this same constant for the actual animation. That way, if you change the duration of the animation at some point, you won't have to make any changes to other components for these changes to be visible:

```
import React from 'react';
import { Animated, Easing } from 'react-native';
+ import { ANIMATION_DURATION } from '../../Screens/Game';

const Filled = ({ filled }) => {
    const [opacityValue] = React.useState(new Animated.Value(0));
    const [scaleValue] = React.useState(new Animated.Value(0));

    React.useEffect(() => {
```

```
        filled && Animated.parallel([
          Animated.timing(
            opacityValue,
            {
              toValue: 1,
-             duration: 1000,
+             duration: ANIMATION_DURATION,
              easing: Easing.linear(),
            }
```

Apart from the slots now being filled in with an animated `Filled` component that executes two parallel animations, when you click on any of them, the functions that set the winner of the game will wait until the slot is filled before firing.

The next section will show how to handle even more advanced animations, such as displaying animated graphics when any of the two players win. For this, we'll use the Lottie package since it supports more functionalities than the built-in Animated API.

Advanced animations with Lottie

The React Native Animated API is great for building simple animations, but building more advanced animations can be harder. Luckily, Lottie offers a solution for creating advanced animations in React Native by making it possible for us to render After Effects animations in real time for iOS, Android, and React Native. Lottie can be installed as a separate package using `npm`, but it is also available from Expo. Since Lottie is still part of Expo's experimental features, you can use it by retrieving it from the `DangerZone` namespace. Therefore, it is currently best to install Lottie from `npm` and import it in the files where you want to use it.

 When using Lottie, you don't have to create these After Effects animations yourself; there's a whole library full of resources that you can customize and use in your project. This library is called `LottieFiles` and is available at `https://lottiefiles.com/`.

Since you've already added animations to the slots of the board game, a nice place to add more advanced animations would be the screen that is displayed when either of the players wins the game. On this screen, a trophy can be displayed instead of the board since the game has ended. Let's do this now:

1. To get started with Lottie, run the following command, which will install Lottie and its dependencies and add it to your `package.json` file:

    ```
    npm install lottie-react-native
    ```

2. After the installation process has completed, you can proceed by creating a component that will be used to render the After Effects animations that have been downloaded as Lottie files. This component can be created in the new `src/Components/Winner/Winner.js` file. In this file, you will need to import React and, of course, Lottie from `lottie-react-native`, which you've just installed:

```
import React from 'react';
import Lottie from 'lottie-react-native';

const Winner = () => ();

export default Winner;
```

3. The imported `Lottie` component can render any Lottie file that you either create yourself or that is download from the `LottieFiles` library. In the `assets` directory, you will find a Lottie file that can be used in this project called `winner.json`. This file can be rendered by the `Lottie` component when you add it to the source, and the width and height of the animation can be set by passing a style object. Also, you should add the `autoPlay` prop to start the animation once the component renders:

```
import React from 'react';
import Lottie from 'lottie-react-native';

const Winner = () => (
+      <Lottie
+          autoPlay
+          style={{
+              width: '100%',
+              height: '100%',
+          }}
+          source={require('../../assets/winner.json')}
+      />
);

export default Winner;
```

4. This component will now start rendering the trophy animation in any of the screens where you'll include this component. Since this animation should be displayed instead of the board when either of the players wins the game, the Board component would be a good place to add this component as you can then use the wrapper styling for the board. The Board component can be found in the src/Components/Board/Board.js file, and is where you can import the Winner component:

```
import React from 'react';
import { View, Dimensions } from 'react-native';
import styled from 'styled-components/native';
import Slot from '../Slot/Slot';
+ import Winner from '../Winner/Winner';


...


const Board = ({ slots, winner, setSlot }) => (
    ...
```

In the return function of this component, you can check whether the winner prop is true or false and, depending on the outcome, display either the Winner component or iterate over slots:

```
const Board = ({ slots, winner, setSlot }) => (
  <BoardWrapper>
    <SlotsWrapper>
-     {slots.map((slot, index) =>
+     {
+       winner
+       ? <Winner />
+       : slots.map((slot, index) =>
            <Slot
              key={index}
              index={index}
              handleOnPress={!winner ? setSlot : () => { }}
              filled={slot.filled}
            />
        )
    }
    </SlotsWrapper>
  </BoardWrapper>
);
```

When the `Board` component receives the `winner` prop with the `true` value, instead of the board, the user will see the trophy animation being rendered. An example of how this will look when you're running the application with the iOS simulator or on an iOS device can be seen here:

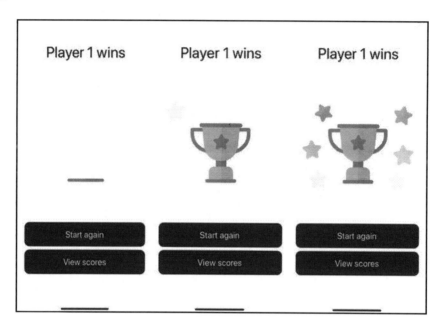

In case you find the speed of this animation too fast, it's possible to change this by combining the Animated API with Lottie. The `Lottie` component can take a `progress` prop that determines the speed of the animation. When passing a value that is created by the Animated API, you can tweak the speed of the animation to your own needs. Adding this to the Lottie animation can be done as follows:

1. First, you'll need to import `Animated` and `Easing` (which you'll use later on) and create a new value using `Animated` and the `useState` Hook at the top of your component:

```
  import React from 'react';
+ import { Animated, Easing } from 'react-native';
  import Lottie from 'lottie-react-native';

- const Winner = () => (
+ const Winner = () => {
+   const [progressValue] = React.useState(new Animated.Value(0));
+   return (
      <Lottie
```

```
        autoPlay
        style={{
           width: '100%',
           height: '100%' ,
        }}
        source={ require('../../assets/winner.json') }
        progress={progressValue}
      />
    );
+ };

export default Winner;
```

2. Within a `useEffect` Hook, you can create the `Animated.timing` method, which will set the `progressValue` over a time frame that you indicate using the `duration` field. The animation should start as soon as the component renders, so the dependency array for the Hook should be empty. You can also add the `Easing.linear` function to the `easing` field to make the animation run smoother:

```
...
const Winner = () => {
    const [progressValue] = React.useState(new Animated.Value(0));

+   React.useEffect(() => {
+     Animated.timing(progressValue, {
+       toValue: 1,
+       duration: 4000,
+       easing: Easing.linear,
+     }).start();
+   }, []);

    return (
      ...
```

3. Now, the `progressValue` value can be passed to the `Lottie` component, which will result in a different behavior for the animation:

```
...
const Winner = () => {
    const [progressValue] = React.useState(new Animated.Value(0));

    ...

    return (
      <Lottie
```

```
              autoPlay
              style={{
                width: '100%',
                height: '100%' ,
              }}
              source={ require('../../assets/winner.json') }
+             progress={progressValue}
              />
          );
      };

      export default Winner;
```

Now, the animation is being slowed down. Instead of the default 3,000 ms, the animation will take 4,000 ms to play from beginning to end. In the next section, you'll add even more complexity to the user experience of this application by handling gestures that are available on mobile devices.

Handling gestures with Expo

Gestures are an important feature of mobile applications as they will make the difference between a mediocre and a good mobile application. In the *Tic-Tac-Toe* game you've created, several gestures could be added to make the game more appealing.

Previously, you used the `TouchableOpacity` element, which gives the user feedback after they press this element by changing the element. Another element that you could have used for this was the `TouchableHighlight` element. Just like `TouchableOpacity`, it can be pressed by the user, but, instead of changing the opacity, it highlights the element. These feedback or highlight gestures give the user an impression of what happens when they make decisions within your application, leading to improved user experience. These gestures can be customized and added to other elements as well, making it possible to have custom Touchable elements as well.

For this, you can use a package called `react-native-gesture-handler`, which helps you access native gestures on every platform. All of these gestures will be run in the native thread, which means you can add complex gesture logic without having to deal with the performance limitations of React Native's gesture responder system. Some of the gestures it supports include tap, rotate, drag, and pan gestures. Any project that's created with the Expo CLI can already use `GestureHandler` from `react-native-gesture-handler` without you having to manually install the package.

You can also use gestures directly from React Native, without having to use an additional package. However, the gesture responder system that React Native currently uses doesn't run in the native thread. Not only does this limit the possibilities of creating and customizing gestures, but you can also run into cross-platform or performance problems. Therefore, it's advised that you use the `react-native-gesture-handler` package, but this isn't necessary for using gestures in React Native.

Handling tap gestures

The first gesture we will implement is a tap gesture, which will be added to the `Slot` component, to give the user more feedback on their actions. Instead of filling the slot when the user taps it, the user will already receive some feedback when the tap event is started and receive feedback when the event is completed. Here, we'll use the `TouchableWithoutFeedback` element from `react-native-gesture-handler`, which runs in the native thread, instead of the `TouchableWithoutFeedback` element from `react-native`, which uses the gesture responder system. Replacing the `react-native` component with the one from `react-native-gesture-handler` can be done by following these steps:

1. `TouchableWithoutFeedback` can be imported from `react-native-gesture-handler` at the top of the `src/components/Slot.js` file:

```
import React from 'react';
- import { TouchableWithoutFeedback, View, Dimensions } from
'react-native';
+ import { View, Dimensions } from 'react-native';
+ import { TouchableWithoutFeedback } from 'react-native-gesture-
handler';
import styled from 'styled-components/native';
import Filled from './Filled';


. . .

const Slot = ({ index, filled, handleOnPress }) => (
    . . .
```

You don't have to change anything in the return function since `TouchableWithoutFeedback` uses the same props as the one from `react-native`. When you tap the slot, nothing will change. This is because the slot will be filled by the `Filled` component, which shows an animation once it appears.

2. When you tap any of the slots and hold your finger on it,
   the handleOnPress function won't be called yet. Only when you complete the
   tap gesture by removing your finger will the gesture end and
   the handleOnPress function will be called. To start the animation when you
   start the tap gesture by touching the slot, you can use the onPressIn callback
   from TouchableWithoutFeedback. Once the tap event starts, a value needs to
   be passed to the Filled component that indicates it should start the animation.
   This value can be created with the useState Hook, so you already have a
   function that can be called to change this value. The handleOnPress function
   should be called when the tap event ends by removing your finger from the
   element. You can do this using the onPressOut callback:

```
import React from 'react';
import { View, Dimensions } from 'react-native';
import { TapGestureHandler, State } from 'react-native-gesture-
handler';
import styled from 'styled-components/native';
import Filled from './Filled';

...

- const Slot = ({ index, filled, handleOnPress }) => (
+ const Slot = ({ index, filled, handleOnPress }) => {
+   const [start, setStart] = React.useState(false);

+   return (
-     <TouchableWithoutFeedback onPress={() => !filled &&
handleOnPress(index)}>
+     <TouchableWithoutFeedback onPressIn={() => setStart()}
onPressOut={() => !filled && handleOnPress(index)}>
        <SlotWrapper>
-         <Filled filled={filled} />
+         <Filled filled={filled} start={start} />
        </SlotWrapper>
      </TouchableWithoutFeedback>
    );
};

export default Slot;
```

3. In the `Filled` component in the `src/Components/Slot/Filled.js` file, you need to check for the `start` prop and start the animation once this prop has a value of `true`. Since you don't want to start the entire animation when the value for `start` is `true`, only the animation that changes `opacityValue` will start:

```
import React from 'react';
import { Animated, Easing } from 'react-native';
import { ANIMATION_DURATION } from '../../utils/constants';

- const Filled = ({ filled }) => {
+ const Filled = ({ filled, start }) => {
    const [opacityValue] = React.useState(new Animated.Value(0));
-   const [scaleValue] = React.useState(new Animated.Value(0));
+   const [scaleValue] = React.useState(new Animated.Value(.8));

+ React.useEffect(() => {
+   start && Animated.timing(
+     opacityValue,
+     {
+         toValue: 1,
+         duration: ANIMATION_DURATION,
+         easing: Easing.linear(),
+     }
+   ).start();
+ }, [start]);

  React.useEffect(() => {
    ...
```

4. Also, the animation that changes the opacity can be removed from the `useEffect` Hook that's checking for the `filled` prop. This `useEffect` Hook only handles the animation that changes the scale. The initial `scaleValue` should be changed because, otherwise, the size of the component will be equal to `0`:

```
+ const Filled = ({ filled, start }) => {
    const [opacityValue] = React.useState(new Animated.Value(0));
-   const [scaleValue] = React.useState(new Animated.Value(0));
+   const [scaleValue] = React.useState(new Animated.Value(.8));

React.useEffect(() => {

  ...

  React.useEffect(() => {
- filled && Animated.parallel([
```

```
-      Animated.timing(
-        opacityValue,
-        {
-          toValue: 1,
-          duration: ANIMATION_DURATION,
-          easing: Easing.linear(),
-        }
-      ),
-      Animated.spring(
+      filled && Animated.spring(
         scaleValue,
         {
           toValue: 1,
           easing: Easing.cubic(),
         }
-      )
-    ]).start()
+    ).start();
   }, [filled]);

   ...
```

When you tap any of the slots after making these changes, the `timing` animation will be started and a square will appear in the slot, which indicates that the slot is being tapped. Once you release your finger from this slot, the square will change in size and fill in the rest of the slot as the `spring` animation starts, which happens when the `onPress` function changes the value for `filled`.

Customizing tap gestures

Now, the slot has different animations, depending on the state of the tap event, which can be useful if the user has second thoughts about which slot to select. The user may remove their finger from the selected slot, in which case the tap event will follow a different flow of states. You can even determine whether the user should click on the slot for a longer time to make the selection definitive or maybe double-tap the slot just like liking a picture on some social media applications.

To create more complex tap gestures such as these, you need to know that the tap event goes through different states. TouchableWithoutFeedback uses TapGestureHandler under the hood and can go through the following states: UNDETERMINED, FAILED, BEGAN, CANCELLED, ACTIVE, and END. The naming of these states is pretty straightforward and, usually, the handler will have the following flow: UNDETERMINED > BEGAN > ACTIVE > END > UNDETERMINED. When you add a function to the onPressIn callback on the TouchableWithoutFeedback element, this function is called when the tap event is in the BEGAN state. The onPressOut callback is invoked when the state is END, while the default onPress callback responds to the ACTIVE state.

To create these complex gestures, you can use the react-native-gesture-handler package by handling the event state yourself, rather than the declarative way of using a touchable element:

1. TapGestureHandler can be imported from react-native-gesture-handler and lets you create customized touchable elements that have gestures that you can define yourself. You'll need to import the State object from react-native-gesture-handler, which holds the constants you'll need to use to handle checking for the state of the tap event:

```
import React from 'react';
- import { TouchableWithoutFeedback } from 'react-native-gesture-
handler';
+ import { TapGestureHandler, State } from 'react-native-gesture-
handler';
import styled from 'styled-components/native';
import Filled from './Filled';

...

const Slot = ({ index, filled, handleOnPress }) => (
   ...
```

2. Instead of event handlers such as `onPress`, the `TouchableWithoutFeedback` element has a callback called `onHandlerStateChange`. This function will be called every time the state of `TapGestureHandler` changes, which is, for example, when the element is tapped. By using `TapGestureHandler` to create the touchable element, you no longer need the `TouchableWithoutFeedback` element. The functionality of this element can be moved to the new element that you'll create:

```
...

const Slot = ({ index, filled, handleOnPress }) => {
...

return (
- <TouchableWithoutFeedback onPressIn={() => setStart()}
onPressOut={() => !filled && handleOnPress(index)}>
+ <TapGestureHandler onHandlerStateChange={onTap}>
    <SlotWrapper>
      <Filled filled={filled} start={start} />
    </SlotWrapper>
- </TouchableWithoutFeedback>
+ </TapGestureHandler>
  );
};

...
```

3. `onHandlerStateChange` takes the `onTap` function, which you still need to create, and checks for the current state of the tap event. When the tap event is in the BEGAN state, which is similar to the `onPressIn` handler, the animation from `Filled` should start. The completion of the tap event has the END state and is like the `onPressOut` handler, where you'll call the `handleOnPress` function, which changes the value for the prop regarding the player that tapped the slot. The `setStart` function will be called to reset the state that starts the animation:

```
import React from 'react';
import { View, Dimensions } from 'react-native';
import { TapGestureHandler, State } from 'react-native-gesture-handler';
import styled from 'styled-components/native';
import Filled from './Filled';

...

const Slot = ({ index, filled, handleOnPress }) => {
```

```
      const [start, setStart] = React.useState(false);

+     const onTap = event => {
+       if (event.nativeEvent.state === State.BEGAN) {
+         setStart(true);
+       }

+       if (event.nativeEvent.state === State.END) {
+         !filled && handleOnPress(index);
+         setStart(false);
+       }
+     }

      return (
        ...
```

When you tap any of the slots and hold your finger on it, the handleOnPress function won't be called. Only when you complete the tap gesture by removing your finger will the gesture end and the handleOnPress function be called.

These gestures can be customized even more since you can use composition to have multiple tap events that respond to each other. By creating so-called **cross-handler interactions**, you can create a touchable element that supports a double-tap gesture and a long-press gesture. By setting and passing down a ref that's been created with the React useRef Hook, you can let the gesture handlers from react-native-gesture-handler listen to the state life cycle of other handlers. That way, you can sequence events and respond to gestures like a double-tap event:

1. To create the ref, you need to place the useRef Hook at the top of your component and pass this ref to TapGestureHandler:

```
import React from 'react';
import { View, Dimensions } from 'react-native';
import { TapGestureHandler, State } from 'react-native-gesture-
handler';
import styled from 'styled-components/native';
import Filled from './Filled';

...

const Slot = ({ index, filled, handleOnPress }) => {
   const [start, setStart] = React.useState(false);
+  const doubleTapRef = React.useRef(null);

   ...
```

```
      return (
  -       <TapGestureHandler onHandlerStateChange={onTap}>
  +       <TapGestureHandler
  +         ref={doubleTapRef}
  +         onHandlerStateChange={onTap}
  +       >
          <SlotWrapper>
             <Filled filled={filled} start={start} />
          </SlotWrapper>
        </TapGestureHandler>
    );
  };

  export default Slot;
```

2. Now, you need to set the number of taps that are needed to start and complete the tap gesture. You don't have to make any changes to the onTap function since the first time you tap the element, the state of the tap event will be BEGAN. Only after you've tapped the element twice will the tap event state change to END:

```
  . . .

  return (
    <TapGestureHandler
      ref={doubleTapRef}
      onHandlerStateChange={onTap}
  +     numberOfTaps={2}
    >
      <SlotWrapper>
        <Filled filled={filled} start={start} />
      </SlotWrapper>
    </TapGestureHandler>
  );

  . . .
```

3. To fill a slot, a user has to tap `TapGestureHandler` two times for the tap event to complete. However, you can also call a function when `TapGestureHandler` is tapped once by adding another `TapGestureHandler` that takes the existing one as its child. This new `TapGestureHandler` should wait for the other handler to have the double-tap gesture, which it can check using `doubleTapRef`. The `onTap` function should be renamed to `onDoubleTap` so that you have a new `onTap` function that will handle the single tap:

```
...

const Slot = ({ index, filled, handleOnPress }) => {
    const [start, setStart] = React.useState(false);
    const doubleTapRef = React.useRef(null);

+   const onTap = event => {};

-   const onTap = event => {
+   const onDoubleTap = event => {
        ...
    }

    return (
+     <TapGestureHandler
+         onHandlerStateChange={onTap}
+         waitFor={doubleTapRef}
+     >
        <TapGestureHandler
          ref={doubleTapRef}
-         onHandlerStateChange={onTap}
+         onHandlerStateChange={onDoubleTap}
          numberOfTaps={2}
        >
          <SlotWrapper>
              <Filled filled={filled} start={start} />
          </SlotWrapper>
        </TapGestureHandler>
+     </TapGestureHandler>
    );
}

...
```

4. When you click on a slot just once, the animation will start, since `TapGestureHandler` will be in the `BEGAN` state. The animation on the double-tap gesture should only start when the state is `ACTIVE` instead of `BEGAN`, so the animation won't start on just a single tap. Also, by adding a `setTimeout` to the functions that are called when the tap gesture has ended, the animation will look smoother since both animations will otherwise occur too soon after each other:

```
 . . .

const Slot = ({ index, filled, handleOnPress }) => {
    const [start, setStart] = React.useState(false);
    const doubleTapRef = React.useRef(null);

    const onTap = event => {};

    const onDoubleTap = event => {
-       if (event.nativeEvent.state === State.BEGAN) {
+       if (event.nativeEvent.state === State.ACTIVE) {
          setStart(true);
        }
        if (event.nativeEvent.state === State.END) {
+         setTimeout(() => {
            !filled && handleOnPress(index);
            setStart(false);
+         }, 100);
        }
    }
}

 . . .
```

Next to having a double-tap gesture to fill a slot, having a long-press gesture could also improve the user's interaction. You can add a long-press gesture by following these steps:

1. Import `LongPressGestureHandler` from `react-native-gesture-handler`.

```
import React from 'react';
import { View, Dimensions } from 'react-native';
- import { TapGestureHandler, State } from 'react-native-gesture-
handler';
+ import { LongPressGestureHandler, TapGestureHandler, State } from
'react-native-gesture-handler';
import styled from 'styled-components/native';
import Filled from './Filled';

 . . .
```

2. On this handler, you can set the minimal duration of the long-press gesture and set the function that should be called after this time frame has passed. The `LongPressGestureHandler` handler has a state life cycle, that you can use together with the `onDoubleTap` function:

```
...

const Slot = ({ index, filled, handleOnPress }) => {
  ...

  return (
+    <LongPressGestureHandler
+      onHandlerStateChange={onDoubleTap}
+      minDurationMs={500}
+    >
        <TapGestureHandler
          onHandlerStateChange={onTap}
          waitFor={doubleTapRef}
        >

          ...
        </TapGestureHandler>
+    </LongPressGestureHandler>
  )
};

export default Slot;
```

If you only want to create a long-press gesture, you can use the `onLongPress` event handler, which is available on the touchable elements from `react-native` and `react-native-gesture-handler`. It's advised that you use the touchable elements from `react-native-gesture-handler` as they will run in the native thread, instead of using the React Native gesture responder system.

3. Maybe not all of your users will understand that they need to use a long-press gesture to fill a slot. Therefore, you can use the `onTap` function, which is called on a single tap, to alert the user about this functionality. For this, you can use the `Alert` API, which works for both iOS and Android and uses the native alert message from either of these platforms. In this alert, you can add a small message for the user:

```
import React from 'react';
- import { View, Dimensions } from 'react-native';
+ import { Alert, View, Dimensions } from 'react-native';
import { LongPressGestureHandler, TapGestureHandler, State } from
```

```
'react-native-gesture-handler';
import styled from 'styled-components/native';
import Filled from './Filled';

...

const Slot = ({ index, filled, handleOnPress }) => {
  const [start, setStart] = React.useState(false);
  const doubleTapRef = React.useRef(null);

  const onTap = event => {
+    if (event.nativeEvent.state === State.ACTIVE) {
+      Alert.alert(
+        'Hint',
+        'You either need to press the slot longer to make your
move',
+      );
+    }
  }

  ...
```

This will show an alert when the user doesn't use the long-press to make a move on the board, thus making it more understandable for them. With these final additions, the game interface has been improved even more. Not only will users see animations based on their actions, but they'll also be notified about which gestures they can use.

Summary

In this chapter, we added animations and gestures to a simple *Tic-Tac-Toe* game that was built with React Native and Expo. The animations were created using the React Native Animated API and Lottie, which is available from the Expo CLI and as a separate package. We also added basic and more complex gestures to the game, which runs in the native thread thanks to the `react-native-gesture-handler` package.

Animations and gestures provide a clear improvement to the user interface of your mobile application, and there's even more we can do. Still, our application will also need to request and display data to your users.

Previously, we used GraphQL alongside React. We will build upon this in the next chapter. The project that you'll create in the next chapter will explore handling real-time data in a React Native application using WebSockets and GraphQL using Apollo.

Further reading

- Various Lottie files: `https://lottiefiles.com/`
- More on the Animated API: `https://facebook.github.io/react-native/docs/animated`

10

Creating a Real-Time Messaging Application with React Native and Expo

Having a real-time connection with a server is crucial when you're developing a real-time messaging application as you want your users to receive their messages as soon as they are sent. What you might have experienced in the previous two chapters is that mobile applications are more intuitive to use than web applications. When you want users to send messages back-and-forth, this is best done by building a mobile application, which you'll do in this chapter.

In this chapter, you'll create a real-time mobile messaging application using React Native and Expo that connects with a GraphQL server. By using WebSockets, you can create real-time connections with a server for web and mobile applications and have a two-way data flow between your application and a GraphQL server. This connection can also be used for authentication by using OAuth and JWT tokens, which is what you did in the Chapter 7, *Build a Full Stack E-Commerce Application with React Native and GraphQL.*

The following topics will be covered in this chapter:

- GraphQL with React Native using Apollo
- Authentication flows in React Native
- GraphQL subscriptions

Project overview

In this chapter, we will create a mobile messaging application build with React Native and Expo that uses a GraphQL server for authentication and to send and receive messages. Messages can be received in real-time as GraphQL subscriptions are used through a WebSocket that was created with Apollo. Users need to be logged in to send messages through the application, for which an authentication flow was built using React Navigation and AsyncStorage to store authentication details in persistent storage.

The build time is 2 hours.

Getting started

The project that we'll create in this chapter builds upon an initial version that you can find on GitHub: `https://github.com/PacktPublishing/React-Projects/tree/ch10-initial`. The complete source code can also be found on GitHub: `https://github.com/PacktPublishing/React-Projects/tree/ch10`.

You need to have the application Expo Client installed on a mobile iOS or Android device to run the project on a physical device. Alternatively, you can install either Xcode or Android Studio on your computer to run the application on a virtual device:

- **For iOS**: Information on how to set up your local machine to run the iOS simulator can be found here: `https://docs.expo.io/versions/v36.0.0/workflow/ios-simulator/`.
- **For Android**: Information on how to set up your local machine to run the emulator from Android Studio can be found here: `https://docs.expo.io/versions/v36.0.0/workflow/android-studio-emulator/`. There's a known issue when running the emulator, which can be prevented by ensuring that the following lines are present in your `~/.bash_profile` or `~/.bash_rc` file:

```
export ANDROID_SDK=ANDROID_SDK_LOCATION
export PATH=ANDROID_SDK_LOCATION/platform-tools:$PATH
export PATH=ANDROID_SDK_LOCATION/tools:$PATH
```

The value for `ANDROID_SDK_LOCATION` is the path to the Android SDK on your local machine and can be found by opening Android Studio and going to **Preferences | Appearance & Behavior | System Settings | Android SDK**. The path is listed in the box that states the Android SDK location and looks like this: `/Users/myuser/Library/Android/sdk`.

 This application was created using **Expo SDK version 33.0.0,** and so, you need to ensure that the version of Expo you're using on your local machine is similar. As React Native and Expo are frequently updated, make sure that you're working with this version so that the patterns described in this chapter behave as expected. In case your application doesn't start or if you encounter errors, refer to the Expo documentation to learn more about updating the Expo SDK.

Checking out the initial project

This project consists of two parts: a boilerplate React Native application and a GraphQL server. The React Native application can be found in the `client` directory, while the GraphQL server can be found in the `server` directory. For this chapter, you'll need to have both the application and the server running at all times, where you'll only make code changes to the application in the `client` directory.

To get started with this chapter, you'll need to run the following command in the `client` and `server` directories in order to install all of the dependencies and start both the server and the application:

```
npm install && npm start
```

For the mobile application, this command will start Expo after installing the dependencies and gives you the ability to start your project from the Terminal or from your browser. In the Terminal, you can either use the QR code to open the application on your mobile device or open the application on a virtual device.

Regardless of whether you've opened the application using the from a physical or virtual iOS or Android device, the application should look something like this:

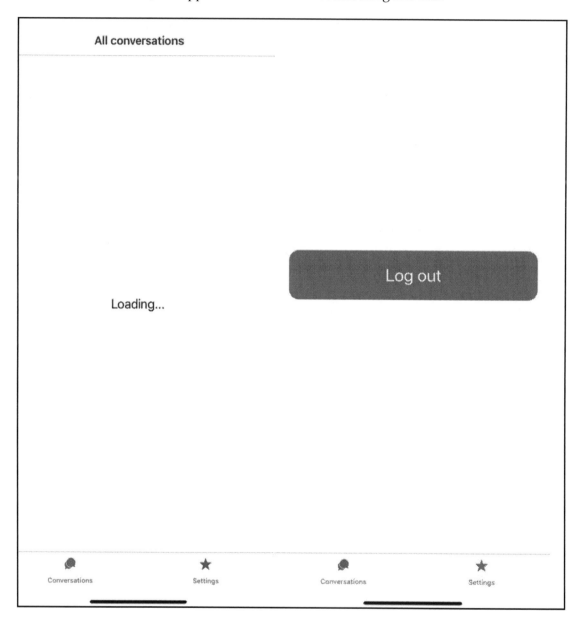

The initial application consists of five screens:
AuthLoading, Conversations, Conversation, Login, and Settings. The
Conversations screen will be the initial screen and shows a loading message, while the
Settings screen contains a non-functioning logout button. For now, the
AuthLoading, Conversation, and Login screens aren't visible yet as you'll add the
routing to these screens later on in this chapter.

The project structure from this React Native application in the client directory is as
follows, where the structure is similar to the projects you've created before in this book:

```
messaging
|-- client
    |-- .expo
    |-- assets
        |-- icon.png
        |-- splash.png
    |-- Components
        |-- // ...
    |-- node_modules
    |-- Screens
        |-- AuthLoading.js
        |-- Conversation.js
        |-- Conversations.js
        |-- Login.js
        |-- Settings.js
    |-- .watchmanconfig
    |-- App.js
    |-- AppContainer.js
    |-- app.json
    |-- babel.config.js
    |-- package.json
```

In the assets directory, you can find the images that are used for the application icon on
the **Home** screen. Once you've installed this application on your mobile device, the image
that will serve as the splash screen will be displayed when you start the application. Details
about your application such as its name, description, and version are placed in app.json,
while babel.config.js holds specific Babel configurations.

The App.js file is the actual entry point of your application, where the
AppContainer.js file is being imported and returned. In AppContainer, all of the routes
for this application are defined and AppContext will contain information that should be
available in the entire application.

All of the components for this application are located in
the `Screens` and `Components` directories, where the first one holds the components that
are rendered by the screens. The child components for these screens can be found in the
`Components` directory, which has the following structure:

```
|-- Components
    |-- Button
        |-- Button.js
    |-- Conversation
        |-- ConversationActions.js
        |-- ConversationItem.js
    |-- Message
        |-- Message.js
    |-- TextInput
        |-- TextInput.js
```

The GraphQL server can be found at: `http://localhost:4000/graphql` and is where
the GraphQL Playground will be visible. From this playground, you can view the schema
for the GraphQL server and introspect all of the available queries, mutations, and
subscriptions. Although you won't be making any code changes to the server, it's important
to know about the schema and how it works.

The server has two queries to retrieve a list of conversations or a single conversation by
using the `userName` parameter as the identifier. These queries will return the
`Conversation` type, which has an `id`, `userName`, and a list of messages of
the `Message` type.

On this GraphQL server, two mutations can be found, which are to either log the user in or
to send a message. The user can be logged in by using the following:

- **Username**: `test`
- **Password**: `test`

Finally, there's one subscription that will retrieve messages that are added to the
conversation. This subscription will enhance the query and can be sent in a document to
retrieve a single conversation.

Creating a real-time messaging application with React Native and Expo

One of the reasons why mobile applications are popular is because they usually provide real-time data, such as updates and notifications. With React Native and Expo, you can create mobile applications that can handle real-time data using WebSockets that synchronize with, for example, a GraphQL server. In this chapter, you'll add GraphQL to a React Native application and add extra features to this application to make it work with real-time data.

Using GraphQL in React Native with Apollo

In Chapter 7, *Build a Full Stack E-Commerce Application with React Native and GraphQL*, you've already set up a connection with the GraphQL server for a web application; similarly, in this chapter, you'll use a GraphQL server for the data in your mobile application. To use GraphQL in a React Native application, you can use Apollo to make the experience of developers smoother.

Setting up Apollo in React Native

The react-apollo package, which you've already used for Apollo in a React web application, can also be used for Apollo in a React Native mobile application. This fits perfectly with the tagline of React and React Native: *learn once, write everywhere*. But before we add Apollo to the application, it's important to know that when you run your application using the Expo application on your mobile, localhost requests aren't supported. The local GraphQL server for this project is running on http://localhost:4000/graphql, but to be able to use this endpoint in the React Native application, you need to find the local IP address of your machine.

To find your local IP address, you'll need to do the following depending on your operating system:

- **For Windows**: Open the Terminal (or command prompt) and run this command:

  ```
  ipconfig
  ```

This will return a list, as follows, with data from your local machine. In this list, you need to look for the field **IPv4 Address**:

```
Windows IP Configuration


Ethernet adapter Ethernet0:

   Connection-specific DNS Suffix  . :
   IPv6 Address. . . . . . . . . . . : 2a02:2f01:5060:9cb:3499:3b63:e8ab:5967
   Temporary IPv6 Address. . . . . . : 2a02:2f01:5060:9cb:e9d9:4dbb:4ddc:a934
   Link-local IPv6 Address . . . . . : fe80::3499:3b63:e8ab:5967%4
   IPv4 Address. . . . . . . . . . . : 192.168.1.107
   Subnet Mask . . . . . . . . . . . : 255.255.255.0
   Default Gateway . . . . . . . . . : fe80::1eb7:2cff:fe74:fef8%4
                                       192.168.1.1

Tunnel adapter Teredo Tunneling Pseudo-Interface:

   Connection-specific DNS Suffix  . :
   IPv6 Address. . . . . . . . . . . : 2001:0:9d38:90d7:285a:3873:3f57:fe94
   Link-local IPv6 Address . . . . . : fe80::285a:3873:3f57:fe94%13
   Default Gateway . . . . . . . . . :
```

- **For macOS**: Open the Terminal and run this command:

  ```
  ipconfig getifaddr en0
  ```

  After running this command, the local `Ipv4 Address` of your machine gets returned, which looks like this:

  ```
  192.168.1.107
  ```

After getting the local IP address, you can use this address to set up the Apollo client for the React Native application. To be able to use Apollo and GraphQL, you need to install several packages from npm using npm with the following command. You need to do this from the `client` directory in a separate Terminal tab:

```
cd client && npm install graphql apollo-client apollo-link-http apollo-cache-inmemory react-apollo
```

In the `App.js`, file, you can now use `apollo-client` to create your GraphQL client using `apollo-link-http` to set up the connection with the local GraphQL server and `apollo-cache-inmemory` to cache your GraphQL requests. Also, the `ApolloProvider` component will use the client you've created to make the GraphQL server available to all of the components that are nested within this Provider. The local IP address must be used to create the value for `API_URL` with the prefix `http://` and suffix `:4000/graphql` that points towards the correct port and endpoint, making it look like `http://192.168.1.107:4000/graphql`.

To do this, add the following lines to `App.js`:

```
 import React from 'react';
 import AppContainer from './AppContainer';
+ import { ApolloClient } from 'apollo-client';
+ import { InMemoryCache } from 'apollo-cache-inmemory';
+ import { HttpLink } from 'apollo-link-http';
+ import { ApolloProvider } from 'react-apollo';

+ const API_URL = 'http://192.168.1.107:4000/graphql';

+ const cache = new InMemoryCache();
+ const client = new ApolloClient({
+   link: new HttpLink({
+     uri: API_URL,
+   }),
+   cache
+ });

- const App = () => <AppContainer />;

+ const App = () => (
+   <ApolloProvider client={client}>
+       <AppContainer />
+   </ApolloProvider>
+ );

 export default App;
```

Now, you're able to send documents with queries and mutations from any of the components nested within `ApolloProvider`, but you aren't able to send subscriptions in your documents yet. Support for subscriptions doesn't come out of the box and requires setting up a WebSocket for a real-time two-way connection between the client React Native application and the GraphQL server. This will be done later on in this chapter, after you've added authentication to the application.

In the next part of this section, you'll use Apollo to get the data from the GraphQL server that you just linked to the Apollo Client in this section.

Using Apollo in React Native

If you look at the application, you will see there are two tabs; one is showing the Conversations screen and the other is showing the Settings screen. The Conversations screen is now displaying the text Loading..., where the conversations that were returned from the GraphQL server should be shown. The components to display the conversations have already been created and can be found in the client/Components/Conversation directory, while the logic to request the conversations still needs to be created.

To add Apollo, follow these steps:

1. The first step is to import the Query component from react-apollo into the client/Screens/Conversations.js file, which you'll use to send a document to the GraphQL server. This Query component will use the GET_CONVERSATIONS query and the ConversationItem component must be imported as well:

   ```
   import React from 'react';
   import { FlatList, Text, View } from 'react-native';
   import styled from 'styled-components/native';
   + import { Query } from 'react-apollo';
   + import { GET_CONVERSATIONS } from '../constants';
   + import ConversationItem from
   '../Components/Conversations/ConversationItem';

   ...

   const Conversations = () => (
     ...
   ```

2. The Conversations screen should now request the GET_CONVERSATIONS query using the Query component. When the request hasn't been resolved, a loading message will be displayed. When the request to the GraphQL server is resolved, a styled Flatlist will return a list of the imported ConversationItem components. The styled Flatlist has already been created and can be found as the ConversationsList component at the bottom of this file:

   ```
   ...

   const Conversations = () => (
     <ConversationsWrapper>
   ```

```
-    <ConversationsText>Loading...</ConversationsText>
+    <Query query={GET_CONVERSATIONS}>
+      {({ loading, data }) => {
+        if (loading) {
+          return <ConversationsText>Loading...</ConversationsText>
+        }

+        return (
+          <ConversationsList
+            data={data.conversations}
+            keyExtractor={item => item.userName}
+            renderItem={({ item }) => <ConversationItem item={item}
/> }
+          />
+        );
+      }}
+    </Query>
     </ConversationsWrapper>
);
```

```
export default Conversations;
```

The `Conversations` screen initially shows the loading message when the
document with the query is sent; after the query has returned data, the
`ConversationsList` component will be displayed. This component renders
`ConversationItem` components that display the data from the query.

3. When you try to click on any of the conversations, nothing will happen, except
   that you'll see a small animation that changes the opacity. This is because the
   `ConversationItem` component is a styled `TouchableOpacity`, which can be
   passed as a function that is called when you tap it. The function to navigate to the
   conversation can be created from the `navigation` prop, which is available in the
   `Conversations` screen. This prop should be passed as a prop to
   `ConversationItem`:

```
    ...

-  const Conversations = () => (
+  const Conversations = ({ navigation ) => (
     <ConversationsWrapper>
       <ConversationsText>Loading...</ConversationsText>
         <Query query={GET_CONVERSATIONS}>
           {({ loading, data }) => {
             if (loading) {
               return
    <ConversationsText>Loading...</ConversationsText>
```

```
                    }

                    return (
                      <ConversationsList
                        data={data.conversations}
                        keyExtractor={item => item.userName}
-                       renderItem={({ item }) => <ConversationItem
item={item} /> }
+                       renderItem={({ item }) => <ConversationItem
item={item} navigation={navigation} />}
                      />
                    );
                  }}
              </Query>
          </ConversationsWrapper>
    );

    export default Conversations;
```

4. The `ConversationItem` component can now navigate to the `Conversation` screen when `TouchableOpacity` is being tapped; this component can be found in the `client/Components/Conversation/ConversationItem.js` file, where the `navigation` prop should be destructured and used to call the `navigate` function on the `onPress` handler. This item is passed with the `navigate` function so that this data can be used in the `Conversation` screen:

```
import React from 'react';
import { Platform, Text, View, TouchableOpacity } from 'react-
native';
import { Ionicons } from '@expo/vector-icons';
import styled from 'styled-components/native';

. . .

- const ConversationItem = ({ item }) => (
+ const ConversationItem = ({ item, navigation }) => (
-   <ConversationItemWrapper>
+   <ConversationItemWrapper
+     onPress={() => navigation.navigate('Conversation', { item })}
+   >
      <ThumbnailWrapper>
        . . .
```

5. This navigates to the `Conversation` screen from
   the `client/Screens/Conversation.js` file, where the full conversation
   should be displayed. To display the conversation, you can either use the item
   data that was just passed to this screen or send another document to the
   GraphQL server that contains the query to retrieve the conversation. To make
   sure the most recent data is displayed, the `Query` component can be used to send
   a query to retrieve the conversation using the `userName` field from the
   `navigation` prop. To do this, you need to import the `Query` component, the
   `GET_CONVERSATION` query that is used by `Query`, and the `Message` component
   to display the messages from the conversation:

```
import React from 'react';
import { Dimensions, ScrollView, Text, FlatList, View } from
'react-native';
+ import { Query } from 'react-apollo';
import styled from 'styled-components/native';
+ import Message from '../Components/Message/Message';
+ import { GET_CONVERSATION } from '../constants';

...

const Conversation = () => (
  ...
```

6. After this, you can add the `Query` component to the `Conversation` screen and
   have it use the `GET_CONVERSATION` query with `userName`, which was retrieved
   from the `navigation` prop. Once the query resolves the `Query` component
   returns a `data` object with a field called `messages`. This value can be passed to a
   `FlatList` component. In this component, you can iterate over this value and
   return `Message` components that display all of the messages from the
   conversation. `FlatList` is already styled and can be found at the bottom of the
   file as `MessagesList`:

```
...

- const Conversation = () => {
+ const Conversation = ({ navigation }) => {
+   const userName = navigation.getParam('userName', '');

+ return (
    <ConversationWrapper>
-       <ConversationBodyText>Loading...</ConversationBodyText>
+       <Query query={GET_CONVERSATION} variables={{ userName }}>
        <ConversationBody>
```

```
+            {({ loading, data }) => {
+              if (loading) {
+                return
<ConversationBodyText>Loading...</ConversationBodyText>;
+              }
+              const { messages } = data.conversation;
+              <MessagesList
+                data={messages}
+                keyExtractor={item => String(item.id)}
+                renderItem={({ item }) => (
+                  <Message align={item.userName === 'me' ? 'left' :
'right'}>
+                    {item.text}
+                  </Message>
+                )}
+              />
+            }}
           </ConversationBody>
+        </Query>
         <ConversationActions userName={userName} />
       </ConversationWrapper>
   );
+ };

  export default Conversation;
```

All of the received messages from this conversation are now being displayed and, using the form at the bottom of this screen, a new message can be added to the conversation.

Depending on the device that you're running the application on, the Conversation and Conversation screens should look something like this on a device running on iOS:

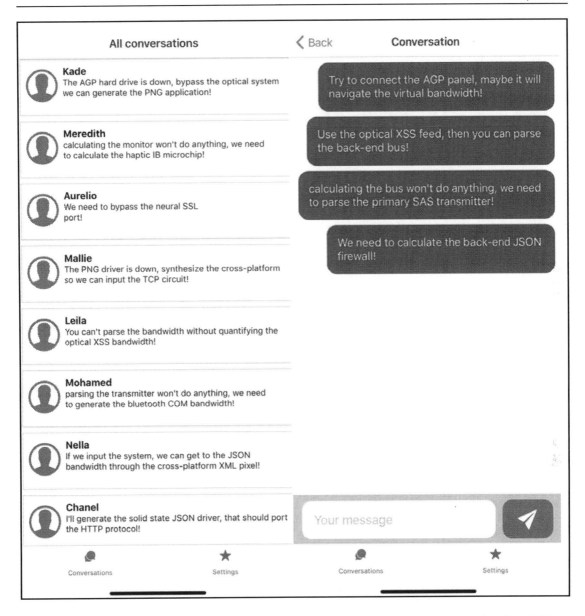

However, to send a message, a document with a mutation should be sent to the GraphQL server and, to do so the user must be authenticated. How to handle authentication for this mutation will be addressed in the next section, where the authentication flow will be added.

Authentication in React Native

Typically, authentication for mobile applications is similar to how you would handle authentication in web applications, although there are some minor differences. The flow for authenticating a user on a mobile application would be as follows:

1. The user opens your application
2. A loading screen is shown that checks for any authentication information in the persistent storage
3. If authenticated, the user will be forwarded to the main screen for the application; otherwise, they will be forwarded to the login screen, where the user can log in
4. Whenever the user signs out, the authentication details will be removed from the persistent storage

One of the biggest caveats of this flow is that the mobile device doesn't support local storage or session storage as these persistent storage solutions are tied to the browser. Instead, you'd need to use the AsyncStorage library from React Native to have persistent storage on both iOS and Android. On iOS, it will use native code blocks to give you the global persistent storage that AsyncStorage offers, while on devices running Android, either RockDB- or SQLite-based storage will be used.

For more complex usages, it's recommended to use an abstraction layer on top of AsyncStorage as encryption isn't supported out of the box by AsyncStorage. Also, the use of a key-value system can give you performance issues if you want to store a lot of information for your application using AsyncStorage. Both iOS and Android will have set limitations on the amount of storage each application can use.

Authentication with React Navigation

To set up the authentication flow we described earlier, you'll use the React Navigation package again. Previously, you used the different types of navigators from React Navigation, but not SwitchNavigator. With this navigator type, you can only display one screen at once, and you can navigate to other screens using the navigation prop. SwitchNavigator should be the main navigator of your application and other navigators such as StackNavigator can be nested inside it.

Adding authentication to the React Native application involves performing the following steps:

1. The first step to using this navigator type is importing `createSwitchNavigator` from `react-navigation`, just like you imported the other navigators into the `client/AppContainer.js` file. Also, import the screen component for the login screen, which can be found at `client/Screens/Login.js`:

```
import React from 'react';
import { Platform } from 'react-native';
import { Ionicons } from '@expo/vector-icons';
import {
+ createSwitchContainer,
  createAppContainer
} from 'react-navigation';
import { createStackNavigator } from 'react-navigation-stack';
import { createBottomTabNavigator } from 'react-navigation-tabs';
import Conversations from './Screens/Conversations';
import Conversation from './Screens/Conversation';
import Settings from './Screens/Settings';
+ import Login from './Screens/Login';

const ConversationsStack = createStackNavigator({
    ...
```

2. Instead of wrapping `TabNavigator` at the bottom of this file with `createAppContainer`, you need to return `SwitchNavigator` instead. To create this, you need to use `createSwitchNavigator`, which you imported in the previous step. This navigator contains the `Login` screen and `TabNavigator`, which is the main screen for this application. For the user to only see the main screen when authenticated, the `Login` screen needs to be the initial screen:

```
    ...

+ const SwitchNavigator = createSwitchNavigator(
+     {
+         Main: TabNavigator,
+         Auth: Login
+     },
+     {
+         initialRouteName: 'Auth',
+     }
+ );
```

```
- export default createAppContainer(TabNavigator);
+ export default createAppContainer(SwitchNavigator);
```

The Login screen that is now displayed in the application will only switch to TabNavigator when the correct authentication details are filled in.

3. However, this form needs to be connected to the GraphQL server first to receive the JWT token that is needed for authentication. The component for the Login screen already has a form, but submitting this form doesn't call any function to authenticate the user yet. Therefore, you need to use a Mutation component from react-apollo and have this component send a document with the correct mutation to the GraphQL server. The mutation that needs to be added to this component can be found in the constants.js file and is called LOGIN_USER. To submit the form, the loginUser function that is returned by the Mutation component should be called when the user presses Button:

```
import React from 'react';
import { View, TextInput } from 'react-native';
import styled from 'styled-components/native';
+ import { Mutation } from 'react-apollo';
import Button from '../Components/Button/Button';
+ import { LOGIN_USER } from '../constants';

...

const Login = () => {
 const [userName, setUserName] = React.useState('');
 const [password, setPassword] = React.useState('');

 return (
+   <Mutation mutation={LOGIN_USER}>
+     {loginUser => (
        <LoginWrapper>
          <StyledTextInput
            onChangeText={setUserName}
            value={userName}
            placeholder='Your username'
            textContentType='username'
          />
          <StyledTextInput
            onChangeText={setPassword}
            value={password}
            placeholder='Your password'
            textContentType='password'
          />
```

```
                    <Button
                      title='Login'
+                     onPress={() => loginUser({ variables: { userName,
password } })}
                    />
                  </LoginWrapper>
+       )}
+     </Mutation>
  );
};

export default Login;
```

Both `TextInput` components are controlled component, and
use `useState` Hooks to control their values. Both
the `userName` and `password` constants that are used by this mutation take two
variables for authentication, which are also `userName` and `password`:

```
...
export const LOGIN_USER = gql`
  mutation loginUser($userName: String!, $password: String!) {
    loginUser(userName: $userName, password: $password) {
      userName
      token
    }
  }
`;
...
```

4. Apart from the `loginUser` function, which sends the mutation in a document,
   the `Mutation` component will also return the `loading`, `error`, and `data`
   variables that are returned by the GraphQL server. The `loading` variable can be
   used to communicate to the user that the document was sent to the server, while
   the `data` and `error` variables are returned when the GraphQL server responds
   to this document:

```
import React from 'react';
import { View, TextInput } from 'react-native';
import styled from 'styled-components/native';
import { Mutation } from 'react-apollo';
import Button from '../Components/Button/Button';
import { LOGIN_USER } from '../constants';

...

const Login = () => {
```

```
    const [userName, setUserName] = React.useState('');
    const [password, setPassword] = React.useState('');

    return (
      <Mutation mutation={LOGIN_USER}>
-        {loginUser => (
+        {(loginUser, { loading }) => (
          <LoginWrapper>
            <StyledTextInput
              onChangeText={setUserName}
              value={userName}
              placeholder='Your username'
              textContentType='username'
            />
            <StyledTextInput
              onChangeText={setPassword}
              value={password}
              placeholder='Your password'
              textContentType='password'
            />
            <Button
-              title='Login'
+              title={loading ? 'Loading...' : 'Login'}
              onPress={() => loginUser({ variables: { userName,
password } })}
            />
          </LoginWrapper>
        }}
      </Mutation>
    );
  };

export default Login;
```

This will change the text of the button at the bottom of the form to
`Loading...` when the document is sent to the GraphQL server and no response
has been returned yet.

5. To use the `error` variable to show an error message when the wrong credentials have been filled in, you won't be destructuring the variable from the output of the `Mutation` component. Instead, the error variable will be retrieved from `Promise` that is returned by the `loginUser` function. For displaying the error, you'll use the `graphQLErrors` method that is available from the `error` variable, which returns an array (since there could be multiple errors) and renders the error within an `Alert` component from React Native:

```
import React from 'react';
- import { View, TextInput } from 'react-native';
+ import { Alert, View, TextInput } from 'react-native';
import styled from 'styled-components/native';
import { Mutation } from 'react-apollo';
import Button from '../Components/Button/Button';
import { LOGIN_USER } from '../constants';

. . .

<Button
    title={loading ? 'Loading...' : 'Login'}
    onPress={() => {
        loginUser({ variables: { userName, password } })
+       .catch(error => {
+           Alert.alert(
+               'Error',
+               error.graphQLErrors.map(({ message }) => message)[0]
+           );
+       });
    }}
/>

. . .
```

6. When the right username and password combination are used, the data variable should be used to store the JWT token that will be returned by the GraphQL server. Just like the `error` variable that was retrieved from the `loginUser` function, the `data` variable can be retrieved from this `Promise` as well. This token is available on the `data` variable and should be stored somewhere safe, which can be done using the `AsyncStorage` library:

```
import React from 'react';
- import { Alert, View, TextInput } from 'react-native';
+ import { AsyncStorage, Alert, View, TextInput } from 'react-native';
import styled from 'styled-components/native';
import { Mutation } from 'react-apollo';
```

```
import Button from '../Components/Button/Button';
import { LOGIN_USER } from '../constants';


...

const Login = ({ navigation }) => {
  ...

  <Button
    title={loading ? 'Loading...' : 'Login'}
    onPress={() => {
      loginUser({ variables: { userName, password } })
+        .then(({data}) => {
+          const { token } = data.loginUser;
+          AsyncStorage.setItem('token', token);
+        })
        .catch(error => {
          if (error) {
            Alert.alert(
              'Error',
              error.graphQLErrors.map(({ message }) => message)[0],
            );
          }
        });
    }}
  />

  ...
```

7. After storing the token, the user should be redirected to the main application, which can be found at the `Main` route and represents the screens linked to `TabNavigator`. To redirect the user, you can use the `navigation` prop that is passed to the `Login` component by `SwitchNavigator`. Since storing something with `AsyncStorage` should be done asynchronously, the navigation function should be called from within the callback of `Promise` that is returned by `AsyncStorage`:

```
import React from 'react';
import { AsyncStorage, Alert, View, TextInput } from 'react-native';
import styled from 'styled-components/native';
import { Mutation } from 'react-apollo';
import Button from '../Components/Button/Button';
import { LOGIN_USER } from '../constants';


...
```

```
- const Login = () => {
+ const Login = ({ navigation }) => {
    ...

  <Button
   title={loading ? 'Loading...' : 'Login'}
   onPress={() => {
   loginUser({ variables: { userName, password } })
    .then(({data}) => {
      const { token } = data.loginUser;
-     AsyncStorage.setItem('token', token)
+     AsyncStorage.setItem('token', token).then(value => {
+       navigation.navigate('Main');
+     });
    })
    .catch(error => {
      if (error) {
        Alert.alert(
          'Error',
          error.graphQLErrors.map(({ message }) => message)[0],
        );
      }
    });
  }}
 />

    ...
```

This, however, only completes a part of the authentication flow since the Login screen will always be displayed when the application first renders. That way, users always have to log in with their authentication details, even when their JWT token is stored in the persistent storage.

To check whether or not the user has logged in before, a third screen has to be added to SwitchNavigator. This screen will determine whether the user has a token stored in the persistent storage and if they do, the user will be redirected to the Main route immediately. If the user hasn't logged in before, the user will be redirected to the Login screen you've just created:

1. This intermediate screen that determines whether there is an authentication token stored in the persistent storage, that is the AuthLoading screen, should be added to SwitchNavigator in App.js. This screen should also become the initial route that is served by the navigator:

```
import React from 'react';
import { Platform } from 'react-native';
```

```
import { Ionicons } from '@expo/vector-icons';
import {
  createSwitchNavigator,
  createAppContainer
} from 'react-navigation';
import { createStackNavigator } from 'react-navigation-stack';
import { createBottomTabNavigator } from 'react-navigation-tabs';
import Conversations from './Screens/Conversations';
import Conversation from './Screens/Conversation';
import Settings from './Screens/Settings';
import Login from './Screens/Login';
+ import AuthLoading from './Screens/AuthLoading';

const ConversationsStack = createStackNavigator({

  ...

const SwitchNavigator = createSwitchNavigator(
  {
    Main: TabNavigator,
    Login,
+   AuthLoading,
  },
  {
-   initialRouteName: 'Login',
+   initialRouteName: 'AuthLoading',
  }
);

export default createAppContainer(SwitchNavigator);
```

2. In this `AuthLoading` screen, the authentication token should be retrieved from the persistent storage, and afterward, the navigation to either the `Login` or `Main` screen should be handled. This screen can be found in the `client/Screens/AuthLoading.js` file, where nothing but a simple interface has been added. The token can be retrieved using the `getItem` method from the `AsyncStorage` library and should be called from a `useEffect` Hook so that it's retrieved when the `AuthLoading` screen is first loaded. From `callback`, and from `Promise` returned by `getItem`, the `navigate` function from the `navigation` prop is used for the actual navigation to either of these screens:

```
import React from 'react';
- import { Text, View } from 'react-native';
+ import { AsyncStorage, Text, View } from 'react-native';
import styled from 'styled-components/native';
```

. . .

```
- const AuthLoading = () => (
+ const AuthLoading = ({ navigation }) => {
+   React.useEffect(() => {
+     AsyncStorage.getItem('token').then(value => {
+       navigation.navigate(value ? 'Main' : 'Auth');
+     });
+   }, [navigation]);

+   return (
      <AuthLoadingWrapper>
        <AuthLoadingText>Loading...</AuthLoadingText>
      </AuthLoadingWrapper>
    );
+ };

  export default AuthLoading;
```

3. The final step in completing the authentication flow is adding the possibility for a user to log out of the application by deleting the token from the persistent storage. This is done in the `client/Screens/Settings.js` file. This renders the `Settings` screen that can be found in `TabNavigator`. The `Settings` screen has a green button, which you can set an `onPress` event on.

   The `removeItem` method from `AsyncStorage` can be used for deleting the token from the persistent storage and returns `Promise`. In the callback of this `Promise`, you can again handle the navigation to return to the `Login` screen as you don't want an unauthenticated user in your application:

```
  import React from 'react';
- import { Text, View } from 'react-native';
+ import { AsyncStorage, Text, View } from 'react-native';
  import styled from 'styled-components/native';
  import Button from '../Components/Button/Button';

  . . .

- const Settings = () => (
+ const Settings = ({ navigation }) => (
      <SettingsWrapper>
-       <Button title='Log out' />
+       <Button
+         title='Log out'
+         onPress={() => {
+           AsyncStorage.removeItem('token').then(() =>
```

```
            navigation.navigate('AuthLoading'));
    +            }}
    +        />
            </SettingsWrapper>
        );

    export default Settings;
```

By adding the logout functionality, you've completed the authentication flow that uses JWT tokens returned by the GraphQL server. This can be requested by filling in a form on the Login screen. If the authentication is successful, the user will be redirected to the Main screen and, by using the **Log out** button on the Settings screen, the user can log out and will be directed back to the Login screen. The final authentication flow will now look something like this, depending on which operating system you're running this application on. The following screenshots have taken taken from a device that's running on iOS:

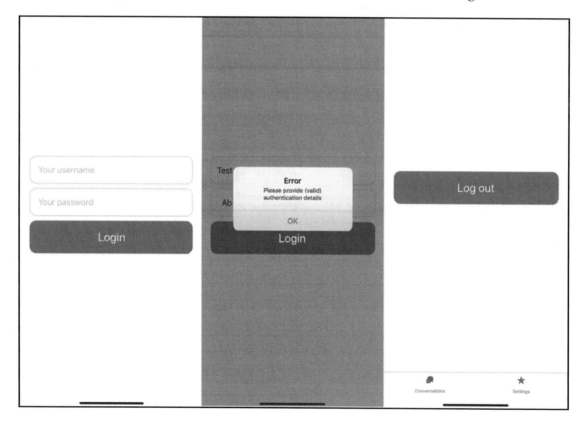

However, for the GraphQL server to know whether this user is authenticated, you need to send a validation token to it. In the next part of this section, you'll learn how to do this by using a **JSON Web Token (JWT)**.

Sending authentication details to the GraphQL server

The authentication details that are now stored in the persistent storage should also be added to the Apollo Client so that they're sent to the GraphQL server with every document. This can be done by extending the setup of Apollo Client with the token information. since the token is a JWT, it should be prefixed with `Bearer`:

1. You need to install an Apollo package to deal with adding values to `context`. The `setContext` method is available from the `apollo-link-context` package, which you can install from `npm`:

   ```
   npm install apollo-link-context
   ```

2. The `apollo-link-context` package should be imported into the `client/App.js` file, where the Apollo client is created. You need to separate the construction of the `HttpLink` object for the client as this one needs to be combined with the created Context:

   ```
   import React from 'react';
   import { ApolloClient } from 'apollo-client';
   import { InMemoryCache } from 'apollo-cache-inmemory';
   + import { setContext }  from 'apollo-link-context';
   import { HttpLink } from 'apollo-link-http';
   import { ApolloProvider } from 'react-apollo';
   import AppContainer from './AppContainer';

   const API_URL = '..';

   + const httpLink = new HttpLink({
   +   uri: API_URL,
   + });

   const cache = new InMemoryCache();

   const client = new ApolloClient({
   - link: new HttpLink({
   -   uri: API_URL,
   - }),
   + link: httpLink,
    cache,
   });
   ```

```
const App = () => (
  ...
```

3. After this, you can use the `setContext()` method to extend the headers that are being sent to the GraphQL server so that you can also include the token that can be retrieved from the persistent storage. This method should be used asynchronously as getting an item from `AsyncStorage` is also asynchronous. The token that will be returned must be prefixed with `Bearer` as the GraphQL server expects the JWT token in that format:

```
import React from 'react';
+ import { AsyncStorage } from 'react-native';
import AppContainer from './AppContainer';
import { ApolloClient } from 'apollo-client';
import { InMemoryCache } from 'apollo-cache-inmemory';
import { setContext } from 'apollo-link-context';
import { HttpLink } from 'apollo-link-http';
import { ApolloProvider } from 'react-apollo';

const API_URL = '...';

const httpLink = new HttpLink({
  uri: API_URL,
});

+ const authLink = setContext(async (_, { headers }) => {
+   const token = await AsyncStorage.getItem('token');
+
+   return {
+     headers: {
+       ...headers,
+       authorization: token ? `Bearer ${token}` : '',
+     }
+   };
+ });

  ...
```

4. The `httpLink` that is used for the `link` field when creating the Apollo Client should now be combined with `authLink` so that the token that is retrieved from `AsyncStorage` will be added to the headers when the request is sent to the GraphQL server:

```
. . .

const cache = new InMemoryCache();

const client = new ApolloClient({
- link: httpLink,
+ link: authLink.concat(httpLink),
  cache
});

const App = () => (
    . . .
```

Now, any document is passed to the GraphQL server will be able to use the token that was retrieved by using the login form of your application—something that you'll need when a mutation is used to send a message in the next section.

Handling subscriptions in React Native with Apollo

Before you can proceed and send documents containing mutations to the GraphQL server, we need to set up Apollo so that we can handle subscriptions. For handling subscriptions, a WebSocket needs to be set up for your application, which enables a real-time two-way connection between the GraphQL server and your application. That way, you'll receive instant feedback when you, for example, send or receive a message using this mobile application.

Setting up Apollo Client for GraphQL subscriptions

To use subscriptions in your React Native application, there are more packages you need to add to the project that, for example, make it possible to add the WebSocket. These packages are as follows:

```
npm install apollo-link-ws subscriptions-transport-ws apollo-
utilities
```

The `apollo-link-ws` package helps you create a link to the GraphQL server running the subscription, like `apollo-link-http` does for queries and mutations. `subscriptions-transport-ws` is a package that is needed to run `apollo-link-ws`, while `apollo-utilities` is added to use a method that is available on those packages so that you can separate requests regarding subscriptions from requests for queries or mutations.

After installing these packages, you need to follow these steps to use subscriptions in your application:

1. You can add the creation of the link to the GraphQL server using `apollo-link-ws`. The URL to the GraphQL server should be prefixed with `ws://` instead of `http://` as it concerns a connection with a WebSocket. The URL to the GraphQL server running on your machine would look like `ws://192.168.1.107/graphql` instead of `http://192.168.1.107/graphql` and must be added to the `SOCKET_URL` constant:

```
import React from 'react';
import { AsyncStorage } from 'react-native';
import { ApolloClient } from 'apollo-client';
import { InMemoryCache } from 'apollo-cache-inmemory';
import { setContext } from 'apollo-link-context';
import { HttpLink } from 'apollo-link-http';
+ import { split } from 'apollo-link';
import { ApolloProvider } from 'react-apollo';
import AppContainer from './AppContainer';

const API_URL = '...';
+ const SOCKET_URL = 'ws://192.168.1.107/graphql';

...

+ const wsLink = new WebSocketLink({
+    uri: SOCKET_URL,
+    options: {
+       reconnect: true,
+    },
+ });

...
```

2. Using the `split` and `getMainDefinition` methods, the distinction between different requests to the GraphQL server can be made by separating queries and mutations from subscriptions. That way, only documents containing subscriptions will be sent using the WebSocket, and queries and mutations will use the default flow:

```
import React from 'react';
import { AsyncStorage } from 'react-native';
import { ApolloClient } from 'apollo-client';
import { InMemoryCache } from 'apollo-cache-inmemory';
import { setContext } from 'apollo-link-context';
import { HttpLink } from 'apollo-link-http';
import { split } from 'apollo-link';
+ import { WebSocketLink } from 'apollo-link-ws';
+ import { getMainDefinition } from 'apollo-utilities';
import { ApolloProvider } from 'react-apollo';
import AppContainer from './AppContainer';

...

+ const link = split(
+    ({ query }) => {
+      const definition = getMainDefinition(query);
+
+      return (
+        definition.kind === 'OperationDefinition' &&
definition.operation === 'subscription'
+      );
+    },
+    wsLink,
+    httpLink,
+ );

const cache = new InMemoryCache();

const client = new ApolloClient({
- link: authLink.concat(httpLink),
+ link: authLink.concat(link),
  cache,
});

const App = () => (
  ...
```

The setup for Apollo now also supports subscriptions, which you'll add in the next part of this section where the `Conversations` screen will be filled with real-time data.

Adding subscriptions to React Native

The local GraphQL server that is running on your machine supports both a query and a subscription so that you can return a conversation from a specific user. Where the query will return the full conversation, the subscription will return any new message that may have been sent or received in that conversation. At the moment, the `Conversation` screen is only sending a document with the query that will return the conversation with a user if you tap on any of the conversations displayed on the `Conversations` screen.

Subscriptions can be added to your application in multiple ways; using the `Subscription` component from `react-apollo` is the most simple one. But since you're already retrieving the conversation using the `Query` component in `client/Screens/Conversation.js`, the `Query` component can be extended to also support subscriptions:

1. The first step in adding the subscriptions to the `Conversation` screen is by splitting the screen into multiple components. You can do this by creating a new component called `ConversationBody` in the `client/Components/Conversation` directory. This file should be called `ConversationBody.js` and contain the following code:

```
import React from 'react';
import styled from 'styled-components/native';
import { Dimensions, ScrollView, FlatList } from 'react-native';
import Message from '../Message/Message';

const ConversationBodyWrapper = styled(ScrollView)`
  width: 100%;
  padding: 2%;
  display: flex;
  height: ${Dimensions.get('window').height * 0.6};
`;

const MessagesList = styled(FlatList)`
 width: 100%;
`;

const ConversationBody = ({ userName, messages }) => {
  return (
    <ConversationBodyWrapper>
      <MessagesList
        data={messages}
        keyExtractor={item => String(item.id)}
        renderItem={({ item }) => (
          <Message align={item.userName === 'me' ? 'left' :
'right'}>
```

```
          {item.text}
        </Message>
      )}
    />
  </ConversationBodyWrapper>
  );
};


export default ConversationBody;
```

2. After creating this new component, it should be imported into the
   `Conversation` screen in the `client/Screens/Conversation.js` file, where it
   can replace the `ContainerBody` component that is already present in that file.
   This also means that some imports become obsolete and that the
   `ContainerBody` styled component can be deleted as well:

   ```
   import React from 'react';
   - import { Dimensions, ScrollView, Text, FlatList, View } from
   'react-native';
   + import { Text, View } from 'react-native';
   import { Query } from 'react-apollo';
   import styled from 'styled-components/native';
   - import Message from '../Components/Message/Message';
   + import ConversationBody from
   '../Components/Conversation/ConversationBody';
   import { GET_CONVERSATION } from '../constants';


   ...


   const Conversation = ({ navigation }) => {
     const userName = navigation.getParam('userName', '');

     return (
       <ConversationWrapper>
         <Query query={GET_CONVERSATION} variables={{ userName }}>
   -         <ConversationBody>
             {(({ loading, data }) => {
               if (loading) {
                 return
   <ConversationBodyText>Loading...</ConversationBodyText>;
               }
               const { messages } = data.conversation;

   -             return (
   -               <MessagesList
   -                 data={messages}
   -                 keyExtractor={item => String(item.id)}
   ```

```
-                   renderItem={(({ item }) => (
-                     <Message align={item.userName === 'me' ? 'left' :
'right'}>
-                       {item.text}
-                     </Message>
-                   )}
-                 />
-               );
-             }}

+           return <ConversationBody messages={messages}
userName={userName} />
            }}
-         </ConversationBody>
        </Query>
        <ConversationActions userName={userName} />
      </ConversationWrapper>
    );
  };

  export default Conversation;
```

3. Now, the logic for retrieving the subscription can be added to the `Query`
   component, by getting the `subscribeToMore` method from it. This method
   should be passed to the `ConversationBody` component, where it will be called
   and thereby retrieve any new messages that are sent or received in the
   conversation:

```
  ...
  return (
    <ConversationWrapper>
      <Query query={GET_CONVERSATION} variables={{ userName }}>
-       {(({ loading, data }) => {
+       {(({ subscribeToMore, loading, data }) => {
          if (loading) {
            return
<ConversationBodyText>Loading...</ConversationBodyText>;
          }
          const { messages } = data.conversation;

-         return <ConversationBody messages={messages}
userName={userName} />
+         return (
+           <ConversationBody
+             messages={messages}
+             userName={userName}
+             subscribeToMore={subscribeToMore}
```

```
+              />
    }}
  </Query>
  <ConversationActions userName={userName} />
</ConversationWrapper>
);
};
```

4. In the `ConversationBody` component, the `subscribeToMore` method can now be used to retrieve any new messages that are added to the conversation, by using a subscription. The subscription to use is called MESSAGES_ADDED and can be found in the `client/constants.js` file. It takes `userName` as a variable:

```
import React from 'react';
import styled from 'styled-components/native';
import { Dimensions, ScrollView, FlatList } from 'react-native';
import Message from '../Message/Message';
+ import { MESSAGE_ADDED } from '../../constants';

...

- const ConversationBody = ({ userName, messages }) => {
+ const ConversationBody = ({ subscribeToMore, userName, messages
}) => {
    return (
      <ConversationBodyWrapper>
        <MessagesList
          data={messages}
          keyExtractor={item => String(item.id)}
          renderItem={({ item }) => (
            <Message align={item.userName === 'me' ? 'left' :
'right'}>
                {item.text}
            </Message>
          )}
        />
    </ConversationBodyWrapper>
  );
};

export default ConversationBody;
```

5. After importing the subscription and destructuring the `subscribeToMore` method from the props, the logic for retrieving the subscription can be added. Calling `subscribeToMore` should be done from a `useEffect` Hook and only when the `ConversationBody` component first mounts. Any newly added messages will cause the `Query` component to rerender, which makes the `ConversationBody` component rerender as well, so it isn't necessary to check for any updates in the `useEffect` Hook:

```
...
const ConversationBody = ({ subscribeToMore, userName, messages })
=> {
+  React.useEffect(() => {
+    subscribeToMore({
+      document: MESSAGE_ADDED,
+      variables: { userName },
+      updateQuery: (previous, { subscriptionData }) => {
+        if (!subscriptionData.data) {
+          return previous;
+        }
+        const messageAdded = subscriptionData.data.messageAdded;
+
+        return Object.assign({}, previous, {
+          conversation: {
+            ...previous.conversation,
+            messages: [...previous.conversation.messages,
messageAdded]
+          }
+        });
+      }
+    });
+  }, []);

   return (
   <ConversationBodyWrapper>

   ...
```

The `subscribeToMore` method will now check for any new messages by using the MESSAGES_ADDED subscription, and the results from that subscription will be added to the `Query` component on an object called `previous`. The local GraphQL server will return a new message every few seconds, so you can see that the subscription is working by opening a conversation and waiting for new messages to appear in that conversation.

Besides queries, you also want to be able to send real-time subscriptions as well. This will be addressed in the final part of this section.

Using mutations with subscriptions

Apart from using a subscription to receive messages in a conversation, they can also be used to display the messages you send yourself. Previously, you used the `refetchQueries` prop on a `Mutation` component to resend documents with any queries that would have been affected by the mutation you've executed. By using subscriptions, you no longer have to refetch, for example, the conversation query, as the subscription will get the new message you've just sent and add it to the query.

In the previous section, you used a `Query` component from `react-apollo` to send a document to the GraphQL server, while in this section, the new React Apollo Hooks will be used.

The React Apollo Hooks can be used from the `react-apollo` package, but if you only want to use the Hooks, you can install `@apollo/react-hooks` instead by executing `npm install @apollo/react-hooks`. The GraphQL components such as `Query` or `Mutation` are available in both the `react-apollo` and `@apollo/react-components` packages. Using these packages will decrease the size of your bundle as you're only importing the features you need.

The Hooks from this package must be used in the `ConversationActions` component. This is used in the `Conversation` screen component, which will consist of the input field to type a message and a button to send the message. When you press this button, nothing will happen as the button isn't connected to a mutation. Let's connect this button and see how the subscription will also display the message you've sent:

1. The `useMutation` Hook should be imported into the `client/Components/Conversation/ConversationActions.js` file, which will be used to send the message from the input field to the GraphQL server. The mutation that will be included in the document that you sent must also be imported and is called `SEND_MESSAGE`; this can be found in the `client/constants.js` file:

```
import React from 'react';
import { Platform, Text, View } from 'react-native';
import styled from 'styled-components/native';
import { Ionicons } from '@expo/vector-icons';
+ import { useMutation } from 'react-apollo';
import TextInput from '../TextInput/TextInput';
import Button from '../Button/Button';
+ import { SEND_MESSAGE } from '../../constants';
```

```
    ...

    const ConversationActions = ({ userName }) => {
      ...
```

2. This `useMutation` Hook can now be used to wrap the `TextInput` and `Button` components, and the `sendMessage` prop from the Hook can be used to send a document with the message to the GraphQL server. The value for `TextInput` is controlled by the `setMessage` function that was created by the `useState` Hook, and this function can be used to clear `TextInput` after the mutation is sent:

```
    ...
    const ConversationActions = ({ userName }) => {
  +   const [sendMessage] = useMutation(SEND_MESSAGE);
      const [message, setMessage] = React.useState('');

      return (
        <ConversationActionsWrapper>
  +       <>
            <TextInput
              width={75}
              marginBottom={0}
              onChangeText={setMessage}
              placeholder='Your message'
              value={message}
            />
            <Button
              width={20}
              padding={10}
  +           onPress={() => {
  +             sendMessage({ variables: { to: userName, text: message
      } });
  +             setMessage('');
  +           }}
              title={
                <Ionicons
                  name={`${Platform.OS === 'ios' ? 'ios' : 'md'}-send`}
                  size={42}
                  color='white'
                />
              }
            />
  +       </>
  +     </ConversationActionsWrapper>
      );
    };
```

Sending a message by typing a value into the text field and pressing the send button afterward will now update the conversation with the message you've just sent. But you might notice that this component is getting lost behind the keyboard, depending on the size of the screen of your mobile device. This behavior can easily be avoided by using the KeyboardAvoidingView component from react-native. This component will make sure that the input field is being displayed outside the area of the keyboard.

3. The KeyboardAvoidingView component can be imported from react-native and used to replace the View component that is currently being styled into the ConversationsActionsWrapper component:

```
import React from 'react';
- import { Platform, Text, View } from 'react-native';
+ import { Platform, Text, KeyboardAvoidingView } from 'react-
native';
import styled from 'styled-components/native';
import { Ionicons } from '@expo/vector-icons';
import { useMutation } from 'react-apollo';
import TextInput from '../TextInput/TextInput';
import Button from '../Button/Button';
import { SEND_MESSAGE } from '../../constants';

- const ConversationActionsWrapper = styled(View)`
+ const ConversationActionsWrapper = styled(KeyboardAvoidingView)`
    width: 100%;
    background-color: #ccc;
    padding: 2%;
    display: flex;
    flex-direction: row;
    align-items: center;
    justify-content: space-around;
`;

const ConversationActions = ({ userName }) => {

  ...
```

4. Depending on which platform your mobile device is running on, the
KeyboardAvoidingView component still might not display the input field
outside the keyboard area. However, the KeyboardAvoidingView component
can be customized using the keyboardVerticalOffset and behavior props.
For iOS and Android, the values for these props should be different; in general,
Android needs a smaller offset than iOS. In this situation,
keyboardVerticalOffset must be set to 190 for iOS and to 140 for Android,
and the behavior of the component for both platforms must be set to padding:

```
...

const ConversationActions = ({ userName }) => {
  const [sendMessage] = useMutation(SEND_MESSAGE);
  const [message, setMessage] = React.useState('');
  return (
-     <ConversationActionsWrapper
+     <ConversationActionsWrapper
+       keyboardVerticalOffset={Platform.OS === 'ios' ? 190 : 140}
+       behavior=;padding'
+     >
        <Mutation mutation={SEND_MESSAGE}>
          ...
```

 KeyboardAvoidingView might not work as expected on the Android
Studio emulator or on devices running Android, as there are a lot of
different possible screen sizes for devices that can run the Android
operating system.

When you press the input field, the keyboard will no longer be hidden behind the keyboard
and you should be able to type and send a message that will send a document with a
mutation to the GraphQL server. Your message will also appear in the conversation that
was being displayed previously.

Summary

In this chapter, you built a mobile messaging application that can be used to send and receive messages from a GraphQL server. The messages are received in real time as GraphQL subscriptions were used to receive the messages through a WebSocket. Also, a mobile authentication flow was added, meaning users should be logged in to send and receive messages. For this, `AsyncStorage` was used to store the JWT token returned by the GraphQL server in persistent storage.

The project you've built in this chapter was pretty challenging, but the project you'll create in the next chapter will be even more advanced. So far, you've handled most of the core features for a React Native mobile application, but there's more to come. The next chapter will explore how to build a full stack application with React Native and GraphQL as you'll be adding notifications and more to a social media application.

Further reading

For more information about what was covered in this chapter, check out the following resources:

- WebSockets: `https://developer.mozilla.org/en-US/docs/Web/API/WebSocket`
- Apollo React Hooks: `https://www.apollographql.com/docs/react/api/react-hooks/`

Build a Full Stack Social Media Application with React Native and GraphQL

By now, you can almost call yourself an expert with React Native, as you're about to start working on the most complex application of the React Native sections. A great advantage of mobile applications is that you can send direct notifications to the people that have your application installed. That way, you can target users when there's an important event taking place in your application or when someone hasn't used the application for a while. Also, mobile applications can directly use the camera of the device it's running on to take photos and videos.

In the previous chapter, you created a mobile messaging application that has an authentication flow and real-time data and uses GraphQL with React Native. These patterns and techniques will also be used in this chapter to create a mobile social media application that lets you post images to a social feed and allows you to star and comment on these posts. Not only will using the camera be an important section in this chapter, but you'll also add the possibility to send notifications to the user with Expo.

The following topics will be covered in this chapter:

- Using the camera with React Native and Expo
- Refreshing data with React Native and GraphQL
- Sending mobile notifications with Expo

Project overview

A mobile social media application that is using a local GraphQL server to request and add posts to the social feed, including using the camera on the mobile device. Basic authentication is added using the local GraphQL server and React Navigation, while Expo is used for access to the camera (roll) and for sending notifications when new comments are added to your posts.

The build time is 2 hours.

Getting started

The project that we'll create in this chapter builds upon an initial version that you can find on GitHub: `https://github.com/PacktPublishing/React-Projects/tree/ch11-initial`. The complete source code can also be found on GitHub: `https://github.com/PacktPublishing/React-Projects/tree/ch11`.

You need to have the application Expo Client installed on a mobile iOS or Android device to run the project on a physical device.

It's **highly recommended** to use the Expo Client application to run the project from this chapter on a physical device. Receiving notifications is currently only supported on physical devices, and running the project on either the iOS simulator or Android Studio emulator will result in error messages.

Alternatively, you can install either Xcode or Android Studio on your computer to run the application on a virtual device:

- **For iOS**: Information on how to set up your local machine to run the iOS simulator can be found here: `https://docs.expo.io/versions/v36.0.0/workflow/ios-simulator/`.
- **For Android**: Information on how to set up your local machine to run the emulator from Android Studio can be found here: `https://docs.expo.io/versions/v36.0.0/workflow/android-studio-emulator/`. There's a known issue when running the emulator, which can be prevented by ensuring that the following lines are present in your `~/.bash_profile` or `~/.bash_rc` file:

  ```
  export ANDROID_SDK=ANDROID_SDK_LOCATION
  export PATH=ANDROID_SDK_LOCATION/platform-tools:$PATH
  export PATH=ANDROID_SDK_LOCATION/tools:$PATH
  ```

The value for `ANDROID_SDK_LOCATION` is the path to the Android SDK on your local machine and can be found by opening Android Studio and going to **Preferences** | **Appearance & Behavior** | **System Settings** | **Android SDK**. The path is listed in the box that states the Android SDK location and looks like this: `/Users/myuser/Library/Android/sdk`.

 This application was created using **Expo SDK version 33.0.0,** and so, you need to ensure that the version of Expo you're using on your local machine is similar. As React Native and Expo are frequently updated, make sure that you're working with this version so that the patterns described in this chapter behave as expected. In case your application doesn't start or if you encounter errors, refer to the Expo documentation to learn more about updating the Expo SDK.

Checking out the initial project

This project consists of two parts, a boilerplate React Native application and a GraphQL server. The React Native application can be found in the `client` directory, while the GraphQL server is placed in the `server` directory. For this chapter, you'll need to have both the application and the server running at all times, while you only make code changes to the application in the `client` directory.

To get started you'll need to run the following command in both the `client` and `server` directories to install all of the dependencies and start both the server and application:

```
npm install && npm start
```

For the mobile application, this command will start Expo after installing the dependencies, and it gives you the ability to start your project both from the Terminal or your browser. In the Terminal, you can now either use the QR code to open the application on your mobile device or open the application in a simulator.

The local GraphQL server for this project is running on `http://localhost:4000/graphql/`, but to be able to use this endpoint in the React Native application, you need to find the local IP address of your machine.

To find your local IP address, you'll need to do the following depending on your operating system:

- **For Windows**: Open the Terminal (or command prompt) and run this command:

  ```
  ipconfig
  ```

  This will return a list like the one you see below with data from your local machine. In this list, you need to look for the field **IPv4 Address**:

```
Windows IP Configuration


Ethernet adapter Ethernet0:

   Connection-specific DNS Suffix  . :
   IPv6 Address. . . . . . . . . . . : 2a02:2f01:5060:9cb:3499:3b63:e8ab:5967
   Temporary IPv6 Address. . . . . . : 2a02:2f01:5060:9cb:e9d9:4dbb:4ddc:a934
   Link-local IPv6 Address . . . . . : fe80::3499:3b63:e8ab:5967%4
   IPv4 Address. . . . . . . . . . . : 192.168.1.107
   Subnet Mask . . . . . . . . . . . : 255.255.255.0
   Default Gateway . . . . . . . . . : fe80::1eb7:2cff:fe74:fef8%4
                                       192.168.1.1

Tunnel adapter Teredo Tunneling Pseudo-Interface:

   Connection-specific DNS Suffix  . :
   IPv6 Address. . . . . . . . . . . : 2001:0:9d38:90d7:285a:3873:3f57:fe94
   Link-local IPv6 Address . . . . . : fe80::285a:3873:3f57:fe94%13
   Default Gateway . . . . . . . . . :
```

- **For macOS**: Open the Terminal and run this command:

  ```
  ipconfig getifaddr en0
  ```

  After running this command, the local `Ipv4 Address` of your machine gets returned, which looks like this:

  ```
  192.168.1.107
  ```

  The local IP address must be used to create the value for `API_URL` in the file `client/App.js`, with the prefix `http://` and suffix `/graphql`, making it look like `http://192.168.1.107/graphql`:

  ```
  ...

  - const API_URL = '';
  + const API_URL = 'http://192.168.1.107/graphql';
  ```

```
const httpLink = new HttpLink({
  uri: API_URL,
});
const authLink = setContext(async (_, { headers }) => {

    ...
```

No matter whether you've opened the application from virtual or physical device, the application at this point should look something like this:

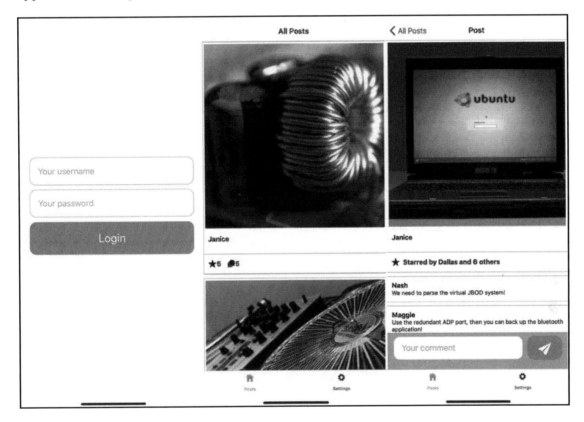

This application was created using **Expo SDK version 33.0.0** and therefore you need to make sure the version of Expo you're using on your local machine is similar. As React Native and Expo are updated frequently, make sure that you're working with this version to ensure the patterns described in this chapter are behaving as expected. If your application won't start or you're receiving errors, make sure to check the Expo documentation to learn more about updating the Expo SDK.

The initial application consists of seven screens: AddPost, AuthLoading, Login, Notifications, Post, Posts, and Settings. The Login screen will be the first screen you'll see when first starting the application, where you can log in using the following credentials:

- **Username**: test
- **Password**: test

The Posts screen will be the initial screen when logged in and shows a list of posts on which you can tap to continue to the Post screen, while the Settings screens shows a non-functioning logout button. For now, the AddPost and Notification screens aren't visible yet, as you'll add the routing to these screens later on in this chapter.

The project structure from this React Native application in the directory client is as follows, where the structure is similar to the projects you've created before in this book:

```
messaging
|-- client
    |-- .expo
    |-- assets
        |-- icon.png
        |-- splash.png
    |-- Components
        |-- // ...
    |-- node_modules
    |-- Screens
        |-- AddPost.js
        |-- AuthLoading.js
        |-- Login.js
        |-- Notifications.js
        |-- Post.js
        |-- Posts.js
        |-- Settings.js
    |-- .watchmanconfig
    |-- App.js
    |-- AppContainer.js
    |-- app.json
    |-- babel.config.js
    |-- package.json
```

In the assets directory, you can find the images that are used as the application icon on the home screen once you've installed this application on your mobile device, and the image that will serve as the splash screen that is displayed when you start the application. For example, configurations in the App Store for the name of your application are placed in app.json, while babel.config.js holds specific Babel configurations.

The `App.js` file is the actual entry point of your application, where the `AppContainer.js` file is being imported and returned. In `AppContainer`, all of the routes for this application are defined and `AppContext` will contain information that should be available in the entire application.

All of the components for this application are located in the `Screens` and `Components` directories, where the first one holds the components that are rendered by the screens. The child components for these screens can be found in the `Components` directory, which has the following structure:

```
|-- Components
    |-- Button
        |-- Button.js
    |-- Comment
        |-- Comment.js
        |-- CommentForm.js
    |-- Notification
        |-- Notification.js
    |-- Post
        |-- PostContent.js
        |-- PostCount.js
        |-- PostItem.js
    |-- TextInput
        |-- TextInput.js
```

The GraphQL server can be found at the `http://localhost:4000/graphql` URL, where GraphQL Playground will be visible. From this playground, you can view the schema for the GraphQL server and inspect all of the available queries, mutations, and subscriptions. Although you won't be making any code changes to the server, it's important to know about the schema and its workings.

The server has two queries to retrieve a list of posts or a single post by using the `userName` parameter as the identifier. These queries will return the `Post` type that has `id`, `userName`, `image`, a counted value of `stars` and `comments`, a list of stars of the `stars` type, and a list of `comments` with the `Comment` type. The query to retrieve a single post will look like this:

```
export const GET_POST = gql`
  query getPost($userName: String!) {
    post(userName: $userName) {
      id
      userName
      image
      stars {
        userName
```

```
      }
      comments {
        id
        userName
        text
      }
    }
  }
`;
```

After this, three mutations can be found for the GraphQL server, which are to either log in the user, store a push token from Expo, or add a post.

 If you're receiving an error stating `Please provide (valid) authentication details`, you'll need to log in to the application again. Probably, the JWT from the previous application is still available in `AsyncStorage` of Expo, and this will not validate on the GraphQL server for this chapter.

Building a full stack social media application with React Native, Apollo, and GraphQL

The application that you're going to build in this chapter will use a local GraphQL server to retrieve and mutate data that is available in the application. This application will display data from a social media feed and let you respond to these social media posts.

Using the camera with React Native and Expo

Next to displaying the posts that were created by the GraphQL server, you can also add a post yourself using a GraphQL mutation and send a text and an image as variables. Uploading images to your React Native application can be done by using either the camera to take an image or by selecting an image from your camera roll. For both use cases, there are APIs available from React Native and Expo, or numerous packages that are installable from npm. For this project, you'll use the ImagePicker API from Expo, which combines these functionalities into just one component.

To add the feature to create new posts to your social media application, the following changes need to be made to create the new screen to add the post:

1. The GraphQL mutation that can be used to add a post to the feed you see in the `Main` screen sends the image variable to the GraphQL server. This mutation has the following form:

```
mutation {
  addPost(image: String!) {
    image
  }
}
```

The `image` variable is `String` and is the URL to the absolute path of the image for this post. This GraphQL mutation needs to be added to the bottom of the `client/constants.js` file so it can be used from a `useMutation` Hook later on:

```
export const GET_POSTS = gql`
  ...
`;

+ export const ADD_POST = gql`
+   mutation addPost($image: String!) {
+     addPost(image: $image) {
+       image
+     }
+   }
+ `;
```

2. With `Mutation` in place, the screen for adding the post must be added to `SwitchNavigator` in the `client/AppContainer.js` file. The `AddPost` screen component can be found in the `client/Screens/AddPost.js` file and should be added as a modal in the navigator:

```
import React from 'react';
import { Platform } from 'react-native';
import { Ionicons } from '@expo/vector-icons';
import {
  createSwitchNavigator,
  createAppContainer
} from 'react-navigation';
import { createStackNavigator } from 'react-navigation-stack';
import { createBottomTabNavigator } from 'react-navigation-tabs';
import Posts from './Screens/Posts';
import Post from './Screens/Post';
import Settings from './Screens/Settings';
```

```
  import Login from './Screens/Login';
  import AuthLoading from './Screens/AuthLoading';
+ import AddPost from './Screens/AddPost';
  ...

  const SwitchNavigator = createSwitchNavigator(
    {
      Main: TabNavigator,
      Login,
      AuthLoading,
+     AddPost,
    },
    {
+     mode: 'modal',
      initialRouteName: 'AuthLoading',
    },
  );

  export default createAppContainer(SwitchNavigator);
```

3. And of course, the user must be able to open this modal from somewhere in your application, for example, from the tab navigator at the bottom of the screen or the header. For this scenario, you can add the navigation link to the AddPost screen in the header—that way, the user can add a new post from the Posts screen only by tapping a link in the header. This link can be added by setting navigationOptions in the client/Screens/Posts.js file:

```
  ...

+ Posts.navigationOptions = ({ navigation}) => ({
+   headerRight: (
+     <Button onPress={() => navigation.navigate('AddPost')}
title='Add Post' />
+   ),
+ });

  export default Posts;
```

By setting the headerRight field in navigationOptions, only the right part of the header will be changed and the title that has been set from the navigator will keep in place. Tapping the Add Post link will now navigate to the AddPost screen, where a title and button to close the modal are displayed.

As you've now added the `AddPost` screen, the ImagePicker API from Expo should be added to this screen. To add `ImagePicker` to the `AddPost` screen, follow the next steps to enable the selection of photos from the camera roll in the `client/Screens/AddPost.js` file:

1. Before the user can select photos from the camera roll, the right permission should be set for the application when the user is using an iOS device. To request permissions, you can use the permissions API from Expo, which should request `CAMERA_ROLL` permissions. The permissions API used to be available directly from Expo, but has been moved to a separate package called `expo-permissions` that can be installed from the Expo CLI by running this:

   ```
   expo install expo-permissions
   ```

2. After this, you can import the permissions API and create the function to check whether the right permissions have been granted for the camera roll:

   ```
   import React from 'react';
   import { Dimensions, TouchableOpacity, Text, View } from 'react-native';
   + import { Dimensions, Platform, TouchableOpacity, Text, View } from 'react-native';
   import styled from 'styled-components/native';
   import Button from '../Components/Button/Button';
   + import * as Permissions from 'expo-permissions';


   ...


   const AddPost = ({ navigation }) => {
   +   const getPermissionAsync = async () => {
   +     if (Platform.OS === 'ios') {
   +       const { status } = await Permissions.askAsync(Permissions.CAMERA_ROLL);
   +
   +       if (status !== 'granted') {
   +         alert('Sorry, you need camera roll permissions! Go to 'Settings > Expo' to enable these.');
   +       }
   +     }
   +   };


     ...
   ```

3. This `getPermissionAsync` function is asynchronous and can be called from a `Button` or `Touchable` element. At the bottom of this file, the `UploadImage` component can be found, which is a styled `TouchableOpacity` element that can take an `onPress` function. This component must be added to the return function of `AddPost` and should call the `getPermissionAsync` function when tapped:

```
. . .

const AddPost = ({ navigation }) => {
  const getPermissionAsync = async () => {
    if (Platform.OS === 'ios') {
      const { status } = await
Permissions.askAsync(Permissions.CAMERA_ROLL);

      if (status !== 'granted') {
        alert('Sorry, you need camera roll permissions! Go to
'Settings > Expo' to enable these.');
      }
    }
  };

  return (
    <AddPostWrapper>
      <AddPostText>Add Post</AddPostText>

+     <UploadImage onPress={() => getPermissionAsync()}>
+       <AddPostText>Upload image</AddPostText>
+     </UploadImage>

      <Button onPress={() => navigation.navigate('Main')}
title='Cancel' />
    </AddPostWrapper>
  );
};

. . .
```

When tapped, a popup requesting permission to access the camera roll will be opened on iOS devices. When you don't accept the request, you can't select photos from the camera roll.

TIP You can't ask the user for permission a second time; instead, you'd need to manually grant the permission to the camera roll. To set this permission again, you should go to the setting screen from iOS and select the Expo application. On the next screen, you're able to add the permission to access the camera.

4. When the user has granted permission to access the camera roll, you can call the ImagePicker API from Expo to open the camera roll. Just like the permissions API, this used to be part of Expo's core, but has now been moved to a separate package that you can install using the Expo CLI:

```
expo install expo-image-picker
```

This is again an asynchronous function that takes some configuration fields such as the aspect ratio. If the user has selected an image, the ImagePicker API will return an object containing the field URI, which is the URL to the image on the users' device that can be used in an Image component. This result can be stored in a local state by creating one with the useState Hook, so it can be sent to the GraphQL server later on:

```
import React from 'react';
import { Dimensions, Platform, TouchableOpacity, Text, View } from
'react-native';
import styled from 'styled-components/native';
import Button from '../Components/Button/Button';
+ import * as ImagePicker from 'expo-image-picker';
import * as Permissions from 'expo-permissions';

...

const AddPost = ({ navigation }) => {
+   const [imageUrl, setImageUrl] = React.useState(false);

+   const pickImageAsync = async () => {
+     const result = await ImagePicker.launchImageLibraryAsync({
+       mediaTypes: ImagePicker.MediaTypeOptions.All,
+       allowsEditing: true,
+       aspect: [4, 4],
+     });
+     if (!result.cancelled) {
+       setImageUrl(result.uri);
+     }
+   };

    return (
      ...
```

And this `pickImageAsync` function can then be called from the function to get the users' permissions when they've been granted for the camera roll:

```
. . .

const AddPost = ({ navigation }) => {
  . . .

  const getPermissionAsync = async () => {
    if (Platform.OS === 'ios') {
      const { status } = await
Permissions.askAsync(Permissions.CAMERA_ROLL);

      if (status !== 'granted') {
        alert('Sorry, you need camera roll permissions! Go to
'Settings > Expo' to enable these.');
+      } else {
+        pickImageAsync();
      }
    }
  };

  return (
```

5. As the URL to the image is now stored in the local state to the `imageUrl` constant, you can display this URL in an `Image` component. This `Image` component takes `imageUrl` as value for the source and has been set to use a 100% `width` and `height`:

```
  . . .

  return (
    <AddPostWrapper>
      <AddPostText>Add Post</AddPostText>

      <UploadImage onPress={() => getPermissionAsync()}>
+        {imageUrl ? (
+          <Image
+            source={{ uri: imageUrl }}
+            style={{ width: '100%', height: '100%' }}
+          />
+        ) : (
            <AddPostText>Upload image</AddPostText>
+        )}
      </UploadImage>

      <Button onPress={() => navigation.navigate('Main')}
```

```
    title='Cancel' />
      </AddPostWrapper>
    );
  };
```

```
  ...
```

With these changes, the `AddPost` screen should look something like the following screenshot, which was taken from a device running iOS. There might be slight differences in the appearance of this screen if you're using the Android Studio emulator or a device that runs Android:

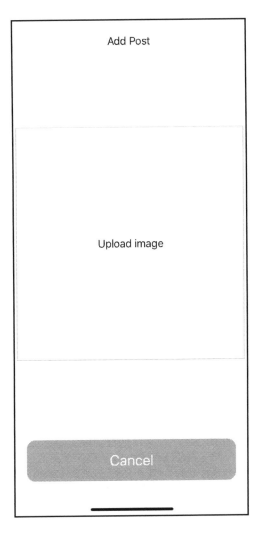

These changes will make it possible to select a photo from your camera roll, but your users should also be able to upload an entirely new photo by using their camera. With the ImagePicker from Expo, you can handle both scenarios, as this component also has a `launchCameraAsync` method. This asynchronous function will launch the camera, and return it the same way as it returns a URL to the image from the camera roll.

To add the functionality to directly use the camera on the user's device to upload an image, you can make the following changes:

1. As the user needs to grant your application permission to access the camera roll, the user needs to do the same for using the camera. Permission to use the camera can be requested by sending `Permissions.CAMERA` with the `Permissions.askAsync` method. The check for the granted permission for the camera roll must be extended to also check for the camera permission:

```
...

  const getPermissionAsync = async () => {
    if (Platform.OS === 'ios') {
-     const { status } = await
Permissions.askAsync(Permissions.CAMERA_ROLL);
-     if (status !== 'granted') {
+       const { status: statusCamera } = await
Permissions.askAsync(Permissions.CAMERA);
+       const { status: statusCameraRoll } = await
Permissions.askAsync(Permissions.CAMERA_ROLL);

+       if (statusCamera !== 'granted' || statusCameraRoll !==
'granted') {
        alert(
          `Sorry, you need camera roll permissions! Go to 'Settings
> Expo' to enable these.`
        );
      } else {
        pickImageAsync();
      }
    }
  };

  return (
    ...
```

This will ask the user for permission to use the camera on iOS, which can also be granted manually by going to **Settings | Expo**.

2. With the permission granted, you can continue by creating the function to launch the camera by calling `launchCameraAsync` from `ImagePicker`. The functionality is the same as for the `launchCameraAsync` function that you created to open the camera roll; therefore, the `pickImageAsync` function can be edited to also be able to launch the camera:

```
const AddPost = ({ navigation }) => {
  const [imageUrl, setImageUrl] = React.useState(false);
- const pickImageAsync = async () => {
+ const addImageAsync = async (camera = false) => {
-   const result = await ImagePicker.launchCameraAsync({
-     mediaTypes: ImagePicker.MediaTypeOptions.All,
-     allowsEditing: true,
-     aspect: [4, 4]
-   });

+   const result = !camera
+     ? await ImagePicker.launchImageLibraryAsync({
+         mediaTypes: ImagePicker.MediaTypeOptions.All,
+         allowsEditing: true,
+         aspect: [4, 4]
+       })
+     : await ImagePicker.launchCameraAsync({
+         allowsEditing: true,
+         aspect: [4, 4]
+       })
    if (!result.cancelled) {
      setImageUrl(result.uri);
    }
  };
```

If you now send a parameter to the `addImageAsync` function, `launchCameraAsync` will be called. Otherwise, the user will be directed to the camera roll on their device.

3. When the user clicks on the image placeholder, the image roll will be opened by default. But you also want to give the user the option to use their camera. Therefore, a selection must be made between using the camera or the camera roll for uploading the image, which is a perfect use case for implementing an ActionSheet component. React Native and Expo both have an ActionSheet component; it's advisable to use the one from Expo as it will use the native UIActionSheet component on iOS and a JavaScript implementation for Android. The ActionSheet component is available from Expo's react-native-action-sheet package, which you can install from npm:

```
npm install @expo/react-native-action-sheet
```

After this, you need to wrap your top-level component in the client/App.js file with Provider from the package, which is comparable to adding ApolloProvider:

```
import React from 'react';
import { AsyncStorage } from 'react-native';
import { ApolloClient } from 'apollo-client';
import { InMemoryCache } from 'apollo-cache-inmemory';
import { setContext } from 'apollo-link-context';
import { HttpLink } from 'apollo-link-http';
import { ApolloProvider } from '@apollo/react-hooks';
+ import { ActionSheetProvider } from '@expo/react-native-action-sheet';
import AppContainer from './AppContainer';

...

const App = () => (
  <ApolloProvider client={client}>
+    <ActionSheetProvider>
      <AppContainer />
+    </ActionSheetProvider>
  </ApolloProvider>
);

export default App;
```

And create `ActionSheet` in `client/Screens/AddPost.js` by importing the `connectActionSheet` function from `react-native-action-sheet`, which needs to wrap the `AddPost` component before you export it. Wrapping the `AddPost` component with `connectActionSheet()` adds the `showActionSheetWithOptions` prop to the component, which you'll use in the next step to create `ActionSheet`:

```
import React from 'react';
import {
  Dimensions,
  Image,
  Platform,
  TouchableOpacity,
  Text,
  View
} from 'react-native';
import styled from 'styled-components/native';
import * as ImagePicker from 'expo-image-picker';
import * as Permissions from 'expo-permissions';
+ import { connectActionSheet } from '@expo/react-native-action-
sheet';
import Button from '../Components/Button/Button';


...

- const AddPost = ({ navigation }) => {
+ const AddPost = ({ navigation, showActionSheetWithOptions }) => {
    ...

- export default AddPost;
+ const ConnectedApp = connectActionSheet(AddPost);
+ export default ConnectedApp;
```

4. To add `ActionSheet`, a function to open this `ActionSheet` must be added, and by using the `showActionSheetWithOptions` prop and the options, `ActionSheet` should be constructed. The options are `Camera`, `Camera roll`, and `Cancel`, where selecting the first option should call the `addImageAsync` function with a parameter, the second should call that function without a parameter, and the last option is to close `ActionSheet`. The function to open `ActionSheet` must be added to the `getPermissionsAsync` function and be called when the permissions for both `Camera` and `Camera roll` are granted:

```
   ...

+  const openActionSheet = () => {
+    const options = ['Camera', 'Camera roll', 'Cancel'];
+    const cancelButtonIndex = 2;
+
+    showActionSheetWithOptions(
+      {
+        options,
+        cancelButtonIndex
+      },
+      buttonIndex => {
+        if (buttonIndex === 0 || buttonIndex === 1) {
+          addImageAsync(buttonIndex === 0);
+        }
+      },
+    );
+  };

   const getPermissionAsync = async () => {
     if (Platform.OS === 'ios') {
       const { status: statusCamera } = await
Permissions.askAsync(Permissions.CAMERA);
       const { status: statusCameraRoll } = await
Permissions.askAsync(Permissions.CAMERA_ROLL);

       if (statusCamera !== 'granted' || statusCameraRoll !==
'granted') {
         alert(
           `Sorry, you need camera roll permissions! Go to 'Settings
> Expo' to enable these.`
         );
       } else {
-        pickImageAsync();
+        openActionSheet();
       }
```

```
        }
    };

    return (
        ...
```

Tapping the image placeholder will give the user the option to either use `Camera` or `Camera roll` to add an image to the `AddPost` component. This can be done from `ActionSheet`, which will look different on iOS and Android. In the following screenshot, you can see what this will look like when using the iOS simulator or a device that runs on iOS:

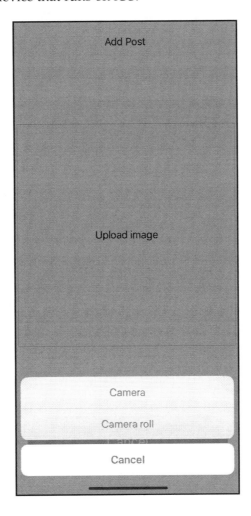

5. This, however, is not all as the image must still be sent to the server to appear in the feed of the application, by adding a `useMutation` Hook from `@apollo/react-hooks` and using the returned `addPost` function to send the `imageUrl` variable in a document to the GraphQL server. The mutation to add the post has been mentioned at the beginning of this section and can be imported from the `client/constants.js` file:

```
import React from 'react';
import {
  Dimensions,
  Image,
  Platform,
  TouchableOpacity,
  Text,
  View
} from 'react-native';
import styled from 'styled-components/native';
import * as ImagePicker from 'expo-image-picker';
import * as Permissions from 'expo-permissions';
import { connectActionSheet } from '@expo/react-native-action-
sheet';
+ import { useMutation } from '@apollo/react-hooks';
+ import { ADD_POST } from '../constants';
import Button from '../Components/Button/Button';

...

const AddPost = ({ navigation, showActionSheetWithOptions }) => {
+ const [addPost] = useMutation(ADD_POST);
  const [imageUrl, setImageUrl] = React.useState(false);

...

  return (
    <AddPostWrapper>
      <AddPostText>Add Post</AddPostText>
        <UploadImage onPress={() => getPermissionAsync()}>
          {imageUrl ? (
            <Image
              source={{ uri: imageUrl }}
              style={{ width: '100%', height: '100%' }}
            />
          ) : (
            <AddPostText>Upload image</AddPostText>
          )}
        </UploadImage>
```

```
+         {imageUrl && (
+           <Button
+             onPress={() => {
+               addPost({ variables: { image: imageUrl } }).then(()
=>
+                 navigation.navigate('Main')
+               );
+             }}
+             title='Submit'
+           />
+         )}
          <Button onPress={() => navigation.navigate('Main')}
title='Cancel' />
        </AddPostWrapper>
      );
    };

export default AddPost;
```

The image will be added as a post after tapping the Submit button, and the user
will be redirected to the Main screen.

6. By setting a query on the refetchQueries variable to the useMutation Hook,
   the posts on the Main screen can be reloaded and the post you've just added will
   be displayed in this list. The posts can be retrieved by fetching the GET_POSTS
   query from client/constants.js:

```
import React from 'react';
import {
  Dimensions,
  Image,
  Platform,
  TouchableOpacity,
  Text,
  View
} from 'react-native';
import styled from 'styled-components/native';
import * as ImagePicker from 'expo-image-picker';
import * as Permissions from 'expo-permissions';
import { connectActionSheet } from '@expo/react-native-action-
sheet';
import { useMutation } from '@apollo/react-hooks';
- import { ADD_POST } from '../constants';
+ import { ADD_POST, GET_POSTS } from '../constants';
import Button from '../Components/Button/Button';

...
```

```
const AddPost = ({ navigation, showActionSheetWithOptions }) => {
- const [addPost] = useMutation(ADD_POST);
+ const [addPost] = useMutation(ADD_POST, {
+   refetchQueries: [{ query: GET_POSTS }]
+ });
  const [imageUrl, setImageUrl] = React.useState(false);

  ...

  return (
    <AddPostWrapper>
      ...
```

Your post will now be displayed at the top of the Main screen, meaning you've added the post successfully and other users can view, star, and comment on it. As your users might be sending posts while the application is opened, you want them to be able to receive these posts. Therefore, the next section will explore how to achieve near real-time data from GraphQL.

Retrieving near real-time data using GraphQL

Other than with the messaging application, you don't want the feed with posts to reload every time a new post has been posted by any of the people in your network. Besides subscriptions, there are other ways to have (near) real-time data flows with GraphQL and Apollo, namely, polling. With polling, you can retrieve a query from a useQuery Hook once every n milliseconds, saving you the complexity of setting up subscriptions.

Polling can be added to the useQuery Hook, like this one in client/Screens/Posts.js. By setting a pollInterval value on the object parameter from the useQuery Hook, you can specify how often the document with the GET_POSTS query should be resent by the Hook:

```
...

const Posts = ({ navigation }) => {
- const { loading, data } = useQuery(GET_POSTS);
+ const { loading, data } = useQuery(GET_POSTS, { pollInterval: 2000 });

  return (
    <PostsWrapper>
      {loading ? (
        <PostsText>Loading...</PostsText>;
      ) : (
        ...
```

This causes your `Posts` component to send a document with the `GET_POSTS` query every 2 seconds (2,000 milliseconds), and as the GraphQL server is returning mocked data, the posts that are displayed will be different on every re-fetch. In comparison to subscriptions, polling will resend the documents to retrieve the posts even when there is no new data—something that isn't very useful for an application displaying mock data or data that changes often.

Next to setting a `pollInterval` variable on the `useQuery` Hook, you can also manually call the `refetch` function that sends a document with the query. A common interaction for social media feeds is being able to pull down the displayed component to refresh the data on the screen.

This pattern can also be added to your application by making the following changes to the `Posts` screen component:

1. The `pollInterval` prop can be set to `0`, which disables the polling for now. Besides the `loading` and `data` variables, more variables can be retrieved from the `useQuery` Hook. One of those variables is the `refetch` function, which you can use to manually send the document to the server:

   ```
   . . .

   const Posts = ({ navigation }) => {
   - const { loading, data } = useQuery(GET_POSTS, { pollInterval:
   2000 });
   + const { loading, data, refetch } = useQuery(GET_POSTS, {
   pollInterval: 0 });
     return (
       <PostsWrapper>
         {loading ? (
           <PostsText>Loading...</PostsText>;
         ) : (
            . . .
   ```

2. There's a React Native component to create the pull-to-refresh interaction, which is called `RefreshControl` and which you should import from `react-native`. Also, you should import a `ScrollView` component as the `RefreshControl` component only works with either a `ScrollView` or `ListView` component:

   ```
   import React from 'react';
   import { useQuery } from '@apollo/react-hooks';
   - import { FlatList, Text, View } from 'react-native';
   + import { FlatList, Text, View, ScrollView, RefreshControl } from
   'react-native';
   import styled from 'styled-components/native';
   ```

```
import { GET_POSTS } from '../constants';
import PostItem from '../Components/Post/PostItem';


...


const Posts = ({ navigation }) => {
  ...
```

3. This `ScrollView` component should be wrapped around the `PostsList` component, which is a styled `FlatList` component that iterates over the posts created by the GraphQL server. As a value for the `refreshControl` prop, the `RefreshControl` component must be passed to this `ScrollView` and a `style` prop must be set, to lock the width to 100%, which makes sure you can only scroll vertically:

```
    const Posts = ({ navigation }) => {
      const { loading, data, refetch } = useQuery(GET_POSTS, {
    pollInterval: 0 });
      return (
        <PostsWrapper>
          {loading ? (
            <PostsText>Loading...</PostsText>;
          ) : (
+           <ScrollView
+             style={{ width: '100%' }}
+             refreshControl={
+               <RefreshControl />
+             }
+           >
              <PostsList
                data={data.posts}
                keyExtractor={item => String(item.id)}
                renderItem={({ item }) => (
                  <PostItem item={item} navigation={navigation} />
                )}
              />
+           </ScrollView>
          )}
        </PostsWrapper>
      );
    };
```

4. If you now pull down the `Posts` screen, a loading indicator will be displayed at the top of the screen that keeps spinning. With the `refreshing` prop, you can control whether or not the loading indicator should be displayed by passing a value that is created by a `useState` Hook. Besides a `refreshing` prop, the function that should be called when the refreshing starts can be passed to the `onRefresh` prop. You should pass the `refetch` function to this function, which should set the `refreshing` state variable to `true` and call the `refetch` function that was returned by the `useQuery` Hook. After the `refetch` function resolves, the callback can be used to set the `refreshing` state to `false` again:

```
...
const Posts = ({ navigation }) => {
  const { loading, data, refetch } = useQuery(GET_POSTS, {
pollInterval: 0 });
+ const [refreshing, setRefreshing] = React.useState(false);

+ const handleRefresh = (refetch) => {
+   setRefreshing(true);
+
+   refetch().then(() => setRefreshing(false));
+ }

  return (
    <PostsWrapper>
    {loading ? (
      <PostsText>Loading...</PostsText>;
    ) : (
      <ScrollView
        style={{ width: '100%' }}
        refreshControl={
-         <RefreshControl />
+         <RefreshControl
+           refreshing={refreshing}
+           onRefresh={() => handleRefresh(refetch)}
+         />
        }
      >
        <PostsList
          ...
```

5. Finally, when you pull down the `Posts` screen, the loading message returned from the `useQuery` Hook interferes with the loading indicator from `RefreshControl`. By also checking for the value of `refreshing` in the if-else statement, you can prevent this behavior:

```
. . .
const Posts = ({ navigation }) => {
  const { loading, data, refetch } = useQuery(GET_POSTS, {
pollInterval: 0 });
  const [refreshing, setRefreshing] = React.useState(false);

  const handleRefresh = (refetch) => {
    setRefreshing(true);

    refetch().then(() => setRefreshing(false));
  }

  return(
    <PostsWrapper>
-       {loading ? (
+       {loading && !refreshing ? (
        <PostsText>Loading...</PostsText>
      ) : (
        . . .
```

After these last changes, the interaction of pulling to refresh the data is implemented for the `Posts` screen, making it possible for your users to retrieve the latest data by pulling down the screen. When you're using iOS as the operating system for the virtual or physical device that runs the application, this will look something like this screenshot:

In the next section, you'll add notifications to this social media application, by using Expo and GraphQL servers.

Sending notifications with Expo

Another important feature for a mobile social media application is the ability to send users notifications of important events, for example, when their post gets starred or a friend has uploaded a new post. Sending notifications can be done with Expo and requires you to add both server- and client-side code, as the notifications are sent from the server. The client needs to retrieve a local identifier for the users' device, which is called the Expo push code. This code is needed to identify which device belongs to the user and how a notification should be sent to either iOS or Android.

 Testing notifications can only be done by using the Expo application on your mobile device. iOS and Android simulators cannot receive push notifications, as they don't run on an actual device.

Retrieving the push code is the first step in sending notifications to your users, which consists of the following steps:

1. To be able to send notifications, users should permit your application to push these notifications. To ask for this permission, the same permissions API should be used to get permission for the camera. The function to request this permission can be added in a new file called `registerForPushNotificationsAsync.js`. This file must be created in the new `client/utils` directory, in which you can paste the following code that also retrieves the push code using the Notifications API:

```
import { Notifications } from 'expo';
import * as Permissions from 'expo-permissions';

async function registerForPushNotificationsAsync() {
  const { status: existingStatus } = await Permissions.getAsync(
    Permissions.NOTIFICATIONS
  );
  let finalStatus = existingStatus;

  if (existingStatus !== 'granted') {
    const { status } = await
Permissions.askAsync(Permissions.NOTIFICATIONS);
    finalStatus = status;
  }

  if (finalStatus !== 'granted') {
    return;
  }
```

```
        const token = await Notifications.getExpoPushTokenAsync();
        return token;
    }

    export default registerForPushNotificationsAsync;
```

2. When you're using an iOS device, the
   `registerForPushNotificationAsync` function should be called when the
   application opens, as you should ask for permission. On Android devices, the
   request for whether or not a user wants you to send them notifications is sent
   during the installation process. This function should, therefore, be fired when the
   user opens the application, after which this function will return the Expo push
   token on Android or launch the popup to ask for permission on iOS. As you only
   want to ask registered users for their token, this is done in the
   `client/Screens/Posts.js` file by using an `useEffect` Hook:

```
    import React from 'react';
    import { useQuery } from '@apollo/react-hooks';
    import {
      Button,
      FlatList,
      Text,
      View,
      ScrollView,
      RefreshControl
    } from 'react-native';
    import styled from 'styled-components/native';
    import { GET_POSTS } from '../constants';
    import PostItem from '../Components/Post/PostItem';
    + import registerForPushNotificationsAsync from
    '../utils/registerForPushNotificationsAsync';

    ...

    const Posts = ({ navigation }) => {
      const { loading, data, refetch } = useQuery(GET_POSTS, {
    pollInterval: 0 });
      const [refreshing, setRefreshing] = React.useState(false);

    + React.useEffect(() => {
    +   registerForPushNotificationsAsync();
    + });

    ...
```

If you see this error, `Error: The Expo push notification service is supported only for Expo projects. Ensure you are logged in to your Expo developer account on the computer from which you are loading your project.`, it means you need to make sure you're logged in to your Expo developer account. By running `expo login` from the Terminal, you can check whether you're logged in and otherwise, it will prompt you to log in again.

3. In the Terminal, the Expo push token for this user will now be displayed, which looks like `ExponentPushToken[AABBCC123]`. This token is unique for this device and can be used to send the notification. To test how a notification will look, you can go to the `https://expo.io/dashboard/notifications` URL in the browser to find the Expo dashboard. In here, you can enter the Expo push token together with a message and a title for the notification; depending on the mobile operating system, there are different options you can select, such as the ones that follow:

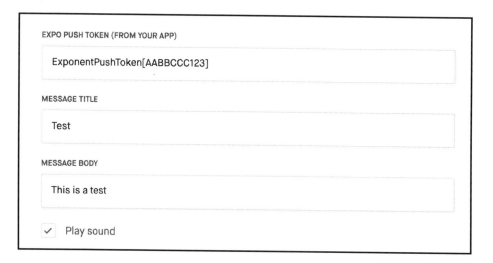

This will send a notification to your device, with the title `Test` and the body `This is a test`, and try to play a sound when the notification is sent.

However, this notification won't be visible on devices running on iOS when the application is foregrounded. So, when you're using the Expo application on an Apple device, make sure the Expo application is running in the background.

The next part of this section will show how you can also receive notifications when the application is running in the foreground.

Handling foreground notifications

Handling notifications when the application is foregrounded is more complex, and requires us to add a listener that checks for new notifications and afterward, these notifications should be stored somewhere. Expo's Notifications API has a listener available that can help you to check for new notifications, while the notifications can be stored using Apollo by having a local state. This local state extends the data returned by the GraphQL server by adding any new notifications that were found by the listener.

When the notifications are stored in the local state, this data can be queried and shown in either a component or a screen in your application. Let's create a notifications screen that will display these notifications that were sent when the application was loaded in the foreground.

Adding the support for foreground notifications requires you to make these changes:

1. The setup for Apollo Client in `client/App.js` should be extended in a way that you could query for notifications and can add new notifications when these are spotted by the listener. A new type for `Query` should be created that is called `notifications` and returns a list of the `Notification` type. Also, an initial value for this `Query` must be added in the form of an empty array that will be written to `cache`:

```
. . .

  const client = new ApolloClient({
    link: authLink.concat(link),
    cache,
+   typeDefs: `
+     type Notification {
+       id: Number!
+       title: String!
+       body: String!
+     }
+     extend type Query {
+       notifications: [Notification]!
+     }
+   `
  });

+ cache.writeData({
+   data: {
+     notifications: []
+   }
+ });
```

```
const App = () => {
    ...
```

2. Now, you're able to send a document with the query to retrieve the list of notifications including the `id`, `title`, and `body` fields. This query must also be defined in the `client/constants.js` file so it can be used from a `useQuery` Hook in the next step:

```
    ...

export const ADD_POST = gql`
  mutation addPost($image: String!) {
    addPost(image: $image) {
      image
    }
  }
`;

+ export const GET_NOTIFICATIONS = gql`
+    query getNotifications {
+      notifications {
+        id @client
+        title @client
+        body @client
+      }
+    }
+ `;
```

3. In the `client/Screens` directory, the `Notifications.js` file can be found, which must be used as the screen to display the notifications for the user. This screen component should be imported in the `client/AppContainer.js` file where a new `StackNavigator` object must be created:

```
import React from 'react';
import { Platform } from 'react-native';
import { Ionicons } from '@expo/vector-icons';
import {
  createSwitchNavigator,
  createAppContainer
} from 'react-navigation';
import { createStackNavigator } from 'react-navigation-stack';
import { createBottomTabNavigator } from 'react-navigation-tabs';
import Posts from './Screens/Posts';
import Post from './Screens/Post';
```

```
import Settings from './Screens/Settings';
import Login from './Screens/Login';
import AuthLoading from './Screens/AuthLoading';
import AddPost from './Screens/AddPost';
+ import Notifications from './Screens/Notifications';

...

+ const NotificationsStack = createStackNavigator({
+   Notifications: {
+     screen: Notifications,
+     navigationOptions: { title: 'Notifications' },
+   }
+ });
```

After `StackNavigator` for the `Notifications` screen is created, it needs to be added to `TabNavigator` so it will be displayed next to the `Posts` and `Settings` screens:

```
...

const TabNavigator = createBottomTabNavigator(
  {
    Posts: PostsStack,
+   Notifications: NotificationsStack,
    Settings
  },
  {
    initialRouteName: 'Posts',
    defaultNavigationOptions: ({ navigation }) => ({
    tabBarIcon: ({ tintColor }) => {
      const { routeName } = navigation.state;
      let iconName;
      if (routeName === 'Posts') {
        iconName = `${Platform.OS === 'ios' ? 'ios' : 'md'}-home`;
      } else if (routeName === 'Settings') {
        iconName = `${Platform.OS === 'ios' ? 'ios' : 'md'}-
settings`;
+     } else if (routeName === 'Notifications') {
+       iconName = `${Platform.OS === 'ios' ? 'ios' : 'md'}-
notifications`;
+     }

      return <Ionicons name={iconName} size={20} color={tintColor}
/>;
    },

    ...
```

4. The `Notifications` screen is now being displayed in `TabNavigator` and displays the text **Empty!** as there aren't any notifications to display. To add any notifications that have been sent to the user, you need to create a local resolver for the GraphQL client. This local resolver will be used to create `Mutation`, which can be used to add any new notifications to the local state. You create the local resolver by adding the following code to `client/App.js`:

```
. . .

import AppContainer from './AppContainer';
+ import { GET_NOTIFICATIONS } from './constants';

. . .

const client = new ApolloClient({
  link: authLink.concat(link),
  cache,
+ resolvers: {
+   Mutation: {
+     addNotification: async (_, { id, title, body }) => {
+       const { data } = await client.query({ query:
GET_NOTIFICATIONS })
+
+         cache.writeData({
+           data: {
+             notifications: [
+               ...data.notifications,
+               { id, title, body, __typename: 'notifications' },
+             ],
+           },
+         });
+       }
+     }
+ },
  typeDefs: `
    type Notification {
      id: Number!
      title: String!
      body: String!
    }
    extend type Query {
      notifications: [Notification]!
    }
  `
}));

. . .
```

This will create the `addNotification` mutation, which takes the `id`, `title`, and `body` variables and adds these values to the data for the `Notification` type. The notifications that are currently in the local state are requested using the `GET_NOTIFICATIONS` query that you created before. By calling the `query` function on the GraphQL `client` constant, you send the document containing this query to the server. Together with the notification that has been sent together with a document containing the mutation, these will be written to the local state by `cache.writeData`.

5. This mutation must be added to the `client/constants.js` file, where the other GraphQL queries and mutations are also placed. It's important to also add that `client` should be used to resolve this mutation, by using the `@client` tag:

```
. . .

export const GET_NOTIFICATIONS = gql`
  query getNotifications {
    notifications {
      id @client
      title @client
      body @client
    }
  }
`;

+ export const ADD_NOTIFICATION = gql`
+   mutation {
+     addNotification(id: $id, title: $title, body: $body) @client
+   }
+ `;
```

6. Finally, the listener from the `Notifications` API is added to the `client/App.js` file, which will look for new notifications when the application is foregrounded. New notifications are added to the local state using the preceding mutation from `client/constants.js`. The `mutate` function that is called on the client will use the information from the Expo notification and adds this to mutation; the mutation will make sure it's added to the local state by writing this information to `cache`:

```
. . .

import { ActionSheetProvider } from '@expo/react-native-action-sheet';
+ import { Notifications } from 'expo';
```

```
import AppContainer from './AppContainer';
- import { GET_NOTIFICATIONS } from './constants';
+ import { ADD_NOTIFICATIONS, GET_NOTIFICATIONS } from
'./constants';

...

const App = () => {
+ React.useEffect(() => {
+   Notifications.addListener(handleNotification);
+ });

+ const handleNotification = ({ data }) => {
+   client.mutate({
+     mutation: ADD_NOTIFICATION,
+     variables: {
+       id: Math.floor(Math.random() * 500) + 1,
+       title: data.title,
+       body: data.body,
+     },
+   });
+ };

  return (

    ...
```

In the previous code block, you cannot use the useMutation Hook to
send the ADD_NOTIFICATION mutation in a document, as React Apollo
Hooks can only be used from a component nested within
ApolloProvider. Therefore, the mutate function on the client object is
used, which also provides the functionality to send documents with
queries and mutations without using a Query or Mutation component.

7. By importing the `Notifications` API from Expo, the `handleNotification` function can access the data object from the notification that was sent. This data object is different from the message title and message body you've sent using the Expo dashboard, therefore you need to also add JSON data when sending the notification from `https://expo.io/dashboard/notifications`. A test notification can be sent by adding the body in the form:

EXPO PUSH TOKEN (FROM YOUR APP)

ExponentPushToken[AABBCC123]

MESSAGE TITLE

Test

MESSAGE BODY

This is a test

☐   Play sound

JSON DATA

{"title": "Test", "body": "This is a test"}

By submitting the form, a notification with the title `Test` and the body `This is a test` will be sent to the user when the application is foregrounded, but also when the application is running in the background.

In a mobile application that is running in production, you'd expect the notifications to be sent from the GraphQL server instead of the Expo dashboard. The local GraphQL server that is handling the data flow for this application is already configured to send notifications to the user but would need the user's Expo push token to send. This token should be stored in the server and linked to the current user, as this token is unique for this device. The token should be sent in a document to the GraphQL server from a mutation that would take the token and can get information about the user from the headers in the mutation:

1. First, the mutation that will store the Expo push token on the GraphQL server must be created in the `client/constants.js` file along with the other queries and mutations. The only variable this mutation takes is the push token, as the OAuth token that is sent with every document to the GraphQL server is used to identify the user:

```
import gql from 'graphql-tag';

export const LOGIN_USER = gql`
  mutation loginUser($userName: String!, $password: String!) {
    loginUser(userName: $userName, password: $password) {
      userName
      token
    }
  }
`;

+ export const STORE_EXPO_TOKEN = gql`
+   mutation storeExpoToken($expoToken: String!) {
+     storeExpoToken(expoToken: $expoToken) {
+       expoToken
+     }
+   }
+ `;

...
```

2. Sending the document with this mutation with the Expo push token must be done from the `client/Posts.js` file where the token is retrieved by calling the `registerForPushNotificationsAsync` function. This function will return the push token, which you can send along with the mutation's document. To send this document, the `useMutation` Hook from `@apollo/react-hooks` can be used, which you must import together with the `STORE_EXPO_TOKEN` constant:

```
import React from 'react';
- import { useQuery } from '@apollo/react-hooks';
+ import { useQuery, useMutation } from '@apollo/react-hooks';
```

. . .

```
- import { GET_POSTS } from '../constants';
+ import { GET_POSTS, STORE_EXPO_TOKEN } from '../constants';
import PostItem from '../Components/Post/PostItem';
import registerForPushNotificationsAsync from
'../utils/registerForPushNotificationsAsync';
```

. . .

Before React Apollo Hooks were available, it was complicated to use a mutation without the usage of a `Mutation` component, as sending mutations was only possible from the `client` object or the `Mutation` component. Accessing the `client` object from a React component is possible by importing an `ApolloConsumer` component that can read the client value from `ApolloProvider` that wraps your application.

3. The `useMutation` Hook can now be called with the `STORE_EXPO_TOKEN` mutation with `expoToken` from `registerForPushNotificationsAsync` as a parameter, which returns a function to store the token called `storeExpoToken`. This function can be called from the callback of the asynchronous `registerForPushNotificationsAsync` function with the token as a variable:

    . . .

```
const Posts = ({ client, navigation }) => {
+ const [storeExpoToken] = useMutation(STORE_EXPO_TOKEN);
  const [refreshing, setRefreshing] = React.useState(false);

  React.useEffect(() => {
-    registerForPushNotificationsAsync();
+    registerForPushNotificationsAsync().then(expoToken => {
+      return storeExpoToken({ variables: { expoToken } });
+    });
  }, []);
```

    . . .

This Expo push token will be sent to the GraphQL server whenever the `Posts` screen gets mounted, something you can force by switching between the `AddPosts` and `Posts` screens, for example. When the content of the `Posts` screen gets requested from the GraphQL server, the server will send a random notification to your application, which you can view from the `Notifications` screen. Also, you're still able to send any notification from the Expo dashboard, both when the application is in the foreground or the background.

Summary

In this chapter, you've created a mobile social media application with React Native and Expo that uses a GraphQL server to send and receive data as well for authentication. Using Expo, you've learned how to have the application request access to use the device's camera or camera roll to add new photos to posts. Also, Expo is used to receive notifications from the Expo dashboard or the GraphQL server. These notifications will be received by the user no matter whether the application is running on the back- or foreground.

In completing this social media application, you've completed the final React Native chapter of this book and are now ready to start with the very last chapter. In this last chapter, you'll be exploring another use case of React, which is React 360. With React 360, you can create 360-degree 2D and 3D experiences by writing React components.

Further reading

- Expo camera: https://docs.expo.io/versions/latest/sdk/camera/
- Notifications: https://docs.expo.io/versions/v33.0.0/sdk/notifications/

12
Creating a Virtual Reality Application with React 360

You're almost there—only one more chapter to go and then you can call yourself a React expert that has experienced React on every platform. Throughout this book, you've built 11 applications with React and React Native, and for the grande dessert, you get to use React 360. The final part of the *learn once, write everywhere* strategy of React and React Native will be best demonstrated in this chapter. With React 360, you can create dynamic 3D and **Virtual Reality (VR)** experiences using principles from React and, more specifically, React Native-like life cycles and UI components. Although VR is still an emerging technology, the best use cases for VR are, for example, retail stores that want their customers to experience their stores or games online.

In this chapter, you'll explore the very basics of what's possible with React 360 and how it relates to React and React Native. The application you will build will be able to render 360 degree panorama images and use state management to render between screens. Animated 3D objects will also be displayed inside the scenes you build with React 360.

The following topics will be covered in this chapter:

- Getting started with React 360
- Creating a panorama viewer with React 360
- Building clickable elements

Project overview

In this chapter, you will build a VR application with React 360 that uses principles from both React and React Native. Both 2D panorama images and 3D objects will be added to this application and the project can be run in the browser using the **Metro bundler**.

The build time is 1.5 hours.

Getting started

The application for this chapter will be built from scratch and uses assets that can be found on GitHub at `https://github.com/PacktPublishing/React-Projects/tree/ch12-assets`. These assets should be downloaded to your computer so that you can use them later on in this chapter. The complete code for this chapter can be found on GitHub at `https://github.com/PacktPublishing/React-Projects/tree/ch12`.

React 360 requires the same versions of Node.js and `npm` as the React and React Native projects. If you haven't installed Node.js on your machine, please go to `https://nodejs.org/en/download/`, where you can find the download instructions for macOS, Windows, and Linux.

After installing Node.js, you can run the following commands in your command line to check the installed versions:

- For Node.js (should be v10.16.3 or higher), use the following command:

    ```
    node -v
    ```

- For npm (should be v6.9.0 or higher), use the following command:

    ```
    npm -v
    ```

Creating a VR application with React 360

React 360 uses principles from React and is heavily based on React Native. React 360 allows you to create applications using UI components without having to deal with complex setups for mobile or VR devices, which is similar to how React Native works.

Getting started with React 360

It doesn't matter whether you're creating a project with React, React Native, or React 360—there are tools to easily get you started with any of these technologies. You've used Create React App as the starting point for the React web applications in this book and the Expo CLI for the React Native projects. This React 360 project will be started using the React 360 CLI, which will help you create and manage your React 360 application.

Setting up React 360

The React 360 CLI can be installed from npm by running the following command:

```
npm install -g react-360-cli
```

This will globally install the React 360 CLI from the npm package registry. After the installation process has completed, you can use it to create your first React 360 project by executing the following command:

```
react-360 init virtual-reality
```

By executing this command, a new React 360 project will be created called virtual-reality. All the packages that are required to run a React 360 application will be installed, such as react, react-native, react-360, react-360-web, and three. The three package installs three.js, a lightweight and easy to use JavaScript 3D library that comes with a default WebGL renderer. This renderer is used by React 360 to render 3D graphics, which it does by adding a layer that allows you to create declarative UI components.

Also, all the files that you will need to build the project are created in a directory with the same name. This directory has the following structure, where the following files are of importance:

```
virtual-reality
|-- __tests__
    |-- index-test.js
|-- node_modules
|-- static_assets
    |-- 360_world.jpg
.babelrc
client.js
index.html
index.js
package.json
```

The __tests__ directory is where you can create test files using the react-test-renderer package. The node_modules directory is where your packages are installed, while the static_assets directory holds the files that are used statically in development mode that may be transferred to a CND later on. To use React 360 in the browser (or mobile devices), you need to use Babel, which transpiles your code. The configuration for this can be found in the .babelrc file. The most important files that were created by react-360-cli are client.js, index.html, and index.js since these files are where you develop and serve your application. The client.js file contains the code that you use to execute the application, while index.js holds the actual code that is rendered by the application that is mounted to the DOM in index.html.

Instead of webpack, another JavaScript bundler is used for React 360 called **Metro**. This was created by Facebook, just like React was. Metro is a bundler for React Native projects and since React 360 takes a lot of principles from React Native to run on VR devices as well, Metro is the preferred bundler for React 360 applications. Just like webpack, all your source code is bundled into one big file in a readable format for web browsers. When you're developing your application, the Metro bundler will run a local development server that allows you to view the application in the browser. Files are compiled or processed at request time and when your application is complete, it can be used to create a production-ready build. You can start the bundler to initiate the development server with the following command:

```
npm start
```

This starts the Metro bundler and compiles your source code, which will be mounted to the DOM in the index.html file and makes it available
at http://localhost:8081/index.html.

When you first visit the project in your browser, the bundler may take a longer time to load as it will need to read your filesystem to get more information on how to render. If you make changes to the source code of the project, these changes will become visible faster to increase your development speed. The initial application that was created by the React 360 CLI is now visible at http://localhost:8081/index.html, which shows a 360 degree viewer that explores the dark landscape that can be found in the static_assets/360_world.jpg file. It looks as follows:

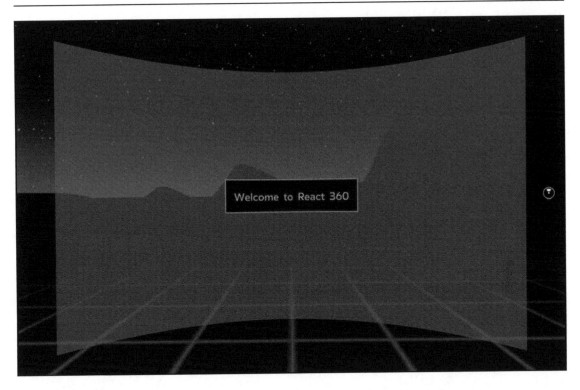

React 360 applications can display a 360 degree (or 3D) image or video as a background and render both 2D and 3D UI components on top of this background. In the client.js file, the image from the static_assets directory is used as a 360 degree 2D background image with the following line of code:

```
function init(bundle, parent, options = {}) {
  ...
  // Load the initial environment
  r360.compositor.setBackground(r360.getAssetURL('360_world.jpg'))
}

window.React360 = {init};
```

The getAssetUrl function points to the static_assets directory and can later be used to point to a CDN or other URL where your background image is hosted when your application is in production.

In case you have 3D glasses in your possession, you can replace the initial 360 degree 2D image with a 3D 360 image to create a 3D effect. NASA's website is a good source for finding 360 degree 3D images from any of the Mars missions, for example. Images from this mission can be found at https://mars.nasa.gov/3d/images and the downloaded files can be placed in static_assets. This should be used in the client.js file instead of the 360_world.jpg file.

Your application that was created by react-360 init also displays some UI components; in the next section we'll explore how to use UI components in React 360 in more detail.

React 360 UI components

Previously, we mentioned that React 360 uses a lot of concepts from React Native. One of them is the use of UI components that can be rendered. Out of the box, four UI components are offered by React 360, that is, View, Text, Entity, and VrButton. First, the View and Text components are 2D and used in the index.js file to create the panel and greeting message that you can see in the application. The other two components are more complex and can be used to render 3D objects in the case of the Entity component, or respond to user actions such as pressing a key down, in the case of the VrButton component.

From the client.js file, these components can be placed on cylinder surfaces from the index.js file since these are rendered by the renderToSurface from client.js. Here, the default surface that is declared refers to a 2D cylinder surface showing the UI components from index.js:

```
function init(bundle, parent, options = {}) {
  ...
  // Render your app content to the default cylinder surface
  r360.renderToSurface(
    r360.createRoot('virtual_reality', { /* initial props */ }),
    r360.getDefaultSurface()
  );
  ...

}

window.React360 = {init};
```

In the index.js file, we have the View and Text components, which are used to render the default surface with the welcome message you see when you start the application. The default export from index.js is called virtual_reality, which refers to the project name and is the same name that's used by the createRoot function in client.js.

The initial structure and naming of the application may get a bit confusing as the application grows. To combat this, you can split the components and make a distinction between the entry point of the application in index.js and the actual UI components. The following changes need to made for this:

1. Move the index.js file to a new directory called Components and call this file Panel.js. Here, you need to change the name of this class component from virtual_reality to Panel:

> Unfortunately, the current version of React 360 doesn't work well with React 16.8+, so you need to use a class component to use life cycles.

```
import React from 'react';
import {
- AppRegistry,
  StyleSheet,
  Text,
  View,
} from 'react-360';

- export default class virtual_reality extends React.Component {
+ export default class Panel extends React.Component {
    render() {
      return (
        <View style={styles.panel}>
          <View style={styles.greetingBox}>
            <Text style={styles.greeting}>Welcome to React
360</Text>
          </View>
        </View>
      );
    }
  };

const styles = StyleSheet.create({
  ...
});

- AppRegistry.registerComponent('virtual_reality', () =>
virtual_reality);
```

2. This newly created `Panel` component can be imported into the `index.js` file, where you need to delete all the code that's already in there and replace it with the following code block:

```
import {
  AppRegistry,
} from 'react-360';
import Panel from './Components/Panel';

AppRegistry.registerComponent('virtual_reality', () => Panel);
```

3. To see the changes you've made, you need to refresh the browser at `http://localhost:8081/index.html`, after which the Metro bundler will compile the code again. Since you made no visible changes, you'll need to look at the output in the Terminal to see if it was successful. To see these changes directly in the browser, you can make some changes to the text displayed in the `Panel` component by changing the value within the `Text` component:

```
import React from 'react';
import {
  StyleSheet,
  Text,
  View,
} from 'react-360';

export default class Panel extends React.Component {
  render() {
    return (
      <View style={styles.panel}>
        <View style={styles.greetingBox}>
-          <Text style={styles.greeting}>Welcome to React 360</Text>
+          <Text style={styles.greeting}>Welcome to this
world!</Text>
        </View>
      </View>
    );
  };
};

...
```

When you refresh the browser after this change, the text *"Welcome to this world!"* will be displayed instead of the initial message.

These `View` and `Text` components are simple 2D elements that can be styled using `StyleSheet`, which you've also used in React Native. By using this method to style your React 360 components, the learning curve for React 360 becomes less steep and the *learn once, write anywhere* principle is applied. The styles for the `View` and `Text` components are placed at the bottom of the `scr/Panel.js` file. The styling rules that can be used for the `View` and `Text` components are limited since not every style rule applies to each of these components. You can make some small changes to this styling, such as the ones we've made in the following code block:

```
. . .

const styles = StyleSheet.create({
  panel: {
    // Fill the entire surface
    width: 1000,
    height: 600,
    backgroundColor: 'rgba(255, 255, 255, 0.4)',
    justifyContent: 'center',
    alignItems: 'center',
  },
  greetingBox: {
-   padding: 20,
-   backgroundColor: '#000000',
-   borderColor: '#639dda',
+   padding: 25,
+   backgroundColor: 'black',
+   borderColor: 'green',
    borderWidth: 2,
  },
  greeting: {
    fontSize: 30,
  }
});
```

The following screenshot shows what your application will look like after these changes, where the box inside the panel that's showing the welcome message has changed a little:

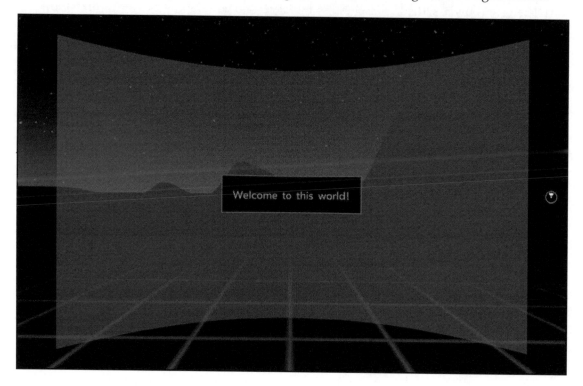

Also, the first view that's using the panel styling is created in client.js and is the default surface with a cylinder shape and a default width of 1000px and a height of 600px. It's also possible to change the shape and size of this surface, which we'll do in the upcoming sections.

In this section, you learned about the basics of how to get started with React 360. Now, we will learn how to interact with React 360.

Interactions in React 360

In the previous section, you set up the basics of React 360 and made some changes to the initial surface that was displaying the welcome message. With React 360, it's possible to create other surfaces that even have some interaction with the user. These surfaces can have different shapes and sizes, such as a flat or a circular shape, which makes it possible to add actionable buttons on these surfaces.

Using local state and VrButton

In this section, you'll add some buttons to the surface so that your users can close the welcome message or switch the background image scenery. First, let's start by creating a button that lets us close the welcome message surface:

1. The `Panel` component is a class component that gives you access to life cycles and local state management. Since you want to be able to close the welcome message, a local state can be used. At the top of the declaration of the `Panel` component, you must add a `constructor` that will have the initial state:

```
import React from 'react';
import {
  StyleSheet,
  Text,
  View,
} from 'react-360';

export default class Panel extends React.Component {
+ constructor() {
+   super();
+   this.state = {
+     open: true
+   }
+ }

  render() {
    return (


      . . .
```

If you're not very familiar with using class components for life cycles, you can look back at the few first chapters of this book. In these chapters, class components are used for life cycles instead of Hooks, which you've primarily used in the last few chapters.

2. The initial state has now been set, and you can use it to modify the styles of the panel by using an array of `styles` instead of just a single object. Apart from passing a `style` object in this array, you can also directly insert a styling rule by using a conditional spread. If the open state isn't true, a `display: 'none'` styling rule will be added to the styling for the panel. Otherwise, an empty array will be spread into the `style` array:

```
. . .

export default class Panel extends React.Component {
    constructor() {
        super();
        this.state = {
            open: true,
        };
    }

    render() {
+       const { open } = this.state;
        return (
-           <View style={styles.panel}>
+           <View style={[styles.panel, ...(!open ? [{ display: 'none' }]
:  [])]}>
                <View style={styles.greetingBox}>
                    <Text style={styles.greeting}>Welcome to this
world!</Text>
                </View>
            </View>
        );
    };
};
```

3. After adding this `state` variable to the style prop of the panel, you can create the button that will change the value of the open state. You may recall that React 360 has four default UI components and that one of them is called `VrButton`. This component is similar to `TouchableOpacity` in React Native and has no styling whatsoever by default. `VrButton` can be imported from `react-360` and can be placed inside a `Text` (or `View`) component. Clicking on this `VrButton` will change the open state since it uses the `setState` method:

```
import React from 'react';
import {
    StyleSheet,
    Text,
    View,
+   VrButton,
```

```
    } from 'react-360';

export default class Panel extends React.Component {

    ...

    render() {
      return (
        <View style={[styles.panel, ...(!open ? [{ display: 'none' }]
: [])]}>
            <View style={styles.greetingBox}>
              <Text style={styles.greeting}>Welcome to this
world!</Text>
            </View>
+           <VrButton
+             onClick={() => this.setState({ open: false })}
+           >
+             <Text>Close X</Text>
+           </VrButton>
        </View>
      );
    };
};
```

4. We can also add some styling to `VrButton` and `Text`. The styling for these
   components can be placed in the same `StyleSheet` that the styling for the other
   components in this file were placed:

```
    ...

    render() {
      return (
        <View style={[styles.panel, ...(!open ? [{ display: 'none' }]
: [])]}>
            <View style={styles.greetingBox}>
              <Text style={styles.greeting}>Welcome to this
world!</Text>
            </View>
            <VrButton
              onClick={() => this.setState({ open: false })}
+             style={styles.closeButton}
            >
-             <Text>Close X</Text>
+             <Text style={styles.close}>Close X</Text>
            </VrButton>
        </View>
      );
    };
```

```
     };

     const styles = StyleSheet.create({

        . . .

  +     closeButton: {
  +        position: 'absolute',
  +        top: 20,
  +        right: 20,
  +     },
  +     close: {
  +        fontSize: 40,
  +        color: 'black',
  +     },
     });
```

Now, when you refresh the application in your browser, the panel will have a button that says `Close X` at the top right. When you click this button, the panel will close and you can freely explore the entire background surface. Besides closing the panel, you can also change the scenery of the entire application, which will be added in the final part of this section.

Dynamically changing scenes

The application is using a default background that is displayed for the surface, but it's also possible to dynamically change this background image. The initial application comes with a default 360 degree background image. To change this, you'd need to either make your own 360 degree panorama images or download some from the internet. Creating your own 360 degree images is possible with special cameras or by downloading an application on your mobile device. Online images can be found on numerous stock photo websites. In this book's GitHub repository, in the `ch12-assets` branch, you can find a selection of 360 degree panorama images.

At the moment, your application only has the one default surface, which is a circular one that is displaying the welcome panel from the `Panel` component. It's also possible to add flat components so that the user can change the scenery using buttons. This requires you to make the following changes:

- Create a component that's displaying the specified buttons
- Import and register the component from `index.js`
- Set the new surface in `client.js`

Before making these changes, you must download the images from the GitHub repository and place them in the `static_assets` directory so that they can be used from within your application. Now, make the following changes to change the scenery:

1. Create a new component called `Navigation` in the `Components` directory and place the following code block inside it. This will return a component with basic styling for the surface, which is where the buttons will be placed later on:

```
import React from 'react';
import { StyleSheet, View } from 'react-360';

export default class Navigation extends React.Component {
  render() {
    return <View style={styles.navigation} />;
  }
}

const styles = StyleSheet.create({
  navigation: {
    width: 800,
    height: 100,
    backgroundColor: 'blue',
    justifyContent: 'space-between',
    alignItems: 'center',
    flexDirection: 'row',
  }
});
```

2. In the `index.js` file, you must import the `Navigation` component and register it with the `AppRegistry` method. This will ensure that the component can be rendered to a surface:

```
import { AppRegistry } from 'react-360';
import Panel from './Components/Panel';
+ import Navigation from './Components/Navigation';

AppRegistry.registerComponent('Panel', () => Panel);
+ AppRegistry.registerComponent('Navigation', () => Navigation);
```

3. In the `client.js` file, this `Navigation` component must be added to a surface; in this case, this is a flat surface. A new surface can be created using the `Surface` method from `react-360` and you must specify the shape and the size of the component. You can also set an angle to position the component:

```
function init(bundle, parent, options = {}) {
    const r360 = new ReactInstance(bundle, parent, {
        // Add custom options here
        fullScreen: true,
        ...options
    });

+ const navigationPanel = new Surface(1000, 100,
Surface.SurfaceShape.Flat);
+ navigationPanel.setAngle(0, -0.3);

+ r360.renderToSurface(r360.createRoot('Navigation'),
navigationPanel);

    // Render your app content to the default cylinder surface
    r360.renderToSurface(
        r360.createRoot('virtual_reality', { /* initial props */ }),
        r360.getDefaultSurface(),
    );
    ...

}

window.React360 = {init};
```

By refreshing the project in your browser, you will see a blue block being rendered at the bottom of the screen. To add buttons to this block, you can use the `VrButton` component and place the currently selected background in the local state. Let's do this now:

1. In the `Components/Navigation.js` file, you can add the necessary buttons to the `Navigation` component. To do this, you need to import the `VrButton` and `Text` components from `react-360` and place them in the `View` component that's being rendered. They'll get styling props since you want the buttons to have a margin on either the left- or right-hand side:

```
import React from 'react';
- import { StyleSheet, View } from 'react-360';
+ import {
+     StyleSheet,
+     Text,
+     View,
```

```
+    VrButton,
+  } from 'react-360';

export default class Navigation extends React.Component {
   render() {
-    return <View style={styles.navigation} />;
+    return (
+      <View style={styles.navigation}>
+        <VrButton style={[styles.button, styles.buttonLeft]}>
+          <Text style={styles.buttonText}>{'< Prev'}</Text>
+        </VrButton>
+        <VrButton style={[styles.button, styles.buttonRight]}>
+          <Text style={styles.buttonText}>{'Next >'}</Text>
+        </VrButton>
+    );
   }
}


...
```

2. These styling objects can be added to the StyleSheet method at the bottom of this file, right below the styling for navigation:

```
...

const styles = StyleSheet.create({
   navigation: {
     width: 800,
     height: 100,
     backgroundColor: 'blue',
     justifyContent: 'space-between',
     alignItems: 'center',
     flexDirection: 'row',
   },
+  button: {
+    padding: 20,
+    backgroundColor: 'white',
+    borderColor: 'black',
+    borderWidth: 2,
+    alignItems: 'center',
+    width: 200,
+  },
+  buttonLeft: {
+    marginLeft: 10,
+  },
+  buttonRight: {
+    marginRight: 10,
+  },
```

```
+ buttonText: {
+    fontSize: 40,
+    fontWeight: 'bold',
+    color: 'blue',
+ },
});
```

3. The different 360 degree panorama background images that you've downloaded from the GitHub repository and placed in `static_assets` can be imported into this file later on using the `assets` method from `react-360`. To do this, you need to create a constant that's an array of all the filenames of these images, including the initial image that was added by `react-360-cli`. Also, the `assets` and `Environment` methods must be imported here as you'll need these to change the background image:

```
import React from 'react';
import {
+ assets,
+ Environment,
  StyleSheet,
  Text,
  View,
  VrButton,
} from 'react-360';

+ const backgrounds = [
+   '360_world.jpg',
+   'beach.jpg',
+   'landscape.jpg',
+   'mountain.jpg',
+   'winter.jpg',
+ ];

export default class Navigation extends React.Component {

  ...
```

4. Just like we did for the `Panel` component, we need to create an initial state that defines which background is being displayed. This will be the first background of the backgrounds array, meaning 0. Also, a function must be created that can change `currentBackground` using the `setState` method. When the state for `currentBackground` has been changed, the background image will be updated using the `Environment` method, which selects one of the backgrounds from the `static_assets` directory using the `assets` method:

```
. . .

export default class Navigation extends React.Component {
+ constructor() {
+   super();
+   this.state = {
+     currentBackground: 0
+   };
+ }

+ changeBackground(change) {
+   const { currentBackground } = this.state;

+   this.setState(
+     {
+       currentBackground: currentBackground + change
+     },
+     () => {
+       Environment.setBackgroundImage(
+         asset(backgrounds[this.state.currentBackground], { format:
'2D' })
+       );
+     }
+   );
+ }

. . .
```

5. The newly created `changeBackground` function can be called when the `Navigation` component mounts and uses the first background image, but when the user clicks the button, the `changeBackground` function must be called as well. This can be done by adding a `componentDidMount` life cycle and calling the function with the `onClick` event on the buttons:

```
. . .

export default class Navigation extends React.Component {
```

```
  . . .

+ componentDidMount() {
+   this.changeBackground(0);
+ }

  render() {
    return (
      <View style={styles.navigation}>
+       <VrButton style={[styles.button, styles.buttonLeft]}>
+       <VrButton
+         onClick={() => this.changeBackground(-1)}
+         style={[styles.button, styles.buttonLeft]}
+       >
          <Text style={styles.buttonText}>{`< Prev`}</Text>
        </VrButton>
+       <VrButton style={[styles.button, styles.buttonRight]}>
+       <VrButton
+         onClick={() => this.changeBackground(1)}
+         style={[styles.button, styles.buttonRight]}
+       >
          <Text style={styles.buttonText}>{`Next >`}</Text>
        </VrButton>
      </View>
    );
  }
}

  . . .
```

6. When you refresh the project in your browser, you may notice that you get an error when you press the left button once or the right button multiple times. To prevent this error from happening, you need to scope the maximum and minimum values of the currentBackground state. The value can't go below zero or above the length of the backgrounds array. You can do this by making the following change to the changeBackground function:

```
  . . .

export default class Navigation extends React.Component {

  . . .

  changeBackground(change) {
    const { currentBackground } = this.state;

    this.setState(
```

```
       {
  −        currentBackground: currentBackground + change
  +        currentBackground:
  +          currentBackground + change > backgrounds.length − 1
  +            ? 0
  +            : currentBackground + change < 0
  +            ? backgrounds.length − 1
  +            : currentBackground + change
       },
       () => {
         Environment.setBackgroundImage(
           asset(backgrounds[this.state.currentBackground], { format:
   '2D' })
         );
       }
     );
   }


   . . .
```

The value of the `currentBackground` state will always be a value that can be found within the length of the `backgrounds` array, which makes it possible for you to navigate back and forth between the different background images. After clicking on the **Prev** or **Next** button a couple of times, your application will look as follows:

Another thing you can do with React 360 is add animated components, just like we did when we looked at React Native. You will learn how to add these animations in the next section.

Animations and 3D

So far, all the components you've added in this chapter were 2D and didn't have animations; however, you can also animate components with React 360 and even add 3D objects. These 3D objects must be pre-built in special 3D modeling software or downloaded from the internet and can be added to a surface in your application. For animations, the Animated API must be imported, which is similar to the Animated API we used for React Native.

Animations

Before getting into using 3D objects in React 360, let's learn how to use the Animated API from React 360 to create animations. The Animated API uses the Animated API from React Native and can be used to create both simple and advanced animations for UI components. With the Animated API, you can easily create animations that fade in and out or rotate, just by using values that are affected by the local state.

One of the components that can be animated is the `Panel` component, which displays a welcome message, since this component has an element that the user can click on to close the surface. When the user clicks the **Close X** button, the display styling rule of the component will be set to `none`, making the component disappear suddenly. Instead of this, you can change this into a smooth animation by doing the following:

1. The `panel` component is created in the `Components/Panel.js` file and is where the `Animated` API must be imported, which you can do from `react-360`:

```
import React from 'react';
- import { StyleSheet, Text, View, VrButton } from 'react-360';
+ import {
+   Animated,
+   StyleSheet,
+   Text,
+   View,
+   VrButton,
+ } from 'react-360';

export default class Panel extends React.Component {
```

2. In `constructor()`, an initial value for the `Animated` value should be set. Call it `opacity` in this case since you want the `opacity` of the `Panel` component to change to zero to make it disappear. Initially, the `opacity` should be 1 since the welcome message must be displayed when the user opens the application:

```
    ...

    export default class Panel extends React.Component {
      constructor() {
        super();
        this.state = {
          open: true,
+         opacity: new Animated.Value(1),
        };
      }

      render() {
        ...
```

3. When the user clicks `VrButton` in the `Panel` component, the state for `open` will be changed, after which the animation should start. Therefore, a `componentDidUpdate()` life cycle method must be created, where you can check for changes in the `state` for `open` and start the animation afterward. When the value for `open` changes from `true` to `false`, the animation should start to change the value for `opacity` from 1 to 0, which makes it disappear:

```
    export default class Panel extends React.Component {
      constructor() {
        super();
        this.state = {
          open: true,
          opacity: new Animated.Value(1),
        };
      }

+   componentDidUpdate() {
+     const { open, opacity } = this.state;
+     Animated.timing(opacity, {
+       toValue: open ? 1 : 0,
+       duration: 800,
+     }).start();
+   }

      render() {

        ...
```

4. Finally, this value should be passed to the `style` prop of an `Animated` component, meaning you need to change the `View` component into an `Animated.View` component that can handle the animation. The `display` styling rule can be deleted from the `style` props and replaced with `opacity` since this controls whether the component is visible to the user or not:

```
render() {
- const { open, opacity } = this.state;
+ const { opacity } this.state;
  return (
-   <View style={[styles.panel, ...(!open ? [{ display: 'none' }] :
[])]}>
+   <Animated.View style={[styles.panel, { opacity }]}>
      <View style={styles.welcomeBox}>
        <Text style={styles.welcome}>Welcome to this world!</Text>
      </View>
      <VrButton
        onClick={() => this.setState({ open: false })}
        style={styles.closeButton}
      >
        <Text style={styles.close}>Close X</Text>
      </VrButton>
-   </View>
+   </Animated.View>
  );
}
```

Now, when you click on the `VrButton` that closes the `Panel` component with the welcome message, the component will slowly dissolve into the background and disappear. The same sort of animation can be added to the `Navigation` component since you want to ensure that our users know that they can navigate through the different backgrounds. You can highlight the option to click on, for example, the **Next** button by having it repeatedly fade in and out. A lot of the logic for this is the same as it is for the `Panel` component:

1. The Animated API should be imported at the top of the `Components/Navigation.js` file and an initial value for the `opacity` state must be created:

```
import React from 'react';
import {
+ Animated,
  asset,
  Environment,
  StyleSheet,
  Text,
```

```
    View,
    VrButton,
  } from 'react-360';

  . . .

  export default class Navigation extends React.Component {
    constructor() {
      super();
      this.state = {
        currentBackground: 0,
+       opacity: new Animated.Value(0),
      };
    }
    changeBackground(change) {
      . . .
```

2. The animation should start as soon as the component mounts, so the
   Animated.timing method, which is used to change the value of opacity, must
   be placed in a componentDidMount() life cycle method. This will start the
   animation of opacity from 0 to 1, making the text inside the button blink:

```
  . . .

  componentDidMount() {
+ const { opacity } = this.state;
    this.changeBackground(0);

+ Animated.timing(opacity, {
+   toValue: 1,
+   duration: 800
+ }).start()
  }

  render() {

    . . .
```

3. The `Text` component inside `VrButton` for the button so that the user can navigate to the next background image can now be changed into an `Animated.Text` component and the `opacity` styling rule must be added to the `style` prop. This will add the animation to this component, making the text blink once when the application is mounted:

```
render() {
+ const { opacity } = this.state;
  return (
    <View style={styles.navigation}>
      <VrButton
        onClick={() => this.changeBackground(-1)}
        style={[styles.button, styles.buttonLeft]}
      >
        <Text style={styles.buttonText}>{`< Prev`}</Text>
      </VrButton>
      <VrButton
        onClick={() => this.changeBackground(1)}
        style={[styles.button, styles.buttonRight]}
      >
-       <Text style={styles.buttonText}>{`Next >`}</Text>
+       <Animated.Text style={[styles.buttonText, { opacity
}]}>{`Next >`}</Animated.Text>
      </VrButton>
    </View>
  );
}
```

. . .

4. You don't want the button text to blink just once. To make it blink repeatedly, you can use the `loop` and `sequence` methods from `Animated` to get multiple iterations of this animation. To make it smoother, we can add a small delay to the animation. This will iterate 10 times, after which the button will stop blinking:

. . .

```
componentDidMount() {
  const { opacity } = this.state;
  this.changeBackground(0);

+ Animated.loop(
+   Animated.sequence([
+     Animated.delay(400),
      Animated.timing(opacity, {
        toValue: 1,
        duration: 800
```

```
  -       }).start()
  +       })
  +   ]),
  +   {
  +     iterations: 10
  +   }
  + ).start();
    }

    render() {

      . . .
```

Now, the **Next** button will blink 10 times when the application mounts, thereby emphasizing to the user that it's possible to navigate between background scenes. However, these animations aren't the only animated features you can add. In the next section, you'll learn how to add animated 3D objects.

Rendering 3D objects

To use 3D objects in React 360, you need you to have prebuilt 3D objects, which you can create with special 3D modeling software or download from the internet. In this section, we'll use a 3D object from the GitHub repository for this chapter, where you can find a `.obj` file that's supported by React 360. Apart from OBJ, GLTF models are also supported as 3D objects by React 360.

OBJ files is a standard format for 3D model files that can be exported and imported by numerous 3D tools. Please keep in mind that React 360 doesn't support lighting and that you will need to include more advanced packages to render complex textures in a 3D model. Due to this, the 3D model that will be used in this example is just in one color, which is white.

Adding 3D objects to React 360 can be easily done with the `Entity` object while using a 3D model that is stored in the `static_assets` directory. By using `Entity`, the 3D model can be transformed into a component that you need to register in `index.js`, so that it can be used in `client.js` and added to the application.

To add 3D objects, make the following changes:

1. First, make sure you've copied the `helicopter.obj` file from this chapter's GitHub repository into the `static_assets` directory and create a new file called `Helicoper.js` in the `Components` directory. In this file, the 3D model can be imported using the `asset` method and added as the source for an `Entity` object. To do this, use the following code:

```
import React from 'react';
import { asset } from 'react-360';
import Entity from 'Entity';

export default class Helicopter extends React.Component {
  render() {
    return (
      <Entity
        source={{
          obj: asset('helicopter.obj'),
        }}
        style={{
          transform: [
            { rotate: 90 },
            { scaleX: 0.02 },
            { scaleY: 0.02 },
            { scaleZ: 0.02 },
          ]
        }}
      />
    );
  }
}
```

The scaling for the `Entity` object in the `style` prop will decrease the size of the 3D model; otherwise, it would be way too big to display properly. Also, the value for `rotateY` will rotate the helicopter 90 degrees on the *y* axis.

2. This `Helicopter` component should be displayed in your application, but this can only be done if you register it to `AppRegistry` in the `index.js` file:

```
import { AppRegistry } from 'react-360';
import Panel from './Components/Panel';
import Navigation from './Components/Navigation';
+ import Helicopter from './Components/Helicopter';

AppRegistry.registerComponent('Panel', () => Panel);
AppRegistry.registerComponent('Navigation', () => Navigation);
+ AppRegistry.registerComponent('Helicopter', () =>
Helicopter);
```

3. This component can be mounted to the application in the `client.js` file using the `renderToLocation` method. Previously, you used the `renderToSurface` method to mount the `Panel` and `Navigation` components, but, for 3D objects, this won't work. Apart to the component itself, the `renderToLocation` method also takes the location of where the object will be placed:

```
- import { ReactInstance, Surface } from 'react-360-web';
+ import { ReactInstance, Surface, Location } from 'react-360-web';

function init(bundle, parent, options = {}) {

    ...

+ const location = new Location([-100, 10, -2]);
+ r360.renderToLocation(r360.createRoot('Helicopter'), location);

    // Render your app content to the default cylinder surface
    r360.renderToSurface(

    ...
```

Now, when you open the application, a white helicopter will be visible when you turn 90 degrees to the left. In the preceding code, Location is used to create a location in the application where the 3D model is mounted. This is done with new Location([-100, 10, -2]). This will place the object 100 meters to the left, 10 meters up, and 2 meters in front of the initial location of the user when the application is started. This can be seen in the following screenshot, which was taken in one of the different scenes for this application:

However, React 360 doesn't stop at importing and rendering 3D objects: you can also animate them, just like any other component. For this, the Animated API can be used again. You can use this with the local state to add any animation to the 3D helicopter. The style prop for Entity already has some styling that determines the scale, which is something you can make dynamically by using an Animated value. By decreasing the scale of the helicopter a bit more, it will look as if it's flying and will disappear into the distance. More effects can be added by changing the rotateY value to make it look like the helicopter is turning.

To create an animated 3D object, make the following changes to
`Components/Helicopter.js`:

1. Import `Animated` from `react-360` and create an `Animated` version of `Entity`.
   Since this isn't a predefined `Animated` component, we can't do this by typing
   `Animated.Entity`. Instead, we need to create a customer `Animated` component
   using the `createAnimatedComponent` method:

```
import React from 'react';
- import { asset } from 'react-360';
+ import { Animated, asset } from 'react-360';
import Entity from 'Entity';

+ const AnimatedEntity = Animated.createAnimatedComponent(Entity);

export default class Helicopter extends React.Component {
   ...
```

2. A `constructor` must be added to the `Helicopter` component, where the initial
   `Animated` values for both the `scale` and `rotateY` are set as local state values.
   The initial value for `scale` is `0.02`, which is the same as the current scale of the
   helicopter, while `rotateY` will get the same value that it currently has:

```
   ...

export default class Helicopter extends React.Component {
+ constructor() {
+    super();
+    this.state = {
+       scale: new Animated.Value(0.02),
+       rotateY: new Animated.Value(90)
+    };
+ }

   render() {
      ...
```

3. We can create the animation in the `componentDidMount()` life cycle method as a sequence since we want the helicopter to turn and fly away. The first part of the animation is a small delay, so the animation won't start as soon as the application mounts. After 1 second (1,000 ms), the helicopter will start turning for about 8 seconds and fly away after another small delay:

```
. . .

+ componentDidMount() {
+   const { scale, rotateY } = this.state;
+
+   Animated.sequence([
+     Animated.delay(1000),
+     Animated.timing(rotateY, {
+       toValue: 0,
+       duration: 8000
+     }),
+     Animated.delay(800),
+     Animated.timing(scale, {
+       toValue: 0,
+       duration: 8000
+     })
+   ]).start();
+ }

  render() {

    . . .
```

4. The `Entity` component must be replaced with the `AnimatedEntity` component, which handles values from the `Animated` API. These values can be taken from the local state so that they can be added to the `style` prop of the `AnimatedEntity` component:

```
  render() {
+   const { scale, rotateY } = this.state;

    return (
-     <Entity
+     <AnimatedEntity
        source={{
          obj: asset('helicopter.obj')
        }}
        style={{
          transform: [
-           { rotateY: 90 },
```

```
    -                 { scaleX: 0.02 },
    -                 { scaleY: 0.02 },
    -                 { scaleZ: 0.02 },
    +                 { rotateY },
    +                 { scaleX: scale },
    +                 { scaleY: scale },
    +                 { scaleZ: scale },
                    ]
                 }}
              />
            );
          }
        }
```

Now, the helicopter will start turning from 90 to 0 degrees and, over a period of time, it will fly away into the distance and disappear.

Summary

In this final chapter, you've combined all of the knowledge you have gathered from this book to get started with React 360. Although React 360 uses practices from both React and React Native, it serves a different and more niche use case than the other React technologies. At the time of writing, well-known principles such as lifecycle methods for the local state and the Animated API have been used to create a VR application that allows users to explore 2D panorama images. It has basic animations, as well as a 3D helicopter object that flies away into the distance.

With this final chapter, you've completed all 12 chapters of this book and have created 12 projects with React, React Native, and React 360. Now, you have a solid understanding of everything that you can do with React and how to use it across different platforms. While React and React Native are already mature libraries, new features are added continuously. Even as you finish reading this book, there will probably be new features you can check out, starting with **Concurrent Mode**. My only advice would be to never stop learning and keep a close view on the documentation whenever a new feature is announced.

Further reading

- React 360 Native Modules
  examples: `https://facebook.github.io/react-360/docs/example-native-modules.html`
- NASA 3D images: `https://mars.nasa.gov/3d/images`

Other Books You May Enjoy

If you enjoyed this book, you may be interested in these other books by Packt:

Learn React Hooks
Daniel Bugl

ISBN: 978-1-83864-144-3

- Understand the fundamentals of React Hooks and how they modernize state management in React apps
- Build your own custom Hooks and learn how to test them
- Use community Hooks for implementing responsive design and more
- Learn the limitations of Hooks and what you should and shouldn't use them for
- Get to grips with implementing React context using Hooks
- Refactor your React-based web application, replacing existing React class components with Hooks
- Use state management solutions such as Redux and MobX with React Hooks

React Design Patterns and Best Practices - Second Edition
Carlos Santana Roldán

ISBN: 978-1-78953-017-9

- Get familiar with the new React features, like context API and React Hooks
- Learn the techniques of styling and optimizing React components
- Make components communicate with each other by applying consolidate patterns
- Use server-side rendering to make applications load faster
- Write a comprehensive set of tests to create robust and maintainable code
- Build high-performing applications by optimizing components

Leave a review - let other readers know what you think

Please share your thoughts on this book with others by leaving a review on the site that you bought it from. If you purchased the book from Amazon, please leave us an honest review on this book's Amazon page. This is vital so that other potential readers can see and use your unbiased opinion to make purchasing decisions, we can understand what our customers think about our products, and our authors can see your feedback on the title that they have worked with Packt to create. It will only take a few minutes of your time, but is valuable to other potential customers, our authors, and Packt. Thank you!

Index

Made in the USA
Columbia, SC
09 August 2020

15912822R00259